1973

MASTERWORKS OF
PHILOSOPHY
VOLUME 2

MASTERWORKS OF
PHILOSOPHY
VOLUME 2

DIGESTS OF

BARUCH SPINOZA: ETHICS

JOHN LOCKE: AN ESSAY CONCERNING
HUMAN UNDERSTANDING

IMMANUEL KANT: THE CRITIQUE OF
PURE REASON

McGraw-Hill Book Company

New York · St. Louis · San Francisco · London · Düsseldorf
Kuala Lumpur · Mexico · Montreal · Panama · Rio de Janeiro
Sydney · Toronto · Johannesburg · New Delhi · Singapore

Masterworks of Philosophy, Volume II

First McGraw-Hill Paperback Edition, 1972
07-040802-5

1 2 3 4 5 6 7 8 9 MU MU 7 9 8 7 6 5 4 3 2

CONTENTS

ETHICS
Proved in Geometrical Order

by

BARUCH SPINOZA

CONTENTS

Ethics

BARUCH SPINOZA

1632–1677

BARUCH SPINOZA, born into an orthodox Jewish family November 24, 1632, was a Dutch philosopher of Spanish ancestry. His parents were members of a community of Jewish emigrants who had fled from Spain and Portugal to escape religious persecution. Both Spinoza's grandfather and father were leaders among the Jews of Amsterdam. The grandfather was the recognized head of his community in 1628; and the father, Michael Espinoza, was the warden of the synagogue between 1630 and 1650.

This ancestral background and early environment gave to the young philosopher two characteristics which dominated his later thinking. The first characteristic was a thorough knowledge of, and a deep respect for, religion. Young Baruch's education was in the best Jewish tradition. His parents were of comfortable means and able to give the boy a Biblical and Talmudic training under the most noted rabbis in Amsterdam. The other characteristic born of the boy's ancestral heritage and early experience was an abiding love of freedom.

It was this love of freedom that caused him much suffering and misunderstanding. His opposition to the antiquated beliefs of the orthodox synagogue brought about his expulsion from the Jewish fold.

His longing for a broader understanding led him to study with Van den Enden, a physician who was generally believed to be a freethinker. As his knowledge widened, he withdrew more and more from the turmoil of the world to the solitude of his study. He moved to an attic in the Ouwerkerk suburb of

Amsterdam, changed his name from Baruch to Benedict, and took up the polishing of lenses as a means of livelihood, and the pursuit of philosophy as the business of his life.

As the trend of Spinoza's philosophy began to take a definite form, his love for clarity and his passion for freedom became more and more pronounced. He refused to impose his religious point of view upon others, and would not attempt to shake their faith even though it was not his own faith.

In 1661 he moved to Rijnsburg, a small town near Leyden, where he started to formulate his great work, the *Ethics*. Shutting himself in his room "like a silkworm in his cocoon," he rarely went out except for a walk or to buy his simple fare of milk and corn meal and an occasional handful of raisins. His chief relaxation was to watch the "fussing and the fighting" of the spiders as they spun out their webs in his workroom whilst he was spinning out the thread of his philosophy.

It was a new and daring philosophy, and it aroused much concern among the religious fanatics of the day. One attempt had been made to assassinate Spinoza, and a great many persons in high position believed him to be "an instrument of Satan" who ought to be put where he belonged. Several attempts to publish the *Ethics* were frustrated through the fanaticism of his opponents. This opposition only brought a smile of pity to his lips. He was utterly indifferent to abuse, just as he was utterly indifferent to applause. On one occasion he refused a call to a professorial chair at the University of Heidelberg. Dedicated to freedom in thinking and in teaching, he feared that he would be too seriously restricted in presenting his ideas at Heidelberg.

Never a strong man, Spinoza finally succumbed to a disease of the lungs and died on February 21, 1677—his *Ethics* still unpublished. Thus ended, at forty-five years of age, the life of one of the greatest of modern philosophers. He was hated by those who feared freedom and loved by those who recognized its true meaning. To the first group he was always an enigma. The pastor Colerue, his most faithful biographer, who despised and feared him intensely but who carefully collected all the items available about his life, failed to understand how a freethinker "could lead so beautiful a life and die so quiet a death."

The philosophy of Spinoza is presented in the form of a treatise on geometry. Beginning with definitions, he lays down a number of axioms (self-evident truths), and then develops his argument through a number of theorems (propositions to be proved by a progressive chain of reasoning).

The general scope of his philosophy embraces three fundamental problems:

1—The structure of the World.
2—The identity of God.
3—The nature of Man.

The world, concludes Spinoza, is infinite. It has no beginning and no ending in space. Let us extend the horizon of our mental vision as far as we possibly can, and we shall still be unable to conceive of "nothingness" beyond the boundaries of space. Space, then, is beginningless, endless, boundless.

Also, declares Spinoza, the world is eternal. It has no beginning and no ending in time. We cannot imagine anything *before* time or *after* time. Just like space, time is all-pervading, everlasting, complete.

And so this world never and nowhere *began,* and never and nowhere will *end*. It simply *is*—everywhere and everlastingly it *exists*.

So much, then, for the structure of the world. And now, what about the identity of God? To this question Spinoza gives a unique and startling answer. God, asserts Spinoza, is identical with the world. He calls this doctrine *Pantheism,* which means that God is in everything and that everything is in God. The visible universe is His body, and the energy (or the harmony) that moves it is His mind.

And what about Man in this scheme of things? The body of Man, of every individual man, is part of God's body; and the mind of Man, of every individual man, is part of God's mind. Each of us, maintains Spinoza, is but a *small part* of God; but—and here is a message of great hope for us all—each of us is an *equally important part*. Even the so-called failures in life are essential notes in the symphony of creation. Let no one therefore despair. No life has ever been in vain. From God we come—to God we return. All humanity is one body and one soul. We live in *one world*. If we hurt a single individual, we hurt all mankind. In striking against any man, we strike against God. We are more than brothers of a single human family. We are related members of a single divine body and a single divine mind.

ETHICS

Proved in Geometrical Order

FIRST PART: CONCERNING GOD

DEFINITIONS

I. I UNDERSTAND that to be CAUSE OF ITSELF whose essence involves existence and whose nature cannot be conceived unless existing.

II. That thing is said to be FINITE IN ITS KIND which can be limited by another thing of the same kind.

III. I understand SUBSTANCE to be that which is in itself and is conceived through itself: I mean that, the conception of which does not depend on the conception of another thing from which it must be formed.

IV. An ATTRIBUTE I understand to be that which the intellect perceives as constituting the essence of a substance.

V. By MODE I understand the Modifications of a substance or that which is in something else through which it may be conceived.

VI. GOD I understand to be a being absolutely infinite, that is, a substance consisting of infinite attributes, each of which expresses eternal and infinite essence.

VII. That thing is said to be FREE which exists by the mere necessity of its own nature and is determined in its actions by itself alone. That thing is said to be NECESSARY, or rather COMPELLED, when it is determined in its existence and actions by something else in a certain fixed ratio.

VIII. I understand ETERNITY to be existence itself, in so far as it is conceived to follow necessarily from the definition of an eternal thing.

AXIOMS

I. All things which are, are in themselves or in other things.

II. That which cannot be conceived through another thing must be conceived through itself.

III. From a given determined cause an effect follows of necessity, and on the other hand, if no determined cause is granted, it is impossible that an effect should follow.

IV. The knowledge of effect depends on the knowledge of cause, and involves the same.

V. Things which have nothing in common reciprocally cannot be comprehended reciprocally through each other, or, the conception of the one does not involve the conception of the other.

VI. A true idea should agree with its ideal, i.e., what it conceives.

VII. The essence of that which can be conceived as not existing does not involve existence.

PROPOSITIONS

PROP. I. A substance is prior in its nature to its modifications.
Proof.—This is obvious from Def. 3 and 5.

PROP. II. Two substances, having different attributes, have nothing in common between them.
Proof.—This also is obvious from Def. 3. For each of them must be in itself and through itself be conceived, or the conception of one of them does not involve the conception of the other.

PROP. III. Of two things having nothing in common between them, one cannot be the cause of the other.
Proof.—If they have nothing in common reciprocally, therefore they cannot be known through each other, and therefore one cannot be the cause of the other. *Q.e.d.*

PROP. IV. Two or three distinct things are distinguished one from the other either by the difference of the attributes of the substances or by the difference of their modifications.
Proof.—All things that are, are either in themselves or in other things, that is, beyond the intellect nothing is granted save substances and their modifications. Nothing therefore is granted beyond the intellect, through which several things may be distinguished one from the other except substances, or what is the same thing, their attributes or modifications. *Q.e.d.*

PROP. V. In the nature of things, two or more things may not be granted having the same nature or attribute.
Proof.—If several distinct substances are given, they must be distinguished one from the other either by the difference of their attributes or their modifications. If, then, they are to be distinguished by the difference of their attributes, two or more cannot be granted having the same attribute. But if they are to be distinguished by the difference of their

modifications, since a substance is prior in its nature to its modifications, therefore let the modifications be laid aside and let the substance itself be considered in itself, that is, truly considered, and it could not then be distinguished from another, that is, two or more substances cannot have the same nature or attribute. *Q.e.d.*

PROP. VI. One substance cannot be produced by another.

Proof.—In the nature of things two substances cannot be granted with the same attribute, that is, which have anything in common, and accordingly one of them cannot be the cause of the other or one cannot be produced by the other. *Q.e.d.*

Corollary.—Hence it follows that a substance cannot be produced from anything else. For in the nature, of things nothing is given save substances and their modifications, as is obvious from Ax. 1 and Def. 3 and 5: and it cannot be produced from another substance. Therefore a substance cannot in any way be produced from anything else. *Q.e.d.*

PROP. VII. Existence appertains to the nature of substance.

Proof.—A substance cannot be produced from anything else: it will therefore be its own cause, that is, its essence necessarily involves existence, or existence appertains to the nature of it. *Q.e.d.*

PROP. VIII. All substance is necessarily infinite.

Proof.—No two or more substances can have the same attribute, and it appertains to the nature of substance that it should exist. It must therefore exist either finitely or infinitely. But not finitely. For it would then be limited by some other substance of the same nature which also of necessity must exist: and then two substances would be granted having the same attribute, which is absurd. It will exist, therefore, infinitely. *Q.e.d.*

PROP. IX. The more reality or being a thing has, the more attributes will it have.

Proof.—This is obvious from Def. 4.

PROP. X. Each attribute of the one substance must be conceived through itself.

Proof.—An attribute is that which the intellect perceives of a substance as constituting its essence, therefore it must be conceived through itself. *Q.e.d.*

PROP. XI. God or a substance consisting of infinite attributes, each of which expresses eternal and infinite essence, necessarily exists.

Proof.—If you deny it, conceive, if it be possible, that God does not exist. Then his essence does not involve existence. But this is absurd. Therefore God necessarily exists. *Q.e.d.*

PROP. XII. No attribute of a substance can be truly conceived, from which it would follow that substance can be divided into parts.

Proof.—The parts into which substance so conceived may be divided will either retain the nature of substance or not. In the first case, then each part must be infinite and its own cause, and must possess different attributes; and so from one substance several can be made, which is absurd. Again, the parts would have nothing in common with the whole, and the whole could exist and be conceived without the parts which go to make it, which no one will doubt to be absurd. But in the second case, when the parts do not retain the nature of substance, then, when a substance is divided into equal parts, it will lose the nature of substance and will cease to be, which is absurd.

PROP. XIII. Substance absolutely infinite is indivisible.

Proof.—If it is divisible, the parts into which it is divided will either retain the nature of substance or will not. In the first case, several substances would be given having the same nature, which is absurd. In the second case, a substance absolutely infinite could cease to be, which is also absurd.

Corollary.—From this it follows that no substance, and consequently no corporeal substance, in so far as it is substance, can be divided into parts.

PROP. XIV. Except God no substance can be granted or conceived.

Proof.—As God is a being absolutely infinite, to whom no attribute expressing the essence of substance can be denied, and as he necessarily exists, if any other substance than God be given, it must be explained by means of some attribute of God, and thus two substances would exist possessing the same attribute, which is absurd; and so no other substance than God can be granted, and consequently not even be conceived. For if it can be conceived it must necessarily be conceived as existing, and this by the first part of this proof is absurd. Therefore except God no substance can be granted or conceived. *Q.e.d.*

Corollary I.—Hence it distinctly follows that (1) God is one alone, i.e., there is none like him, or in the nature of things only one substance can be granted, and that is absolutely infinite.

Corollary II.—It follows, in the second place, that extension and thought are either attributes of God or modifications of attributes of God.

PROP. XV. Whatever is, is in God, and nothing can exist or be conceived without God.

Proof.—Save God no substance is granted or can be conceived, that is, a thing which is in itself and through itself is conceived. But modifications cannot exist or be conceived without substance, wherefore these can only exist in divine nature, and through that alone be conceived. But nothing is granted save substances and their modifications. Therefore nothing can exist or be conceived without God. *Q.e.d.*

PROP. XVI. Infinite things in infinite modes must necessarily follow from the necessity of divine nature.

Proof.—This proposition must be manifest to every one who will but consider this, that from a given definition of everything the intellect gathers certain properties, which in truth necessarily follow from the definition, and so the more reality the definition of a thing expresses, i.e., the more reality the essence of a definite thing involves, the more properties the intellect will gather. But as divine nature has absolutely infinite attributes, each of which expresses infinite essence in its kind, infinite things in infinite modes must necessarily follow its necessity. *Q.e.d.*

Corollary I.—Hence it follows that God is the effecting cause of all things which can be perceived by infinite intellect.

Corollary II.—Hence it follows that God is the cause through himself, and not indeed by accident.

Corollary III.—Hence it follows that God is absolutely the first cause.

PROP. XVII. God acts merely according to his own laws, and is compelled by no one.

Proof.—That infinite things must follow from the mere necessity of divine nature, or what is the same thing, by the mere laws of divine nature, we have just shown, and we have shown that nothing can be conceived without God, but that everything exists in God. Therefore nothing outside God can exist by which he could be determined or compelled in his actions; and therefore God acts merely according to the laws of his nature, and is compelled by no one. *Q.e.d.*

Corollary I.—Hence it follows that no cause can be given except the perfection of God's nature which extrinsically or intrinsically incites him to action.

Corollary II.—Hence it follows that God alone is a free cause. For God alone exists from the mere necessity of his own nature, and by the mere necessity of his nature he acts. And therefore he is the only free cause. *Q.e.d.*

PROP. XVIII. God is the indwelling and not the transient cause of all things.

Proof.—All things that are, are in God, and through God must be conceived, and therefore God is the cause of all things which are in him: which is the first point. Again, beyond God no substance, that is, a thing which outside God is in itself, can be granted: which was the second point. Therefore God is the indwelling and not the transient cause of all things. *Q.e.d.*

PROP. XIX. God and all the attributes of God are eternal.

Proof.—God is a substance, which necessarily exists, that is, to whose nature existence appertains, or from whose definition existence itself follows: accordingly it is eternal. Again, by the attributes of God must be understood that which expresses the essence of divine substance, that is, that which appertains to substance: that itself, I say, must involve the attributes themselves. But eternity appertains to the nature of substance. Therefore each of the attributes must involve eternity, and therefore they are all eternal. *Q.e.d.*

PROP. XX. God's existence and his essence are one and the same thing.

Proof.—God and all his attributes are eternal, that is, each of his attributes expresses existence. Therefore the same attributes of God, which explain the eternal essence of God, explain at the same time his existence, that is, whatever forms the essence of God, forms also his existence: therefore the essence and existence of God are one and the same thing. *Q.e.d.*

Corollary I.—Hence it follows that the existence of God, like his essence, is an eternal truth.

Corollary II.—Hence it follows that God and all his attributes are immutable. For if they were changed with regard to existence, they must also be changed with regard to essence, that is, falsehood would be made from truth, which is absurd.

PROP. XXI. All things which follow from the absolute nature of any attribute of God must exist for ever and infinitely, or must exist eternally and infinitely through that same attribute.

Proof.—Conceive, if it can happen, that anything in any attribute of God following from its absolute nature is finite and has a fixed existence or duration, e.g., the idea of God in thought. But thought, since it is supposed an attribute of God, is necessarily infinite in its nature. In so far as it has the idea of God, it is supposed to be finite. But it cannot be conceived finite unless it is limited by thought itself; but it cannot be limited by thought in so far as it forms the idea of God, for then it would be finite: so it must be limited by thought in so far as it does not form the idea of God, and this idea nevertheless must exist necessarily. A thought is therefore granted which does not form an idea of God, and therefore from its nature, in so far as it is an absolute thought, the idea of God does not necessarily follow: thought is then conceived as forming and not forming the idea of God, which is contrary to the hypothesis. So if the idea of God in thought or anything in any attribute of God follows from the necessity of the absolute nature of that attribute, it must of necessity be infinite: which is the first point.

Again, that which follows from the necessity of the nature of any attribute cannot have a fixed duration. If you deny this, let something which follows from the necessity of the nature of any attribute be supposed to be granted in any attribute of God, e.g., the idea of God in thought, and let it be supposed either not to have existed at some past time, or to cease to exist in some future time. But since thought is supposed to be an attribute of God, it must of necessity exist, and that immutably. Thence it follows that outside the limits of the duration of the idea of God, thought must exist without the idea of God: and this is contrary to the hypothesis, for it is supposed that the idea of God necessarily follows from the given thought. Therefore the idea of God in thought or anything that follows of necessity from the absolute nature of any attribute of God cannot have a fixed duration, but through the attribute itself is eternal: which was the second point. Note that this can be asserted of anything which in any attribute of God follows of necessity from the absolute nature of God.

PROP. XXII. Whatever follows from an attribute of God, in so far as it is modified by such a modification as exists of necessity and infinitely through the same, must also exist of necessity and infinitely.

Proof.—The proof of this proposition proceeds in the same manner as the proof of the last proposition.

PROP. XXIII. Every mode which of necessity and infinitely exists must of necessity have followed either from the absolute nature of some attribute of God, or from some attribute modified by a modification which exists of necessity and infinitely.

Proof.—Now mode is in something else through which it must be conceived, that is, it is in God alone, and can only be conceived through God. If, therefore, mode be conceived to exist of necessity and to be infinite, its existence and infinity must be concluded or perceived through some attribute of God, in so far as this attribute is conceived to express infinity and necessity of existence, or eternity, that is, as far as it is considered absolutely. Mode, therefore, which of necessity and infinitely exists, must have followed from the absolute nature of some attribute of God, and that either immediately or by means of some modification which follows from the absolute nature of the attribute, that is, which necessarily and infinitely exists. *Q.e.d*.

PROP. XXIV. The essence of things produced by God does not involve existence.

Proof.—This is clear from Def. 1. For that whose nature involves existence is its own cause, and exists merely by the necessity of its own nature.

Corollary.—Hence it follows that God is not only the cause that all things begin to exist, but also that they continue to exist, or God is the cause of the being of things. For whether things exist or whether they do not, however often we consider their essence, we will find it to involve neither existence nor duration; and their essence cannot be the cause either of their existence or their duration, but only God, to whose nature alone existence appertains.

Prop. XXV. God is not only the effecting cause of the existence of things, but also of their essence.

Proof.—If you deny it, then let God be not the cause of the essence of things: therefore the essence of things can be conceived without God. But this is absurd. Therefore God is the cause of the essence of things. *Q.e.d.*

Corollary.—Particular things are nothing else than modifications of attributes of God, or modes by which attributes of God are expressed in a certain and determined manner.

Prop. XXVI. A thing which is determined for the performing of anything was so determined necessarily by God, and a thing which is not determined by God cannot determine of itself to do anything.

Proof.—That through which things are said to be determined for performing anything must necessarily be something positive: and therefore God, by the necessity of his nature, is the effecting cause of the essence and existence of this: which was the first point. From which clearly follows that which was proposed in the second place. For if a thing which is not determined by God could determine itself, the first part of this proof would be false: which is absurd, as we have shown.

Prop. XXVII. A thing which is determined by God for the performing of anything cannot render itself undetermined.

Proof.—This is obvious from the third axiom.

Prop. XXVIII. Every individual thing, or whatever thing that is finite and has a determined existence, cannot exist nor be determined for action unless it is determined for action and existence by another cause which is also finite and has a determined existence; and again, this cause also cannot exist nor be determined for action unless it be determined for existence and action by another cause which also is finite and has a determined existence: and so on to infinity.

Proof.—Whatever is determined for existence or action is so determined by God. But that which is finite and has a determined existence cannot be produced from the absolute nature of any attribute of God: for anything that follows from the absolute nature of any attribute of God must be infinite and eternal. It must have followed, therefore, either from God or some attribute of his, in so far as it is considered as modified in some mode: for save substance and modes nothing is granted, and modes are nothing else than modifications of attributes of God. But it also cannot have followed from God or any attribute of his, in so far as it is modified by some modification which is eternal and infinite. It follows, then, that it must have been determined for existence or action by God or some attribute of his, in so far as it is modified by a modification which is finite and has a determined existence: which was the first point. Then again, this cause or mode must also have been determined by another cause which also is finite and has a determined existence; and again, the latter must have been determined by another: and so on to infinity. *Q.e.d.*

PROP. XXIX. In the nature of things nothing contingent is granted, but all things are determined by the necessity of divine nature for existing and working in a certain way.

Proof.—Whatever is, is in God. But God cannot be called a contingent thing: for he exists of necessity and not contingently. Again, the modes of divine nature do not follow from it contingently, but of necessity, and that either in so far as divine nature be considered absolutely or as determined for certain action. Now God is the cause of these modes, not only in so far as they simply exist, but also in so far as they are considered as determined for the working of anything. For if they are not determined by God, it is impossible, not contingent indeed, that they should determine themselves; and on the other hand, if they are determined by God, it is impossible and in no wise contingent for them to render themselves undetermined. Wherefore all things are determined by the necessity of divine nature, not only for existing, but also for existing and working after a certain manner, and nothing contingent is granted. *Q.e.d.*

PROP. XXX. Intellect, finite or infinite in actuality, must comprehend the attributes of God and the modifications of God and nothing else.

Proof.—A true idea must agree with its ideal, that is, that which is contained in the intellect objectively must of necessity be granted in nature. But in nature, only one substance can be granted, and that is God, and only such modifications can be granted as are in God and cannot exist or be conceived without God. Therefore, intellect finite or infinite in actuality must comprehend the attributes and modifications of God and nothing else. *Q.e.d.*

PROP. XXXI. The intellect in actuality, whether it be finite or infinite, as will, desire, love, etc., must be referred not to active, but passive nature.

Proof.—Now by intellect we do not understand absolute thought, but only a certain mode of thinking which differs from other modes, such as desire and love, etc., and therefore must be conceived through absolute thought; moreover, it must be so conceived through some attribute of God which expresses eternal and infinite essence of thought, that without it, it can neither exist nor be conceived. On this account, like the other modes of thinking, the intellect must be referred not to active but passive nature. *Q.e.d.*

PROP. XXXII. Will can only be called a necessary cause, not a free one.

Proof.—Will, like intellect, is only a certain mode of thinking, and therefore any single volition cannot exist or be determined for perform-ing anything unless it be determined by some other cause, and this one again by another, and so on to infinity. Now if will be supposed infinite, it must then be determined for existence and action by God, in so far, not as he is an infinite substance, but as he has an attribute expressing infinite and eternal essence of thought. So in whatever way it be conceived, whether as finite or infinite, it requires a cause by which it is determined for existence or action: and therefore it cannot be said to be a free cause, but only a necessary one. *Q.e.d.*

Corollary I.—Hence it follows that God does not act from freedom of will.

Corollary II.—Hence it follows again that will and intellect hold the same place in the nature of God as motion and rest, and that, absolutely, as with all natural things which must be determined by God in a certain way for existence and action. For will, like all other things, needs a cause by which it is determined in a certain way for existence or action. And although from a given will or intellect infinite things follow, yet it cannot be said on that account that God acts from freedom of will any more than it can be said that, as infinite things follow from motion and rest, God acts from freedom of motion and rest. Wherefore will does not appertain to the nature of God any more than the rest of the things of nature, but holds the same place in God's nature as motion and rest, and all other things which we have shown to follow from the necessity of divine nature, and to be determined by it for existence and action in a certain way.

PROP. XXXIII. Things could not have been produced by God in any other manner or order than that in which they were produced.

Proof.—All things must have followed of necessity from a given nature of God, and they were determined for existence or action in a certain way by the necessity of divine nature. And so if things could have been of another nature or determined in another manner for action so that the order of nature were different, therefore, also, the nature of God could be different than it is now: then another nature of God must exist, and consequently two or more Gods could be granted, and this is absurd. Wherefore things could not have been produced in any other way or order, etc. *Q.e.d.*

PROP. XXXIV. The power of God is the same as his essence.

Proof.—It follows from the mere necessity of the essence of God that God is his own cause, and the cause of all things. Therefore the power of God, by which he and all things are and act, is the same as his essence. *Q.e.d.*

PROP. XXXV. Whatever we conceive to be in the power of God necessarily exists.

Proof.—Now whatever is in the power of God must be so comprehended in his essence that it follows necessarily from it, and so it necessarily exists. *Q.e.d.*

PROP. XXXVI. Nothing exists from whose nature some effect does not follow.

Proof.—Whatever exists expresses in a certain and determined manner either the nature or essence of God, that is, whatever exists expresses in a certain and determined way the power of God, which is the cause of all things, and therefore from it some effect must follow. *Q.e.d.*

SECOND PART: CONCERNING THE NATURE AND ORIGIN OF THE MIND

DEFINITIONS

I. BY BODY I understand that mode which expresses in a certain determined manner the essence of God in so far as he is considered as an extended thing.

II. I say that appertains to the essence of a thing which, when granted, necessarily involves the granting of the thing, and which, when removed, necessarily involves the removal of the thing; or that without which the thing, or on the other hand, which without the thing can neither exist nor be conceived.

III. By IDEA I understand a conception of the mind which the mind forms by reason of its being a thinking thing.

IV. By an ADEQUATE IDEA I understand an idea which in so far as it is considered without respect to the object, has all the properties or intrinsic marks of a true idea.

V. DURATION is indefinite continuation of existing.

VI. REALITY and PERFECTION I understand to be one and the same thing.

VII. By INDIVIDUAL THINGS I understand things which are finite and have a determined existence; but if several of them so concur in one

action that they all are at the same time the cause of one effect, I consider them all thus far as one individual thing.

AXIOMS

I. The essence of man does not involve necessary existence, that is,
in the order of nature it can equally happen that this or that man exists as
that he does not exist.

II. Man thinks.

III. The modes of thinking, such as love, desire, or any other name
by which the modifications of the mind are designated, are not granted
unless an idea in the same individual is granted of the thing loved, desired, etc. But the idea can be granted although no other mode of thinking be granted.

IV. We feel that a certain body is affected in many ways.

V. We neither feel nor perceive any individual things save bodies
and modes of thinking. For Postulates, see after Prop. 13.

PROPOSITIONS

PROP. I. Thought is an attribute of God, or God is a thinking thing.

Proof.—Individual thoughts or this and that thought are modes
which express in a certain and determined manner the nature of God. The
attribute whose conception all individual thoughts involve and through
which they are conceived, belongs to God. Thought, therefore, is one of
the infinite attributes of God which express the eternal and infinite essence of God, or God is a thinking thing. *Q.e.d.*

PROP. II. Extension is an attribute of God, or God is an extended thing.

Proof.—This proof proceeds in the same manner as that of the previous proposition.

PROP. III. In God there is granted not only the idea of his essence, but
also the idea of all the things which follow necessarily from his essence.

Proof.—God can think infinite things in infinite modes, or he can
form an idea of his essence and of all things which follow from it. Now
all that is in the power of God necessarily exists. Therefore such an idea
is granted, and that only in God. *Q.e.d.*

PROP. IV. The idea of God from which infinite things in infinite
modes follow can only be one.

Proof.—Infinite intellect comprehends nothing save the attributes and modifications of God. God is one. Therefore the idea of God from which infinite things in infinite modes follow can only be one. *Q.e.d.*

PROP. V. The formal being of ideas acknowledges God as its cause only in so far as he is considered as a thinking thing, and not in so far as he is revealed in some other attribute: that is, the ideas, not only of the attributes of God, but also of individual things, do not acknowledge their ideals or the objects perceived as their effecting cause, but God himself in so far as he is a thinking thing.

Proof.—This is obvious from Prop. 3 of this part. For there we concluded that God can form an idea of his essence and of all things which follow therefrom necessarily, and that from this alone that he is a thinking thing, and not from the fact that he is the object of his idea. Wherefore the formal being of ideas acknowledges God for its cause in so far as he is a thinking thing. But this can be shown in another manner. The formal being of ideas is a mode of thinking, that is, a mode which expresses in a certain manner the nature of God in so far as he is a thinking thing, and therefore involves the conception of no other attribute of God, and consequently is the effect of no other attribute or thought. Therefore the formal being of ideas acknowledges God as its cause in so far as he is a thinking thing, etc. *Q.e.d.*

PROP. VI. The modes of any attribute of God have God for their cause only in so far as he is considered through that attribute, and not in so far as he is considered through any other attribute.

Proof.—Each attribute is conceived through itself without the aid of another. Wherefore the modes of each attribute involve the conception of their attribute and not that of another; and so the modes of any attribute of God have God for their cause only in so far as he is considered through that attribute, and not in so far as he is considered through any other attribute. *Q.e.d.*

Corollary.—Hence it follows that the formal being of things which are not modes of thinking does not follow from divine nature because it knows things prior to it; but things conceived follow and are concluded from their attributes in the same manner and by the same necessity as we have shown ideas to follow from their attribute of thought.

PROP. VII. The order and connection of ideas is the same as the order and connection of things.

Proof.—This is clear from Ax. 4, Part I. For the idea of everything that is caused depends on the knowledge of the cause of which it is an effect.

Corollary.—Hence it follows that God's power of thinking is equal to his actual power of acting: that is, whatever follows formally from the infinite nature of God, follows also invariably objectively from the idea of God in the same order and connection.

Note.—Before we proceed any further, let us call to mind what we have already shown above: that whatever can be perceived by infinite intellect as constituting the essence of substance, invariably appertains to one substance alone; and consequently thinking substance and extended substance are one and the same thing, which is now comprehended through this and now through that attribute. For example, a circle existing in nature and the idea of an existing circle which is also in God is one and the same thing, though explained through different attributes.

Prop. VIII. The ideas of individual things or modes which do not exist must be comprehended in the infinite idea of God in the same way as the formal essences of individual things or modes are contained in the attributes of God.

Proof.—This proposition is clear from the preceding note.

Corollary.—Hence it follows that as long as individual things do not exist save in so far as they are comprehended in the attributes of God, their objective being or ideas do not exist save in so far as the infinite idea of God exists; and when individual things are said to exist not only in so far as they are comprehended in the attributes of God, but also in so far as they are said to last, their ideas also involve existence, through which they are said to last.

Prop. IX. The idea of an individual thing actually existing has God for its cause, not in so far as he is infinite, but in so far as he is considered as affected by the idea of another individual thing actually existing of which also God is the cause, in so far as he is affected by another third idea, and so on to infinity.

Proof.—The idea of an individual thing actually existing is an individual mode of thinking and distinct from all others; and therefore has God, in so far only as he is a thinking thing, for its cause. But not in so far as he is a thing thinking absolutely, but in so far as he is considered as affected by another mode of thinking, and again he is the cause of this in so far as he is affected by a third, and so on to infinity. And the order and connection of ideas is the same as the order and connection of causes. Therefore the cause of an individual thing is either another idea or God in so far as he is considered as affected by the other idea: and of this idea God is the cause in so far as he is affected by another idea, and so on to infinity. *Q.e.d.*

Corollary.—The knowledge of whatever happens in the individual object of any idea has its knowledge in God, but only in so far as he has the idea of the object.

Proof.—Whatever happens in the object of any idea has its idea in God, not in so far as he is infinite, but only in so far as he is considered as affected by another idea of an individual thing, but the order and connection of ideas is the same as the order and connection of things. Therefore the knowledge of that which happens in any individual object is in God in so far only as he has the idea of the object. *Q.e.d.*

PROP. X. The being of substance does not appertain to the essence of man, or, again, substance does not constitute the form of man.

Proof.—The being of substance involves necessary existence. If therefore the being of substance appertains to the essence of man, substance being granted, man also must necessarily be granted, and consequently man must necessarily exist, which is absurd. Therefore, etc. *Q.e.d.*

Corollary.—Hence it follows that the essence of man is constituted by certain modifications of attributes of God. For the being of substance does not appertain to the essence of man. The latter is therefore something that is in God and which cannot exist or be conceived without God, whether it be a modification or a mode that expresses the nature of God in a certain determined manner.

PROP. XI. The first part which constitutes the actual being of the human mind is nothing else than the idea of an individual thing actually existing.

Proof.—The essence of man is constituted by certain modes of attributes of God; that is, by certain modes of thinking, of all which the idea is prior in nature, and this idea being granted the remaining modes must be in the same individual. And therefore the idea is the first part that constitutes the being of the human mind, but not the idea of a thing not existing: for then that very idea cannot be said to exist. It must therefore be the idea of a thing actually existing. But not of a thing infinite. For an infinite thing must always necessarily exist. But this is absurd. Therefore the first part which constitutes the actual being of the human mind is the idea of an individual thing actually existing. *Q.e.d.*

Corollary.—Hence it follows that the human mind is a part of the infinite intellect of God, and thus when we say that the human mind perceives this or that, we say nothing else than that God, not in so far as he is infinite, but in so far as he is explained through the nature of the human mind, or in so far as he constitutes the essence of the human mind, has this or that idea: and when we say that God has this or that idea not only in so far as he constitutes the nature of the human mind, but also in so far simultaneously with the human mind as he has also the idea of another thing, then we say that the human mind perceives the thing only in part or inadequately.

PROP. XII. Whatever happens in the object of the idea constituting the human mind must be perceived by the human mind, or the idea of that thing must necessarily be found in the human mind: that is, if the object of the idea constituting the human mind be the body, nothing can happen in that body which is not perceived by the mind.

Proof.—Now whatever happens in the object of any idea, the knowledge of it is necessarily granted in God in so far as he is considered as affected by the idea of that object, that is, in so far as he constitutes the mind of anything. Therefore whatever happens in the object of an idea constituting the human mind, knowledge of it must be granted in God in so far as he constitutes the nature of the human mind, that is, the knowledge of this thing will be necessarily in the mind or the mind will perceive it. *Q.e.d.*

PROP. XIII. The object of the idea constituting the human mind is the body, or a certain mode of extension actually existing and nothing else.

Proof.—Now if the body is not the object of the human mind, the ideas of the modifications of the body would not be in God in so far as he constitutes our mind or the mind of some other thing, that is, the ideas of the modifications of the body would not be in our mind. But we have ideas of the modifications of the body. Therefore the object of the idea constituting the human mind is the body, and that actually existing. Further, if there were still another object of the mind besides the body, then since nothing can exist from which some effect does not follow, therefore necessarily there would be found in our mind an idea the effect of that object. But no idea of this is found. Therefore the object of our mind is the existing body and nothing else. *Q.e.d.*

Corollary.—Hence it follows that man consists of mind and body, and that the human body exists according as we feel it.

At this point I must premise a few statements concerning the nature of bodies.

AXIOM I. All bodies are either moving or stationary.

AXIOM II. Each body is moved now slowly now more fast.

LEMMA I. Bodies are reciprocally distinguished with respect to motion or rest, quickness or slowness, and not with respect to substance.

Proof.—The first part of this proposition I suppose to be clear of itself. But that bodies should not be distinguished one from the other with respect to substance, is obvious both from Prop. 5 and Prop. 8, Part I.

LEMMA II. All bodies agree in certain respects.

Proof.—All bodies agree in this, that they involve the conception of one and the same attribute: and again, that they may be moved more quickly or more slowly or be absolutely in motion or absolutely stationary.

LEMMA III. A body in motion or at rest must be determined for motion or rest by some other body, which, likewise, was determined for motion or rest by some other body, and this by a third, and so on to infinity.

Proof.—Bodies are individual things, which are distinguished reciprocally with respect to motion or rest: and, therefore, each must necessarily be determined for motion or rest by some other individual thing, that is, by another body, which also is either in motion or at rest. But this one also, by the same reason, cannot be in motion or at rest unless it was determined for motion or rest by another body, and that again by another, and so on to infinity. *Q.e.d.*

Corollary.—Hence it follows that a moving body continues in motion until it is determined for rest by another body; and that a body at rest continues so until it is determined by another body for motion. This is self-evident. For if I suppose a given body A to be at rest and pay not attention to other moving bodies, I can say nothing concerning the body A save that it is at rest. And if it afterwards comes about that the body A moves, it clearly could not have been brought into motion by the fact that it was at rest: for from this it could only follow that it should remain at rest. If, on the other hand, the body A be supposed in motion, as long as we only have regard to the body A we can assert nothing concerning it save that it is in motion. And if it subsequently comes to pass that the body A comes to rest, it also clearly cannot have evolved from the motion which it had: for from this nothing else can follow than that A should be moved. It therefore comes to pass from something that was not in A, that is, from an external cause, that it was determined for rest.

AXIOM I. All modes in which any body is affected by another follow alike from the nature of the body affected and the body affecting: so that one and the same body may be moved in various ways according to the variety of the natures of the moving bodies, and, on the other hand, various bodies may be moved in various manners by one and the same body.

AXIOM II. When a moving body impinges another body at rest which cannot move, it recoils in order to continue to move: and the angle of the line of recoiling motion with the plane of the body at rest which it impinged will be equal to the angle which the line of the motion of incidence made with the same plane.

Thus far we have been speaking of the most simple bodies, which are distinguished reciprocally merely by motion or rest, by swiftness or slowness: now we pass on to compound bodies.

Definition.—When a number of bodies of the same or different size are driven so together that they remain united one with the other, or if they are moved with the same or different rapidity so that they communicate their motions one to another in a certain ratio, those bodies are called reciprocally united bodies, and we say that they all form one body or individual, which is distinguished from the rest by this union of the bodies.

AXIOM III. According as the parts of an individual or compound body are united on a greater or less surface so the greater is the difficulty or facility with which they are forced to change their position and, consequently, the greater the difficulty or facility with which it is brought about that they assume another form. And hence those bodies whose parts are united over a large surface I shall call hard, and those whose parts are united over a small surface are called soft, and those whose parts are in motion among each other are called fluid.

LEMMA IV. If from a body or individual which is composed of several bodies certain ones are removed, and at the same time the same number of bodies of the same nature succeed to their place, the individual will retain its nature as before without any change of its form.

Proof.—Now bodies are not distinguished with respect to substance. But that which constitutes the form of an individual consists of a union of bodies. But this union, although the change of bodies continue, is retained: the individual will therefore retain as before its nature both with respect to substance and mode. *Q.e.d.*

LEMMA V. If the parts composing an individual become larger or smaller, but in such proportion that they preserve between themselves with respect to motion and rest the same ratio as before, the individual will retain its nature as before without any change of form.

Proof.—This is the same as that of the previous lemma.

LEMMA VI. If certain bodies composing an individual are forced to change their motion which they had in one direction into another, but in such a manner that they can continue their motion and preserve one with the other the same ratio with respect to motion and rest as before, the individual will retain its nature without any change of form.

Proof.—This is self-evident. For it is supposed to retain all that which in its definition we said constituted its form.

LEMMA VII. Moreover, the individual thus composed retains its nature whether as a whole it be moved or remain at rest, whether it be moved in this or that direction, provided that each part retains its motion and communicates it as before to the other parts.

Proof.—This is clear from its definition, which see before.

POSTULATES

I. The human body is composed of many individuals (of different nature), each one of which is also composed of many parts.

II. The individuals of which the human body is composed are some fluid, some soft, and some hard.

III. The individuals composing the human body, and consequently the human body itself, are affected in many ways by external bodies.

IV. The human body needs for its preservation many other bodies from which it is, so to speak, regenerated.

V. When the fluid part of the human body is so determined by an external body that it impinges frequently on another part which is soft, it changes its surface and imprints such marks on it as the traces of an external impelling body.

VI. The human body can move external bodies in many ways, and dispose them in many ways.

PROP. XIV. The human mind is apt to perceive many things, and more so according as its body can be disposed in more ways.

Proof.—Now the human body is affected by external bodies in many ways and disposed to affect external bodies in many ways. But the human mind must perceive all things which happen in the human body. Therefore the human mind is apt to perceive many things, and more so, etc. *Q.e.d.*

PROP. XV. The idea which constitutes the formal being of the human mind is not simple, but composed of many ideas.

Proof.—The idea which constitutes the formal being of the human mind is the idea of the body, which is composed of many individuals, each composed of many parts. But the idea of each individual composing the body is necessarily granted in God. Therefore the idea of the human body is composed of the many ideas of the component parts. *Q.e.d.*

PROP. XVI. The idea of every mode in which the human body is affected by external bodies must involve the nature of the human body and at the same time the nature of the external body.

Proof.—All modes in which any body is affected follow from the nature of the body affected, and at the same time from the nature of the affecting body. Wherefore the idea of them must involve necessarily the nature of each body. Therefore the idea of each mode in which the human body is affected by an external body involves the nature of the human body and that of the external body. *Q.e.d.*

Corollary I.—Hence it follows in the first place that the human mind can perceive the nature of many bodies at the same time as the nature of its own body.

Corollary II.—It follows in the second place that the ideas which we have of external bodies indicate rather the disposition of our body than the nature of the external bodies.

Prop. XVII. If the human body is affected in a mode which involves the nature of any external body, the human mind regards that external body as actually existing, or as present to itself until the body is affected by a modification which cuts off the existence or presence of that body.

Proof.—This is clear. For as long as the human body is thus affected, so long does the human mind regard this modification of the body; that is, it has the idea of the mode actually existing, and the idea involves the nature of the external body, that is, it has an idea which does not cut off the existence or presence of the nature of the external, but imposes it. Therefore the mind regards the external body as actually existing or present, until it is affected, etc. *Q.e.d.*

Corollary.—The mind can regard external bodies by which the human body was once affected, although they do not exist, nor are present, as if they were present.

Proof.—When external bodies so determine the fluid parts of the human body that they often impinge the soft parts, they change the surface of them. Whence it comes about that they are reflected thence in a different manner than before, and as afterwards they impinge on new surfaces by their spontaneous movement, they are reflected in the same manner as if they were driven towards those surfaces by external bodies, and consequently while they continue to be reflected they will affect the human body in the same manner, and the human mind will again think of external bodies, that is, the human mind will regard the external body as present, and that as long as the fluid parts of the human body impinge the same surfaces by their spontaneous motion. Wherefore although the external bodies by which the human body was once affected no longer exist, the mind nevertheless regards them as present as often as this action of the body is repeated. *Q.e.d.*

Prop. XVIII. If the human body has once been affected at the same time by two or more bodies, when the mind afterwards remembers any one of them it will straightway remember the others.

Proof.—The mind imagines any body for this reason, that the human body is affected and disposed by impressions of an external body in the same way as it is affected when certain parts of it are affected by the same external body. But the body was then so disposed that the mind imagined two bodies at once. Therefore it will imagine two bodies at the same time, and the mind when it imagines one of them will also straightway recall the other. *Q.e.d.*

Prop. XIX. The human mind has no knowledge of the human body, nor does it know it to exist save through ideas of modifications by which the body is affected.

Proof.—The human mind is the very idea or knowledge of the human body, which is in God in so far as he is considered as affected by another idea of an individual thing: or because the human body needs many bodies from which it is continuously regenerated, so to speak, and the order and connection of ideas is the same as the order and connection of causes this idea will be in God in so far as he is considered as affected by the ideas of several individual things. God, therefore, has the idea of the human body, or has a knowledge of the human body, in so far as he is considered as affected by many other ideas and not in so far as he con-stitutes the nature of the human mind, that is, the human mind has no knowledge of the human body. But the ideas of the modifications of the human body are in God, in so far as he constitutes the nature of the human mind, or the human mind perceives those modifications, and con-sequently the human body itself, and that as actually existing. The human mind, therefore, perceives only thus far the human body. *Q.e.d.*

PROP. XX. The idea or knowledge of the human mind is granted in God and follows in God, and is referred to him in the same manner as the idea or knowledge of the human body.

Proof.—Thought is an attribute of God, and therefore the idea of this and of all its modifications, and consequently of the human mind, must necessarily be granted in God. Now this idea or knowledge of the human mind is not granted in God in so far as he is infinite, but in so far as he is affected by another idea of an individual thing. But the order and connection of ideas is the same as the order and connection of causes. It follows, therefore, that this idea or knowledge of the human mind is in God and is referred to God in the same manner as the knowledge or idea of the human body. *Q.e.d.*

PROP. XXI. This idea of the mind is united to the mind in the same manner as the mind is united to the body.

Proof.—That the mind is united to the body we have shown from the fact that the body is the object of the mind; and therefore by that same reason the idea of the mind is united to its object, that is, the mind itself, in the same manner as the mind is united to the body. *Q.e.d.*

PROP. XXII. The human mind perceives not only the modifications of the body, but also the ideas of these modifications.

Proof.—The ideas of the ideas of modifications follow in God in the same way and are referred to him in the same way as the ideas of modifica-tion. But the ideas of modifications of the body are in the human mind, that is, in God in so far as he constitutes the essence of the human mind. Therefore, the ideas of these ideas are in God, in so far as he has the knowledge or idea of the human mind, that is, in the human mind itself, which therefore perceives not only the modifications of the human body but also the ideas of them. *Q.e.d.*

PROP. XXIII. The mind has no knowledge of itself save in so far as it perceives the ideas of the modifications of the body.

Proof.—The idea or knowledge of the mind follows in God, and is referred to him in the same manner as the idea or knowledge of the body. But since the human mind does not know the human body, that is, since the knowledge of the human body is not referred to God in so far as he constitutes the nature of the human mind, therefore neither is the knowledge of the mind referred to God in so far as he constitutes the essence of the human mind, and therefore the human mind thus far has no knowledge of itself. Then again the ideas of modifications by which the body is affected involve the nature of the human body itself, that is, they agree with the nature of the mind. Wherefore the knowledge of these ideas necessarily involves the knowledge of the mind. But the knowledge of these ideas is in the human mind itself. Therefore the human mind has only thus far a knowledge of itself. *Q.e.d.*

PROP. XXIV. The human mind does not involve an adequate knowledge of the component parts of the human body.

Proof.—The parts composing the human body do not appertain to the essence of that body save in so far as they reciprocally communicate their motions in a certain ratio, and not in so far as they may be considered as individuals without relation to the human body. For the parts of the human body are individuals very complex, the parts of which can be taken away from the human body without harm to the nature or form of it, and can communicate their motions to other bodies in another ratio. And therefore the idea or knowledge of each part will be in God in so far as he is considered as affected by another idea of an individual thing which is prior in the order of nature to that part. This also can be said of any part of the individual component of the human body, and therefore the knowledge of each component part of the human body is in God in so far as he is affected by many ideas of things, and not in so far as he has only the idea of the human body, that is, the idea which constitutes the nature of the human mind. And therefore the human mind does not involve an adequate knowledge of the component parts of the human body. *Q.e.d.*

PROP. XXV. The idea of each modification of the human body does not involve an adequate knowledge of the external body.

Proof.—We have shown that the idea of the modification of the human body involves the nature of the external body in so far as the external body determines the human body in a certain way. But in so far as the external body is an individual which has no reference to the human body, its idea or knowledge is in God in so far as God is considered as affected by the idea of the other thing which is by nature prior to the external body. Therefore adequate knowledge of the external body is not in God in so far as he has the idea of the modification of the human body, or the idea of the modification of the human body does not involve adequate knowledge of the external body. *Q.e.d.*

PROP. XXVI. The human mind perceives no external body as actually existing save through ideas of modifications of its body.

Proof.—If the human body is affected in no way by any external body, then neither is the idea of the human body, that is, the human mind, affected in any wise by the idea of the existence of the external body, or, in other words, it does not perceive in any way the existence of that external body. But in so far as the human body is affected in any way by any external body, thus far it perceives the external body. *Q.e.d.*

Corollary.—In so far as the human mind imagines an external body, thus far it has no adequate knowledge of it.

Proof.—When the human mind regards external bodies through the ideas of the modifications of its own body, we say it imagines: nor can the human mind in any other way imagine external bodies as actually existing. And therefore in so far as the mind imagines external bodies, it has no adequate knowledge of them. *Q.e.d.*

PROP. XXVII. The idea of each modification of the human body does not involve adequate knowledge of the human body itself.

Proof.—Any idea of each modification of the human body involves the nature of the human body in so far as the human body itself is considered to be affected in a certain manner. But in so far as the human body is an individual which can be affected in many other ways, the idea of the modification, etc.

PROP. XXVIII. The ideas of the modifications of the human body, in so far as they are referred to the human mind alone, are not clear and distinct but confused.

Proof.—The ideas of the modifications of the human body involve both the nature of the external bodies and that of the human body itself: and not only must they involve the nature of the human body, but also that of its parts. For modifications are modes in which parts of the human body, and consequently the whole body, is affected. But adequate knowledge of external bodies, as also of the parts composing the human body, is not in God in so far as he is considered as affected by the human mind, but in so far as he is considered as affected by other ideas. These ideas of modifications, in so far as they have reference to the human mind alone, are like consequences without premises, that is, confused ideas. *Q.e.d.*

PROP. XXIX. The idea of the idea of each modification of the human mind does not involve adequate knowledge of the human mind.

Proof.—The idea of a modification of the human body does not involve adequate knowledge of the body itself, or, in other words, does not express its nature adequately, that is, it does not agree adequately with the nature of the mind. And therefore the idea of this idea does not adequately express the nature of the human mind, or does not involve adequate knowledge of it. *Q.e.d.*

Corollary.—Hence it follows that the human mind, whenever it perceives a thing in the common order of nature, has no adequate knowledge of itself, nor of its body, nor of external bodies, but only a confused and mutilated knowledge thereof. For the mind knows not itself save in so far as it perceives ideas of modifications of the body. But it does not perceive its body save through the ideas of modifications, through which also it only perceives external bodies. And therefore in so far as it has these ideas it has no adequate knowledge of itself, nor of its body, nor of external bodies, but only a confused and mutilated one. *Q.e.d.*

PROP. XXX. We can have only a very inadequate knowledge of the duration of our body.

Proof.—The duration of our body does not depend on its essence, nor even on the absolute nature of God; but it is determined for existence and action by certain causes, which are in their turn determined for existing and acting in a certain determined ratio by other causes, and these by others, and so on to infinity. Therefore the duration of our body depends on the common order of nature and the disposition of things. But there is in God an adequate knowledge of the reason why things are disposed in any particular way, in so far as he has ideas of all things, and not in so far as he has only a knowledge of the human body. Wherefore the knowledge of the duration of our body is very inadequate in God in so far as he is considered as constituting only the nature of the human mind, that is, this knowledge is very inadequate in our mind. *Q.e.d.*

PROP. XXXI. We can only have a very inadequate knowledge of individual things which are outside us.

Proof.—Each individual thing, such as the human body, must be determined for existence or action in a certain manner by another individual thing: and this again by another, and so on to infinity. But as we have shown in the previous proposition that we can only have a very inadequate knowledge of the duration of our body, owing to this common property of individual things, so this must also be concluded concerning the duration of individual things, i.e., that we can only have a very inadequate knowledge thereof. *Q.e.d.*

Corollary.—Hence it follows that all individual things are contingent and corruptible. For we can have no adequate knowledge concerning their duration, and this is what must be understood by the contingency of things and their liability to corruption. For, save this, nothing is granted to be contingent.

PROP. XXXII. All ideas, in so far as they have reference to God, are true.

Proof.—Now all ideas which are in God must entirely agree with their ideals: and therefore they are true. *Q.e.d.*

PROP. XXXIII. There is nothing positive in ideas, wherefore they could be called false.

Proof.—If you deny this, conceive, if possible, a positive mode of thinking which would constitute the form of error or falsity. This mode of thinking cannot be in God, and outside God it cannot exist or be conceived. Therefore there is nothing positive in ideas, wherefore they could be called false. *Q.e.d.*

PROP. XXXIV. Every idea in us which is absolute, or adequate and perfect, is true.

Proof.—When we say that an adequate and perfect idea is granted in us, we say nothing else than that there is granted in God an adequate and perfect idea in so far as he constitutes the essence of our mind, and consequently we say nothing else than that such an idea is true. *Q.e.d.*

PROP. XXXV. Falsity consists in privation of knowledge which is involved by inadequate or mutilated and confused ideas.

Proof.—Nothing positive is granted in ideas which could constitute their form of falsity. But falsity cannot consist in mere privation, nor in mere ignorance: for ignorance and error are two different things. Wherefore it consists in the privation of knowledge which is involved by inadequate knowledge or inadequate or confused ideas. *Q.e.d.*

PROP. XXXVI. Inadequate and confused ideas follow from the same necessity as adequate or clear and distinct ideas.

Proof.—All ideas are in God, and in so far as they have reference to God, they are true and adequate; and therefore none are inadequate or confused save in so far as they have reference to the individual mind of any one. And therefore all ideas, both adequate and inadequate, follow together from the same necessity. *Q.e.d.*

PROP. XXXVII. That which is common to all, and that which is equally in a part and in the whole, do not constitute the essence of an individual thing.

Proof.—If you deny this, conceive, if it can be, that it does constitute the essence of an individual thing, namely, the essence of B. Then it cannot be conceived nor exist without B. And this is contrary to the hypothesis. Therefore it does not appertain to the essence of B, nor can it constitute the essence of any other individual thing. *Q.e.d.*

PROP. XXXVIII. Those things which are common to all, and which are equally in a part and in the whole, can only be conceived as adequate.

Proof.—Let A be anything that is common to all bodies, and which is equally in one part of any body and in the whole. Then I say that A can only be conceived as adequate. For its idea will necessarily be adequate in God both in so far as he has the idea of the human body, and in so far as he has ideas of its modifications, which involve in part both the nature of the human body and that of external bodies, that is, this idea will necessarily be adequate in God in so far as he constitutes the human mind, or in so far as he has ideas which are in the human mind. Therefore the mind necessarily adequately perceives A, and that both in so far as it perceives itself and its own or an external body: nor can A be conceived in any other manner. *Q.e.d.*

Corollary.—Hence it follows that certain ideas or notions are granted common to all men. For all bodies agree in certain things which must adequately or clearly and distinctly be perceived by all.

PROP. XXXIX. That which is common to and a property of the human body, and certain external bodies by which the human body is used to be affected, and which is equally in the part and whole of these, has an adequate idea in the mind.

Proof.—Let A be that which is common to and a property of the human body and certain external bodies, and which is equally in the human body and in the external bodies, and which also is equally in a part and in the whole of each external body. There will be in God an adequate idea of A, both in so far as he has the idea of the human body, and in so far as he has ideas of the given external bodies. Then let it be granted that the human body is affected by an external one through that which it has in common with it, namely, A. The idea of this modification involves the property A: and therefore the idea of this modification, in so far as it involves the property A, will be adequate in God in so far as he is affected by the idea of the human body, that is, in so far as he constitutes the nature of the human mind. And therefore this idea is also adequate in the human mind. *Q.e.d.*

Corollary.—Hence it follows that the mind is the more apt to perceive many things adequately, the more its body has things in common with other bodies.

Prop. XL. Whatever ideas follow in the mind from ideas which are adequate in the mind, are also adequate.

Proof.—This is clear. For when we say that in the mind ideas follow from other ideas which are adequate in the mind, we say nothing else than that an idea is granted in the divine intellect itself whose cause is God, not in so far as he is infinite nor in so far as he is affected by the ideas of many individual things, but in so far only as he constitutes the essence of the human mind.

Note.—From all that has been said above it is now clearly apparent that we perceive many things and form universal notions, first, from individual things represented to our intellect mutilated, confused, and without order, and therefore we are wont to call such perceptions knowledge from vague or casual experience; second, from signs, e.g., from the fact that we remember certain things through having read or heard certain words and form certain ideas of them similar to those through which we imagine things. Both of these ways of regarding things I shall call hereafter knowledge of the first kind, opinion, or imagination. Third, from the fact that we have common notions and adequate ideas of the properties of things. And I shall call this reason and knowledge of the second kind. Besides these two kinds of knowledge there is a third, as I shall show in what follows, which we shall call intuition.

Prop. XLI. Knowledge of the first kind is the only cause of falsity; knowledge of the second and third kinds is necessarily true.

Proof.—We said in the preceding note that all those ideas which are inadequate and confused appertain to knowledge of the first kind: and therefore this knowledge is the only cause of falsity. Then as for knowledge of the second and third kinds, we said that those ideas which are adequate appertained to it; therefore it is necessarily true. *Q.e.d.*

Prop. XLII. Knowledge of the second and third kinds and not of the first kind teaches us to distinguish the true from the false.

Proof.—This proposition is clear of itself. For he who would distinguish the true from the false must have an adequate idea of what is true and false, that is, must know the true and false by the second and third kinds of knowledge.

Prop. XLIII. He who has a true idea, knows at that same time that he has a true idea, nor can he doubt concerning the truth of the thing.

Proof.—A true idea in us is that which is adequate in God in so far as he is explained through the nature of the human mind. Let us suppose, then, that there is in God, in so far as he is explained through the nature of the human mind, an adequate idea A. The idea of this idea must necessarily be granted in God, and it refers to God in the same manner as the idea A. But the idea A is supposed to refer to God in so far as he is explained through the nature of the human mind: therefore also the idea of the idea A must refer to God in the same manner, that is, the adequate idea of the idea A will be in the same mind as has the adequate idea A: and therefore he who has an adequate idea or who knows a thing truly must at the same time have an adequate idea of his knowledge or a true knowledge, that is, he must at the same time be certain. *Q.e.d.*

Prop. XLIV. It is not the nature of reason to regard things as contingent but necessary.

Proof.—It is the nature of reason to perceive things truly, namely, as they are in themselves, that is, not as contingent but necessary. *Q.e.d.*

Corollary I.—Hence it follows that it depends solely on the imagination that we consider things whether in respect to the past or future as contingent.

Corollary II.—It is the nature of reason to perceive things under a certain species of eternity.

Proof.—It is the nature of reason to regard things not as contingent, but as necessary. It perceives this necessity of things truly, that is, as it is in itself. But this necessity of things is the necessity itself of the eternal nature of God. Therefore it is the nature of reason to regard things under this species of eternity. Add to this that the bases of reason are the notions which explain these things which are common to all, and which explain the essence of no individual thing: and which therefore must be conceived without any relation of time, but under a certain species of eternity. *Q.e.d.*

Prop. XLV. Every idea of every body or individual thing actually existing necessarily involves the eternal and infinite essence of God.

Proof.—The idea of an individual thing actually existing necessarily involves both the essence of that thing and its existence. But individual things cannot be conceived without God: and forasmuch as they have God for a cause in so far as he is considered under the attribute, of which these things are modes, their ideas must necessarily involve the conception of their attribute, that is, they must involve the eternal and infinite essence of God. *Q.e.d.*

Prop. XLVI. The knowledge of the eternal and infinite essence of God which each idea involves is adequate and perfect.

Proof.—The proof of the previous proposition is of universal application, and whether the thing be considered as a part or a whole, its idea, whether it be of the part or whole, involves the eternal and infinite essence of God. Wherefore that which gives knowledge of the eternal and infinite essence of God is common to all, and equally in part as in whole, and therefore this knowledge will be adequate. *Q.e.d.*

PROP. XLVII. The human mind has an adequate knowledge of the eternal and infinite essence of God.

Proof.—The human mind has ideas from which it perceives itself and its body and external bodies as actually existing; and therefore it has an adequate knowledge of the eternal and infinite essence of God. *Q.e.d.*

PROP. XLVIII. There is in no mind absolute or free will, but the mind is determined for willing this or that by a cause which is determined in its turn by another cause, and this one again by another, and so on to infinity.

Proof.—The mind is a fixed and determined mode of thinking, and therefore cannot be the free cause of its actions, or it cannot have the absolute faculty of willing and unwilling: but for willing this or that it must be determined by a cause which is determined by another, and this again by another, etc. *Q.e.d.*

PROP. XLIX. There is in the mind no volition or affirmation and negation save that which the idea, in so far as it is an idea, involves.

Proof.—There is not in the mind an absolute faculty of willing and unwilling, but only individual volitions such as this or that affirmation and this or that negation. Let us conceive then any individual volition, namely, the mode of thinking, whereby the mind affirms that the three angles of a triangle are equal to two right angles. This affirmation involves the conception or idea of the triangle, that is, without the idea of the triangle it cannot be conceived. It is the same when I say that A involves the conception of B, as when I say that A cannot be conceived without B. Then this affirmation cannot be without the idea of the triangle. Therefore this affirmation cannot exist or be conceived without the idea of the triangle. Moreover, this idea of the triangle must involve the same affirmation, namely, that its three angles are equal to two right angles. Wherefore, vice versa also, this idea of the triangle cannot exist or be conceived without this affirmation: and therefore this affirmation appertains to the essence of the idea of a triangle, nor is anything else than that. And what we have said of this volition can be said of any other volition, namely, that it is nothing but an idea. *Q.e.d.*

Corollary.—Will and intellect are one and the same thing.

Proof.—Will and intellect are nothing but individual volitions and ideas. But an individual volition and idea are one and the same thing. Therefore will and intellect are one and the same thing. *Q.e.d.*

THIRD PART: CONCERNING THE ORIGIN AND NATURE OF THE EMOTIONS

DEFINITIONS

I. I CALL THAT an ADEQUATE CAUSE whose effect can clearly and distinctly be perceived through it. I call that one INADEQUATE or PARTIAL whose effect cannot be perceived through itself.

II. I say that we act or are active when something takes place within us or outside of us whose adequate cause we are, that is, when from our nature anything follows in us or outside us which can be clearly and distinctly understood through that alone. On the other hand, I say we suffer or are passive when something takes place in us or follows from our nature of which we are only the partial cause.

III. By EMOTION I understand the modifications of the body by which the power of action in the body is increased or diminished, aided or restrained, and at the same time the ideas of these modifications.

Explanation.—Thus if we can be the adequate cause of these modifications, then by the emotion I understand an ACTION, if otherwise a PASSION.

POSTULATES

I. The human body can be affected in many ways whereby its power of acting is increased or diminished, and again in others which neither increase nor diminish its power of action.

II. The human body can suffer many changes and yet retain the impressions or traces of objects, and consequently the same images of things.

PROPOSITIONS

PROP. I. Our mind acts certain things and suffers others: namely, in so far as it has adequate ideas, thus far it necessarily acts certain things, and in so far as it has inadequate ideas, thus far it necessarily suffers certain things.

Proof.—The ideas of every human mind are some adequate and some mutilated and confused. But the ideas which are adequate in the mind of any one are adequate in God in so far as he constitutes the essence of that mind, and those again which are inadequate in the mind of any one are also in God, but adequate, not in so far as he contains in himself the essence of the given mind, but in so far as he contains the minds of other things at the same time. Again, from any given idea some effect must necessarily follow, and of this effect God is the adequate cause, not in so far as he is infinite, but in so far as he is considered as affected by that given idea. But of that effect of which God is the cause, in so far as he is affected by an idea which is adequate in the mind of some one, that same mind is the adequate cause. Therefore our mind, in so far as it has adequate ideas, necessarily acts certain things: which was the first point. Then whatever follows from an idea which is adequate in God, not in so far as he has in himself the mind of one man only, but in so far as he has in himself the minds of other things at the same time with the mind of this man, of that effect the mind of that man is not the adequate but merely the partial cause. And so the mind, in so far as it has inadequate ideas, necessarily suffers certain things: which was the second point. Therefore our mind, etc. *Q.e.d.*

Corollary.—Hence it follows that the mind is more or less subject to passions according as it has more or less inadequate ideas, and, on the other hand, to more action the more adequate ideas it has.

Prop. II. The body cannot determine the mind to think, nor the mind the body to remain in motion, or at rest, or in any other state.

Proof.—All modes of thinking have God for their cause, in so far as he is a thinking thing and not in so far as he is explained through another attribute. Therefore that which determines the mind to think is a mode of thinking and not of extension, that is, it is not a body: which was the first point. Again, the motion and rest of a body must arise from another body, which also was determined for motion or rest by another body, and absolutely everything which arises in a body must have arisen from God in so far as he is considered as affected by some mode of extension and not some mode of thinking, that is, it cannot arise from the mind which is a mode of thinking: which is the second point. Therefore the body cannot, etc. *Q.e.d.*

Prop. III. The actions of the mind arise from adequate ideas alone, but passions depend on inadequate ideas alone.

Proof.—The first thing which constitutes the essence of the mind is nothing else than the idea of the body actually existing, which is composed of many other bodies of which certain are adequate and certain inadequate. Therefore whatever follows from the nature of the mind, and of which the mind is the proximate cause through which it must be understood, must necessarily follow from an idea adequate or inadequate. But in so far as the mind has inadequate ideas, thus far it is necessarily passive. Therefore the actions of the mind follow from adequate ideas alone, and the mind is passive therefore merely because it has inadequate ideas. *Q.e.d.*

PROP. IV. Nothing can be destroyed save by an external cause.

Proof.—This proposition is self-evident. For the definition of anything affirms its essence and does not deny it: or it imposes the essence of the thing and does not take it away. And so while we regard the thing alone, and not the external causes, we can find nothing in it which can destroy it. *Q.e.d.*

PROP. V. Things are contrary by nature, that is, they cannot exist in the same subject in so far as one can destroy the other.

Proof.—If they could agree one with the other, or exist at the same time in the same subject, then something could be found in the subject which could destroy it, which is absurd. Therefore a thing, etc. *Q.e.d.*

PROP. VI. Everything in so far as it is in itself endeavours to persist in its own being.

Proof.—Individual things are modes in which the attributes of God are expressed in a certain determined manner, that is, they are things which express in a certain determined manner the power of God whereby he is and acts. Nor can a thing have anything within itself whereby it can be destroyed, or which takes its existence from it; but on the other hand, it is opposed to everything that could take its existence away. Therefore as much as it can, and is within itself, it endeavours to persist in its being. *Q.e.d.*

PROP. VII. The endeavour wherewith a thing endeavours to persist in its being is nothing else than the actual essence of that thing.

Proof.—From the given essence of a thing certain things necessarily follow, nor can things do anything else than that which follows necessarily from their determined nature. Wherefore the power or endeavour of anything by which it does, or endeavours to do, anything, either alone or with others, that is, the power or endeavour by which it endeavours to persist in its own being, is nothing else than the given or actual essence of that given thing. *Q.e.d.*

PROP. VIII. The endeavour wherewith a thing endeavours to persist in its own being involves no finite time but an indefinite time.

Proof.—If it involves a limited time which must determine the duration of the thing, then it would follow from the power alone by which the thing exists, that the thing after that limited time could exist no longer, but must be destroyed. But this is absurd. Therefore the endeavour wherewith a thing endeavours to exist involves no definite time; but on the other hand, since it is destroyed by no external cause, by the same power by which it now exists it will continue to exist for ever: therefore this endeavour involves no definite time. *Q.e.d.*

PROP. IX. The mind, in so far as it has both clear and distinct and confused ideas, endeavours to persist in its being for an indefinite period, and is conscious of this its endeavour.

Proof.—The essence of the mind is constituted of adequate and inadequate ideas, and therefore, inasmuch as it has the first or the second, it endeavours to persist in its being, and that for an indefinite period. But since the mind is necessarily conscious of the modifications of its body through ideas, therefore the mind is conscious of its endeavour. *Q.e.d.*

PROP. X. The idea which cuts off the existence of our body cannot be given in our mind, but is contrary thereto.

Proof.—Whatever can destroy our body cannot be granted in the same. Therefore the idea of this thing cannot be granted in God in so far as he has the idea of our body, that is, the idea of this thing cannot be given in our mind; but on the other hand, since the first thing which forms the essence of the mind is the idea of the body actually existing, the first and principal endeavour of our mind is to affirm the existence of our body. And therefore the idea which denies the existence of our body is opposed to the mind, etc. *Q.e.d.*

PROP. XI. Whatever increases or diminishes, helps or hinders the power of action of our body, the idea thereof increases or diminishes, helps or hinders the power of thinking of our mind.

Proof.—This proposition is clear from Prop. 7, Part II, or even from Prop. 14, Part II.

PROP. XII. The mind, as much as it can, endeavours to imagine those things which increase or help its power of acting.

Proof.—As long as the human body is affected in a mode which involves the nature of any external body, so long the human mind regards the same body as present; and consequently, as long as the human mind regards any external body as present, that is, as long as it imagines, so long the human mind is affected in a mode which involves the nature of the external body. And therefore as long as the mind imagines those things which increase or help the power of acting of our body, so long the body is affected in modes which increase or help its power of acting, and consequently so long the power of thinking in the mind is increased or helped. And therefore the mind as much as it can endeavours to imagine those things. *Q.e.d.*

PROP. XIII. When the mind imagines things which diminish or hinder the power of acting of the body, it endeavours as much as it can to remember things which will cut off their existence.

Proof.—As long as the mind imagines any such thing, so long the power of the mind and body is diminished or hindered, and, nevertheless,

it will imagine it until the mind recalls some other thing which cuts off
its present existence, that is, the power of the mind and body is decreased
or diminished until the mind imagines some other thing which cuts off
its existence, which, therefore, the mind as much as possible endeavours
to imagine or recall. *Q.e.d.*

Corollary.—Hence it follows that the mind is averse to imagining
those things which diminish or hinder its power and that of the body.

Prop. XIV. If the mind were once affected at the same time by two
emotions, when afterwards it is affected by one of them it will be also
affected by the other.

Proof.—If the human body was affected once by two bodies at the
same time, when the mind afterwards imagines one of them it will immediately recall the other. But the imaginations of our mind indicate
rather the modifications of our body than the nature of external bodies.
Therefore if the body, and consequently the mind, was once affected by
two emotions, when afterwards it may be affected by one it will also be
affected by the other. *Q.e.d.*

Prop. XV Anything can accidentally be the cause of pleasure, pain, or
desire.

Proof.—Let us suppose the mind simultaneously affected by two emotions, by one which neither increases nor diminishes its power of acting,
and the other which increases or diminishes it. It is clear from the previous
proposition that when the mind is afterwards affected by that one through
its true cause which neither increases nor diminishes through itself the
power of thinking, it will be affected at the same time by the other which
increases or diminishes its power of thought, that is, it will be affected
by pleasure or pain; and therefore the former, not through itself, but accidentally, will be the cause of pleasure or pain. And in this way it may
easily be shown that that thing could accidentally be the cause of desire. *Q.e.d.*

Corollary.—From the fact alone that we have regarded something
with the emotion of pleasure or pain, though it were not the effecting
cause, we can love or hate that thing.

Proof.—From this alone it comes to pass that the mind, after imagining the said thing, is affected by the emotion of pleasure or pain, that
is, that the power of the mind or body is increased or diminished: and
consequently that the mind is desirous of, or averse to, imagining it, that
is, that it loves or hates it. *Q.e.d.*

Prop. XVI. From the fact alone that we imagine anything which has
something similar to an object which is wont to affect the mind with
pleasure or pain, although that in which the thing is similar to the object

be not the effecting cause of those emotions, nevertheless we shall hate or love it accordingly.

Proof.—We have regarded that which is similar to the object in the object itself with the emotion of pleasure or pain; and therefore when the mind is affected with its image, at the same time it is also affected with this or that emotion, and consequently a thing which we see to have this will be accidentally the cause of pleasure or pain. And therefore, although that in which it is similar to the object is not the effecting cause of these emotions, we nevertheless will love or hate it. *Q.e.d.*

PROP. XVII. If we imagine a thing which is wont to affect us with the emotion of sadness to have something similar to another thing which equally affects us with the emotion of pleasure, we will hate and love that thing at the same time.

Proof.—This thing is through itself a cause of pain, and in so far as we imagine with that emotion we hate it; and in so far as we imagine it to have something similar to another thing which is wont to affect equally with an emotion of pleasure, we love it equally with an impulse of love. And therefore we hate and love it at the same time. *Q.e.d.*

PROP. XVIII. A man is affected with the same emotion of pleasure or pain from the image of a thing past or future as from the image of a thing present.

Proof.—As often as a man is affected by the image of anything, he regards the thing as present, although it may not exist, nor will he regard it as past or future save in so far as its image is connected with the image of time past or future. Wherefore the image of the thing considered in itself is the same whether it refers to time present, past, or future, that is, the disposition of the body or emotion is the same whether the image of the thing be present, past, or future. And so the emotion of pleasure or pain is the same whether the image of the thing be present, past, or future. *Q.e.d.*

PROP. XIX. He will be saddened who imagines that which he loves to be destroyed: if he imagines it to be preserved he is rejoiced.

Proof.—The mind, in so far as it can, tries to imagine those things which increase or help the power of acting of the body, that is, those things which it loves. But the imagination is aided by those things which impose existence on a thing, and, on the other hand, hindered by those which cut off existence from a thing. Therefore the images of things which impose the existence of a thing that is loved, help the endeavour of the mind wherewith it endeavours to imagine the thing that is loved, that is, they affect the mind with pleasure; and, on the other hand, those things which cut off the existence of a thing that is loved, hinder that endeavour of the mind, that is, they affect the mind with pain. And so he will be saddened who imagines that which he loves to be destroyed, etc. *Q.e.d.*

PROP. XX. He will be rejoiced who imagines what he hates to be destroyed.

Proof.—The mind endeavours to imagine those things which cut off the existence of other things by which the body's power of acting is diminished or hindered, that is, it endeavours to imagine those things which cut off the existence of such things as it hates. And therefore the image of a thing which cuts off the existence of that which the mind hates, helps that endeavour of the mind, that is, affects the mind with joy. And so he will be rejoiced who imagines the destruction of that which he hates. *Q.e.d.*

PROP. XXI. He who imagines that which he loves to be affected by pleasure or pain, will also be affected by pleasure or pain: and these will be greater or less in the lover according as they are greater or less in the thing loved.

Proof.—The images of things which impose existence on the thing loved, help the mental endeavour by which it tries to imagine the thing loved. But pleasure imposes existence on the thing feeling pleasure, and the more so according as the emotion of pleasure is greater, for it is a transition to a greater state of perfection. Therefore the image of pleasure in the thing loved helps the mental effort of the lover, that is, it affects the lover with pleasure, and the more so according as this emotion was greater in the thing loved: which was the first point. Then in so far as a thing is affected with pain, thus far it is destroyed, the more so according to the greatness of the affecting pain: and therefore he that imagines what he loves to be affected with pain will also be affected with pain, and the more so according as the emotion was great in the object loved. *Q.e.d.*

PROP. XXII. If we imagine anything to affect with pleasure what we love, we are affected with love towards it: and, on the other hand, if we imagine anything to affect it with pain, we are affected with hatred towards it.

Proof.—He who affects a thing we love with pleasure or pain, likewise affects us with pleasure or pain, that is, if we imagine that the object loved is affected with pleasure or pain. But this pleasure or pain is supposed to be given in us accompanied by the idea of an external cause. Therefore, if we imagine anything to affect what we love with pleasure or pain, we are affected with love or hatred towards it. *Q.e.d.*

PROP. XXIII. He will be rejoiced who imagines that which he hates to be affected with pain; if, on the other hand, he imagines it to be affected with pleasure, he will be saddened: and these emotions will be greater or less according as the contrary emotions were greater or less in the things hated.

Proof.—In so far as a hateful thing is affected with pain, thus far it is destroyed, and the more so according as it is affected with more pain. Who, therefore, imagines a thing that he hates to be affected with pain, is inversely affected with pleasure, and the more so according as he imagines the thing hated to be affected with greater pain: which was the first point. Again, pleasure imposes existence of the thing affected with pleasure, and the more so according as more pleasure is conceived. If any one then imagines that which he hates to be affected with pleasure, this imagination will hinder his effort of pleasure, that is, he who hates will be affected with pain, etc. *Q.e.d.*

PROP. XXIV. If we imagine any one to affect a thing we hate with pleasure, we are affected with hatred towards that person. If, on the other hand, we imagine him to affect it with pain, we are affected with love towards him.

Proof.—This proposition is proved in the same manner as Prop. 22, Part III, which see.

PROP. XXV. We endeavour to affirm, concerning ourselves or what we love, everything that we imagine to affect what we love or ourselves with pleasure; and, on the other hand, we endeavour to deny, concerning ourselves and the object loved, everything that we imagine to affect us or the object loved with pain.

Proof.—What we imagine to affect a loved thing with pleasure or pain affects us also with pleasure or pain. But the mind endeavours to imagine as much as it can those things that affect us with pleasure, that is, to regard it as present; and, on the other hand, to cut off the existence of those things which affect us with pain. Therefore we endeavour to affirm, concerning ourselves or the thing loved, what we imagine will affect us or the thing loved with pleasure, and contrariwise. *Q.e.d.*

PROP. XXVI. We endeavour to affirm, concerning a thing that we hate, that which we imagine will affect it with pain, and, on the contrary, to deny all that which we imagine will affect it with pleasure.

Proof.—This proposition follows from Prop. 23, as the last one follows Prop. 21.

PROP. XXVII. By the fact that we imagine a thing which is like ourselves, and which we have not regarded with any emotion to be affected with any emotion, we also are affected with a like emotion.

Proof.—The images of things are modifications of the human body the ideas of which represent to us external bodies as present, that is, the ideas of which involve the nature of our body and at the same time the nature of the external body as present. If, therefore, the nature of an external body is similar to that of our own, then the idea of the external body which we imagine will involve a modification of our body similar to the modification of an external body: and consequently if we imagine any one similar to ourselves to be affected with any emotion, this imagination will express a modification of our body similar to that emotion. And therefore from the fact that we imagine a thing similar to ourselves to be affected with any emotion, we are affected in company with it by that emotion. And if we hate a thing similar to ourselves, we shall to that extent be affected with it by a contrary emotion, not a similar one. *Q.e.d.*

Corollary I.—If we imagine any one, whom we have regarded hitherto with no emotion whatever, to affect a thing similar to ourselves with pleasure, we are affected with pleasure towards that person. If, on the other hand, we imagine him to affect it with pain, we are affected with hatred towards him.

Proof.—This is shown from the previous Prop. in the same manner as Prop. 22 from Prop. 21.

Corollary II.—We cannot hate a thing which we pity because its misery affects us with pain.

Proof.—For if we could hate it, then we should be rejoiced at its pain, which is contrary to the hypothesis.

Corollary III.—We endeavour as much as we are able to liberate a thing we pity from its misery.

Proof.—That which affects a thing we pity with pain, affects us also with a similar pain; and therefore we endeavour to recollect everything that can take away its existence or which would destroy it, that is, we desire to destroy it or we are determined for its destruction; and therefore we endeavour to liberate it from its misery. *Q.e.d.*

Prop. XXVIII. We endeavour to promote the being of everything that we imagine conducive to pleasure; but what we find repugnant or conducive to pain we endeavour to remove or destroy.

Proof.—We endeavour to imagine as much as possible what we imagine to be conducive to pleasure, that is, we endeavour as much as possible to regard it as present or actually existing. But the mind's endeavour or its power of thinking is equal and simultaneous in nature with the body's endeavour or power in acting; therefore we endeavour absolutely to bring about its existence, or we desire and strive for it: which was the first point. Again, if that which we think to be the cause of pain, that is, that which we hate, we imagine to be destroyed, we are rejoiced; and therefore we endeavour to destroy or remove it from us, lest we should regard it as present: which was the second point. Therefore everything that is conducive to pleasure, etc. *Q.e.d.*

PROP. XXIX. We also shall endeavour to do everything which we imagine men (let it be understood in this and the following propositions that we mean men for whom we have no particular emotion) to regard with pleasure, and, on the other hand, we shall be averse to doing what we imagine men to turn away from.

Proof.—From the fact that we shall love and hate the same thing as we imagine men to love or hate, we are rejoiced or saddened at the presence of that thing; and therefore we endeavour to do everything which we imagine men to love or to regard with pleasure. *Q.e.d.*

PROP. XXX. If any one has done anything which he imagines to affect others with pleasure, he will be affected with pleasure accompanied by the idea of himself as the cause, or he will regard himself with pleasure. On the other hand, if he has done anything which he imagines to affect the others with pain, he regards himself then with pain.

Proof.—He who imagines that he has affected others with pleasure or pain is himself affected with pleasure or pain. But as a man is conscious of himself through modifications by which he is determined for action, whoever has done anything which he imagines to affect others with pleasure, will be affected with pleasure accompanied by the idea of himself as the cause, or he will regard himself with pleasure, and, on the other hand, the contrary follows. *Q.e.d.*

PROP. XXXI. If we imagine any one to love, desire, or hate anything which we ourselves love, hate, or desire, by that very fact we shall love, hate, or desire it the more. But, on the other hand, if we imagine that what we love is avoided by some one, then we undergo a wavering of the mind.

Proof.—From the very fact that we imagine any one to love anything, we shall also love it ourselves. But we suppose ourselves to love it without this; there is then brought to play a new cause of love whereby our emotion is fostered: and therefore that which we love we shall love with more emotion. Again, from the fact that we imagine any one to turn away from anything, we also shall turn away from it. But if we suppose that we love it at the same time, then at the same time we shall love and turn away from a thing, or we shall undergo a wavering of the mind. *Q.e.d.*

Corollary.—Hence, and from Prop. 28, Part III, it follows that every one endeavours as much as he can to cause every one to love what he himself loves, and to hate what he himself hates: as in the words of the poet, "As lovers let us hope and fear alike: of iron is he who loves what the other leaves."

Prop. XXXII. If we imagine any one to enjoy anything which only one can possess, we shall endeavour to bring it to pass that he does not possess it.

Proof.—From the fact alone that we imagine any one to enjoy anything, we shall love that thing and desire to enjoy it. But (by the hypothesis) we imagine there to be an obstacle to this pleasure inasmuch as another may possess it: we shall therefore endeavour to bring it to pass that another should not possess it. *Q.e.d.*

Prop. XXXIII. When we love a thing similar to ourselves, we endeavour as much as possible to bring it about that it also should love us.

Proof.—We endeavour to imagine a thing that we love as much as we can above all others. If, therefore, the thing is similar to us, we shall endeavour to affect it with joy above the rest, or we shall endeavour as much as possible to bring it about that the thing loved should be affected with pleasure accompanied by the idea of ourselves, that is, that it should love us. *Q.e.d.*

Prop. XXXIV. The greater the emotion with which we imagine a thing loved to be affected towards us, the greater will be our vain-glory.

Proof.—We endeavour as much as we can to make the thing loved love us in return, that is, to bring it about that the thing loved should be affected with pleasure accompanied with the idea of ourselves. And so the more pleasure with which we imagine the thing loved to be affected on our account, the more this endeavour is assisted, that is, the more we are affected with pleasure. But when we are pleased with the fact that we affect another thing similar to ourselves with pleasure, then we regard ourselves with pleasure. Therefore the greater the pleasure with which we imagine the thing loved to be affected on our account, the greater the pleasure with which we regard ourselves, or the more self-complacent or vain we become. *Q.e.d.*

Prop. XXXV. If any one imagines that the thing loved is joined to another than himself with the same or a faster bond of love than that which binds it to him, he will be affected with hatred towards the object loved, and envy towards the other.

Proof.—The greater the love towards himself with which the thing loved is affected, the greater his self-complacency, that is, the greater his pleasure; and therefore he will endeavour to imagine as much as possible the thing loved to be bound to him in the tightest bond of love, and this endeavour or appetite will increase if he imagines any one else to desire the same thing for himself. But this endeavour or appetite is supposed to be hindered by the image of the thing loved, accompanied by the image of him whom the thing loved has joined to itself. Therefore he will be affected with pain accompanied by the idea of the thing loved as the cause, and at the same time the image of the other, that is, he will be affected with hatred towards the object loved, and at the same time towards the other, which by reason that he enjoys the object loved, he will envy. *Q.e.d.*

PROP. XXXVI. He who recollects a thing which he once enjoyed, de-s.res to possess it under the same circumstances as those with which he first enjoyed it.

Proof.—Whatever a man sees in conjunction with a thing which has delighted him will be accidentally to him a cause of pleasure, and therefore he will desire to possess it at the same time as the thing which delights him, or he will desire to possess the thing under the same circumstances as when he first enjoyed it. *Q.e.d.*

Corollary.—A lover will accordingly be saddened if he finds one of those attendant circumstances to be wanting.

Proof.—Now in so far as he finds one circumstance wanting, thus far he imagines something which cuts off its existence. But as he is assumed as a lover to be desirous of that one thing or circumstance, therefore in so far as he imagines it to be wanting he is saddened. *Q.e.d.*

PROP. XXXVII. The desire which arises by reason of sadness, joy, hatred, or love, is greater according as the emotion is greater.

Proof.—Sadness diminishes or hinders a man's power of action, that is, it diminishes or hinders the endeavour with which a man endeavours to persist in his being, and therefore it is contrary to this endeavour, and whatever the power of a man affected by pain is, is directed to remove that pain. But the greater the pain the greater it must be opposed to the man's power of acting. Therefore the greater the pain the more will the man endeavour by his power of acting to remove it, that is, the more desire or appetite with which he will endeavour to remove it. Again, since pleasure increases or helps a man's power of acting, it can easily be shown in that way that a man affected with pleasure desires nothing else than to preserve that pleasure, and that with the greater desire according as the pleasure is greater. Then since love and hatred are the emotions of pleasure and pain, it follows in the same manner that the endeavour, appetite, or desire which arises by reason of love or hatred will be greater according to the love or hatred. *Q.e.d.*

PROP. XXXVIII. If any one begins to hate a thing loved so that his love for it is clearly laid aside, he will bear greater hatred towards it on that very account than if he had never loved it, and the more so according as his former love was greater.

Proof.—Now if any one begins to hate a thing, more of his appetites are hindered than if he had not loved it. For love is a pleasure which man, as much as he can, endeavours to preserve by regarding the thing loved as present, and affecting it with pleasure as much as he can; his endeavour is greater according as his love is greater, and so is his endeavour to bring it to pass that the thing loved should love him in return. But these endeavours are hindered by hatred towards the thing loved. Therefore the lover will be affected with sadness on this account, and the more so according as his love was greater, that is, besides the pain whose cause is hatred there is also another cause, namely, that he loved the thing; and consequently he will regard the thing loved with a greater emotion of pain, that is, he will regard it with more hatred than if he had never loved it, and the more so according as his former love was greater. *Q.e.d.*

PROP. XXXIX. He who hates any one will endeavour to do him harm unless he fears to receive a greater harm from him; and, on the other hand, he who loves some one will by the same law endeavour to do him good.

Proof.—To hate any one is the same as to imagine him the cause of pain, and therefore he who hates anything will endeavour to remove or destroy it. But if thence he fears something more painful, or, what is the same thing, something worse, and thinks that he can avoid it by not inflicting that evil which he intended on the person he hates, he will desire to abstain from inflicting that evil, and that with a greater endeavour than that with which he intended to inflict the evil which hitherto prevailed. The second part of the proof proceeds in the same manner as this. Therefore he who hates, etc. *Q.e.d.*

PROP. XL. He who imagines himself to be hated by another, and believes that he has given the other no cause for hatred, will hate that person in return.

Proof.—He who imagines any one to be affected with hatred will also be affected with hatred, that is, with sadness accompanied with the idea of an external cause. But he (according to the hypothesis) imagines no cause of this pain save the person who hates him. Therefore from the fact that he imagines himself to be hated by any one, he will be affected with pain accompanied with the idea of the person who hates him, or he will hate that person. *Q.e.d.*

Corollary I.—He that imagines that one whom he loves hates him, is a prey to the conflicting passions of love and hatred; for in so far as he imagines himself to be hated by any one, he is determined also to hate him. But he loves him nevertheless. Therefore he is a prey to the conflicting passions of love and hatred.

Corollary II.—If any one imagines that an ill has been inflicted on him by a person to whom he bore no good or evil before, he immediately will endeavour to repay that evil to the person in question.

Proof.—He who imagines any one to be affected with hatred towards himself will hate that person in turn, and he will endeavour to remember everything that can affect him with pain, and will endeavour, moreover, to inflict this injury on the person. But (by the hypothesis) the first evil he recalls is that one done to himself. Therefore he immediately endeavours to inflict that one in return. *Q.e.d.*

PROP. XLI. If any one imagines himself to be loved by some one else, and does not believe that he has given any cause for this love, he shall love that person in return.

Proof.—The proof of this proposition proceeds in the same manner as that of the previous one.

Corollary.—He who imagines he is loved by one whom he hates is a prey to the conflicting emotions of hatred and love. This is shown in the same way as was the corollary of the previous proposition.

PROP. XLII. He who confers a benefit on any one, if moved by love, or by the hope of honour, will be saddened if he sees that the benefit is received with ingratitude.

Proof.—He who loves something similar to himself endeavours as much as possible to bring it about that he is loved in turn by that thing. Therefore he who confers a benefit on any one through love, does so with the desire which holds him to be loved in return, that is, by the hope of honour or of pleasure: and therefore he will endeavour as much as possible to imagine this cause of honour, or regard it as actually existing. But he imagines something else that cuts off the cause of its existence. Therefore by that very fact he will be saddened. *Q.e.d.*

PROP. XLIII. Hatred is increased by reciprocal hatred, and, on the other hand, can be destroyed by love.

Proof.—He who imagines that one whom he hates is affected with hatred towards him will feel to arise in himself a new hatred, while the first hatred still remains. But if, on the contrary, he imagines that one whom he hates is affected with love towards him, in so far as he imagines this he will regard himself with pleasure, and will endeavour to please the object of his hatred, that is, he will endeavour not to hate him and not to affect him with pain: and this endeavour will be greater or less according to the emotion from which it arises. And so if it be greater than that one which arose from hatred, and through which he endeavoured to affect the thing which he hated with pain, it will prevail and will remove hatred from the mind. *Q.e.d.*

PROP. XLIV. Hatred which is entirely conquered by love passes into love, and love on that account is greater than if it had not been preceded by hatred.

Proof.—The proof proceeds in the same manner as that of Prop. 38,

Part III. For he who begins to love a thing which he hated, or which he was wont to regard with pain, by the very fact that he loves will rejoice; and to this pleasure which love involves is added that which arises from the fact that the endeavour to remove pain which hatred involves is aided, accompanied by the idea of him whom he hated as cause.

Prop. XLV. If one imagines that any one similar to himself is affected with hatred towards another thing similar to himself whom he himself loves, then he will hate the first of these two.

Proof.—The thing loved has reciprocal hatred towards him who hates it. And therefore the lover who imagines that any one hates the thing he loves, by that very fact imagines the thing beloved to be affected by hatred, that is, by pain: and consequently he will be saddened, and that accompanied by the idea of him who hates the thing beloved as a cause, that is, he will hate that person. *Q.e.d.*

Prop. XLVI. If any one has been affected with pleasure or pain by another person of a class or nation different to his own, and that accompanied by the idea of that person under the general name of that class or nation as the cause of the pleasure or pain, he will love or hate not only that person, but all of that class or nation.

Proof.—The proof of this is clear from Prop. 16, Part III.

Prop. XLVII. Joy which arises from the fact that we imagine a thing which we hate to be destroyed or affected by some evil never arises without some pain in us.

Proof.—This is clear from Prop. 27, Part III. For in so far as we imagine a thing similar to ourselves to be affected with pain we are saddened.

Prop. XLVIII. Love and hatred, for example, towards Peter, are destroyed, if the pain which the latter involves, and the pleasure which the former involves, are connected to the idea of another thing as a cause; and each of them will be diminished in so far as we imagine Peter not to be the only cause of either.

Proof.—This is obvious from the mere definition of love and hatred. For pleasure is called love towards Peter, and pain hatred towards him merely on this account, that he is regarded as the cause of this or that effect. When this then is either wholly or partly removed, the emotion towards Peter is either wholly or partly removed. *Q.e.d.*

Prop. XLIX. Love or hatred towards a thing which we imagine to be free must be greater than the love or hatred towards a necessary thing, provided both are subject to the same cause.

Proof.—A thing which we imagine to be free must be perceived through itself without any others. If, therefore, we imagine it to be the cause of the aforesaid pleasure or pain, by that very fact we shall love or hate it, and that with the greatest love or hatred that can arise from the given emotion. But if we imagine the thing which is the cause of the given effect to be necessary, then we shall imagine it not alone, but together with other things, to be the cause of the given effect: and therefore our love or hatred towards it will be less. *Q.e.d.*

PROP. L. Anything can be accidentally the cause of hope or fear.
Proof.—This proposition is shown in the same way as Prop. 15, Part III.

PROP. LI. Different men can be affected by one and the same object in different manners, and one and the same man can be affected by one and the same object in different ways at different times.
Proof.—The human body is affected by external bodies in many ways. Therefore two men can be affected in different ways at the same time, and therefore they can be affected in various ways by one and the same object. Again, the human body can be affected now in this mode and now in that, and consequently it can be affected by one and the same object at different times in different ways. *Q.e.d.*

PROP. LII. We cannot regard an object which we have seen before together with some others, or which we imagine to have nothing that is not common to many, as long as one which we imagine to have something singular about it.
Proof.—As soon as we imagine the object which we have seen with others, we immediately recall the others, and thus from regarding one we immediately pass to the regarding of another. And this is the case with an object which we imagine to have nothing that is not common to many. For we suppose by that very fact that we are regarding in it nothing that we have not seen with the others. But when we suppose that we imagine something singular in any object, something that we have never seen before, we say nothing else than that the mind, while it regards that object, has nothing else in itself to the regarding of which it may pass to the regarding of something else. And therefore it is determined for the regarding of that alone. Therefore we cannot regard, etc. *Q.e.d.*

PROP. LIII. When the mind regards itself and its power of acting it is rejoiced, and the more so, the more distinctly it imagines itself and its power of acting.
Proof.—Man does not know himself save through the modifications of his body, and the ideas of these modifications. Therefore when it happens that the mind can regard itself, it is assumed by that very fact

to pass to a greater state of perfection, that is, to be affected with pleasure, and the more so according as it can imagine itself and its power of acting more distinctly. *Q.e.d.*

Corollary.—This pleasure is more and more fostered the more a man imagines himself to be praised by others. For the more he imagines himself to be praised by others, the greater, by that very fact, the pleasure with which he imagines others to be affected, and that accompanied by the idea of himself as cause. And therefore the greater will be the joy accompanied by an idea of himself with which he is affected. *Q.e.d.*

PROP. LIV. The mind endeavours to imagine those things only which impose its power of action on it.

Proof.—The endeavour or power of the mind is the same as the essence of the mind. But the essence of the mind only affirms that which the mind is and can do; and not that which it is not and cannot do. And therefore it endeavours to imagine only that which affirms or imposes its power of acting. *Q.e.d.*

PROP. LV. When the mind imagines its want of power it is saddened by that fact.

Proof.—The essence of the mind affirms only that which the mind is and can do, or it is the nature of the mind only to imagine those things which impose its power of acting (previous Prop.). When therefore we say that the mind, while regarding itself, imagines its weakness, we say nothing else than that, while the mind endeavours to imagine something which imposes its power of acting, that endeavour is hindered or that it is saddened. *Q.e.d.*

Corollary I.—This pain or sadness is fostered more and more if one imagines himself to be reviled by others, which can be proved in the same manner as the Coroll., Prop. 53, Part III.

Corollary II.—No one envies the virtue of any one save his equal.

Proof.—Envy is hatred itself or sadness, that is, a modification by which a man's power of acting or endeavour is hindered. But man endeavours or desires to do nothing save what can follow from his given nature. Therefore man desires to attribute to himself no power of acting or (what is the same thing) no virtue which is proper to another nature and alien to his own. And therefore his desire cannot be hindered nor he himself saddened by the fact that he regards some virtue in some one dissimilar to himself, and consequently he cannot envy him; but he can envy his equal, who is supposed to be of the same nature as himself. *Q.e.d.*

PROP. LVI. There are as many species of pleasure, pain, desire, and consequently any emotion which is composed of these, such as wavering of the mind, or which is derived from these, such as love, fear, hope, hate, etc., as there are species of objects by which we are affected.

Proof.—Pleasure and pain, and consequently the emotions which are composed of or derived from these, are passions; we also are passive in so far as we have inadequate ideas, and in so far as we have them alone are we passive, that is, we are only necessarily passive in so far as we imagine, or in so far as we are affected by an emotion which involves the nature of our body and the nature of an external body. The nature, therefore, of each passion must so be explained necessarily that the nature of the object by which we are affected may be expressed. The pleasure which arises from the object, e.g., A, involves the nature of the object A, and the pleasure which arises from the object B involves the nature of that object B: and therefore these two pleasures are of different nature because they arise from causes of different nature. Thus also the emotion of sadness which arises from one object is different in nature from the sadness which arises from another cause, which also must be understood of love, hate, hope, fear, wavering of the mind, etc.: and therefore there are as many species of pleasure, pain, love, etc., as there are species of objects by which we are affected. But desire is the essence or nature of every one in so far as it is conceived as determined from any given disposition of the person to do anything. Therefore, according as each one is affected by external causes with this or that kind of pleasure, pain, love, hatred, that is, according as his nature is constituted in this or that manner, so will his desire be this or that, and the nature of one desire necessarily different to the nature of another as much as the emotions from which each one has arisen differ one from the other. Therefore there are as many species of desires as there are species of pleasure, pain, love, etc., and consequently as there are species of objects by which we are affected. *Q.e.d.*

PROP. LVII. Any emotion of every individual differs from the emotion of another only in so far as the essence of one differs from the essence of another.

Proof.—All emotions have reference to desire, pleasure, or pain, as the definitions which we gave of them show. But desire is the nature and essence of everything: therefore the desire of one individual differs from the desire of another only inasmuch as the essence of one differs from the essence or nature of the other. Pleasure and pain are passions by which the power or endeavour of every person to persist in his own being is increased or diminished, aided or hindered. But by endeavour to persist in its being, in so far as it refers to the mind and body at the same time, we understand appetite and desire; therefore pleasure and pain are desire itself, or appetite, in so far as it is increased or diminished by external causes, helped or hindered, that is, they are the nature of every one. And therefore the pleasure or pain of one person differs only from the pleasure or pain of another in so far as the nature or essence of one differs from the nature or essence of another: and consequently any emotion of an individual, etc. *Q.e.d.*

PROP. LVIII. Besides pleasure and desire, which are passions, there are other emotions of pleasure and pain which refer to us in so far as we are active.

Proof.—When the mind conceives itself and its power of acting, it rejoices. But the mind necessarily regards itself when it conceives a true or adequate idea. But the mind conceives certain adequate ideas. Therefore it will also rejoice in so far as it conceives adequate ideas, that is, in so far as it is active. Again, the mind endeavours to persist in its being in so far as it has both clear and distinct ideas and confused ones. But by endeavour we understand desire. Therefore desire also has reference to us in so far as we understand, or in so far as we are active. *Q.e.d.*

PROP. LIX. Among all the emotions which have reference to the mind, in so far as it is active, there are none which have not reference to pleasure or desire.

Proof.—All emotions have reference to pleasure, pain, or desire, as the definitions which we gave of them show. But we understand by pain that the mind's power of thinking is diminished or hindered, and therefore the mind in so far as it is saddened has its power of understanding, that is, its power of acting, diminished or hindered. And therefore no emotions of pain can be referred to the mind in so far as it is active, but only emotions of pleasure or desire which thus far have reference to the mind. *Q.e.d.*

FOURTH PART: ON HUMAN SERVITUDE, OR THE STRENGTH OF THE EMOTIONS

DEFINITIONS

I. By GOOD I understand that which we certainly know to be useful to us.

II. But by BAD I understand that which we certainly know will prevent us from partaking any good.

III. I call individual things CONTINGENT in so far as while we regard their essence alone, we find nothing which imposes their existence necessarily, or which necessarily excludes it.

IV. I call the same individual things POSSIBLE in so far as while we regard the causes by which they must be produced, we know not whether they are determined to produce them.

V. In the following propositions I shall understand by CONTRARY EMOTIONS those which draw a man in different directions, although they may be of the same kind, as luxury and avarice, which are species of love, and are contrary not by nature but by accident.

VI. What I understand by emotion towards a thing future, present, or past, I have explained.

But it is the place here to note that we can only distinctly imagine distance of time, like that of space, up to a certain limit, that is, just as those things which are beyond two hundred paces from us, or whose distance from the place where we are exceeds that which we can distinctly imagine, we are wont to imagine equally distant from us and as if they were in the same plane, so also those objects whose time of existing we imagine to be distant from the present by a longer interval than that which we are accustomed to imagine, we imagine all to be equally distant from the present, and refer them all to one moment of time.

VII. By END, with which in view we do anything, I understand a desire.

VIII. By VIRTUE and POWER I understand the same thing, that is, virtue, in so far as it has reference to man, is his essence or nature in so far as he has the power of effecting something which can only be understood by the laws of that nature.

AXIOM. There is no individual thing in nature than which there is none more powerful or stronger; but whatever is given, there is also something stronger given by which that given thing can be destroyed.

PROPOSITIONS

PROP. I. Nothing positive, which a false idea has, is removed from the presence of what is true in so far as it is true.

Proof.—Falsity consists solely of the privation of knowledge which is involved by inadequate ideas. Nor do these have anything positive, by reason of which they are called false; but on the contrary, in so far as they have reference to God, they are true. If, therefore, that which is positive, possessed by a false idea, were removed from the presence of what is true in so far as it is true, then a true idea would be removed from itself, which is absurd. Therefore nothing positive, etc. *Q.e.d.*

PROP. II. We are passive in so far as we are a part of nature which cannot be conceived through itself without others.

Proof.—We are said to be passive when something takes place in us of which we are only the partial cause, that is, something which cannot be deduced solely from the laws of our nature. We are passive, therefore, in so far as we are part of nature which cannot be conceived through itself without other parts. *Q.e.d.*

PROP. III. The force with which man persists in existing is limited, and is far surpassed by the power of external causes.

Proof.—This is clear from the axiom of this part. For with a given man there is given something, say A, stronger than he, and given A, there is given something, say B, stronger than A, and so on to infinity. And therefore the power of man is limited by the power of some other thing, and infinitely surpassed by the power of external causes. *Q.e.d.*

PROP. IV. It cannot happen that a man should not be a part of nature, and that he should be able not to suffer changes, save those which can be understood through his nature alone, and of which he is the adequate cause.

Proof.—The power with which individual things, and consequently man, preserve their being is the very power of God or nature, not in so far as he is infinite, but in so far as he can be explained through actual human essence. Therefore the power of man, in so far as it is explained through its actual essence, is a part of the infinite power of God or nature, that is, of his essence: which was the first point. Again, if it can come to pass that a man can suffer no changes save those that can be understood through the nature alone of that man, it would follow that he cannot perish, and that he will live of necessity for ever. But this must follow from a cause whose power is finite or infinite, namely, from the mere power of man, that he would be able to remove changes which arise from external causes from him, or from the infinite power of nature by which all individual things are so directed that man can suffer no other changes than those which serve for his preservation. But the first point is absurd. Therefore, if it could come to pass that man should suffer no changes save those that can be understood through the mere nature of man himself, and consequently, as we have already shown, that he should exist for ever, this would have to follow from the infinite power of God. Consequently the order of the whole of nature would have to be deduced in so far as it is considered under the attributes of thought and extension from the necessity of divine nature, in so far as it is considered as affected by the idea of some man. And therefore it would follow that man was infinite, which is absurd. It cannot therefore happen that a man should suffer no changes save those of which he is the adequate cause. *Q.e.d.*

Corollary.—Hence it follows that man is always necessarily liable to passions, that he always follows the common order of nature and obeys it, and that he accommodates himself to it as much as the nature of things demands.

Prop. V. The force and increase of any passion, and its persistence in existing, are not defined by the power whereby we endeavour to persist in existing, but by the power of an external cause compared with our own.

Proof.—The essence of passion cannot be explained merely through our essence, that is, the power of passion cannot be defined by the power with which we endeavour to persist in our being; but it must necessarily be defined by the power of some external cause compared with our own. *Q.e.d.*

Prop. VI. The force of any passion or emotion can so surpass the rest of the actions or the power of a man that the emotion adheres obstinately to him.

Proof.—The force and increase of any passion, and its persistence in existing, is defined by the power of an external cause compared with ours: and therefore it can surpass a man's power, etc. *Q.e.d.*

Prop. VII. An emotion can neither be hindered nor removed save by a contrary emotion and one stronger in checking emotion.

Proof.—An emotion, in so far as it has reference to the mind, is an idea wherewith the mind affirms a greater or less force of existing of its body than before. When, therefore, the mind is assailed by any emotion, the body is affected at the same time by a modification whereby its power of acting is either increased or diminished. Now this modification of the body receives from its cause the force for persisting in its being, which therefore can neither be restrained nor removed save by a bodily cause which affects the body with a modification contrary to that one and stronger than it. And therefore the mind is affected by the idea of a modification stronger and contrary to the previous one, that is, the mind will be affected with an emotion stronger and contrary to the former which cuts off the existence of or takes away the former: and thus the emotion can neither be checked nor removed save by a contrary and stronger emotion. *Q.e.d.*

Corollary.—An emotion, in so far as it has reference to the mind, can neither be hindered nor destroyed save through the idea of a contrary modification of the body and one stronger than the modification which we suffer. For the emotion which we suffer cannot be checked or removed save by an emotion stronger than it and contrary to it, that is, save through the idea of a modification of the body stronger than and contrary to the modification which we suffer.

PROP. VIII. The knowledge of good or evil is nothing else than the emotion of pleasure or pain, in so far as we are conscious of it.

Proof.—We call that good or evil which is useful or the contrary for our preservation, that is, which increases or diminishes, helps or hinders our power of acting. And so, in so far as we perceive anything to affect us with pleasure or pain, we call it good or evil; and therefore the knowledge of good or evil is nothing else than the idea of pleasure or pain which follows necessarily from the emotion of pleasure or pain. But this idea is united to the emotion in the same manner as the mind is united to the body, that is, this idea is not distinguished in truth from that emotion or from the idea of the modification of the body save in conception alone. Therefore this knowledge of good and evil is nothing else than emotion itself, in so far as we are conscious of it. *Q.e.d.*

PROP. IX. An emotion whose cause we imagine to be with us at the present is stronger than if we did not imagine it to be present.

Proof.—Imagination is the idea wherewith the mind regards a thing as present which nevertheless indicates rather the disposition of the human body than the nature of the external body. Imagination is therefore an emotion in so far as it indicates the disposition of the body. But imagination is more intense as long as we imagine nothing which cuts off the present existence of the external object. Therefore an emotion also, whose cause we imagine to be with us in the present, is more intense or stronger than if we did not imagine it to be present with us. *Q.e.d.*

Corollary.—The image of a thing future or past, that is, of a thing which we regard with reference to time future or past, to the exclusion of time present, is, under similar conditions, weaker than the image of a thing present, and consequently the emotion towards a thing future or past is, *cæteris paribus,* less intense than the emotion towards a thing present.

PROP. X. Towards a future thing which we imagine to be close at hand we are more intensely affected than if we imagine the time of its existing to be further distant from the present; and by the recollection of a thing which we imagine to have passed not long ago we are more intensely affected also than if we imagine it to have passed long ago.

Proof.—For in so far as we imagine a thing to be close at hand or just to have past, we imagine that which will exclude the presence of the thing less than if we imagine its future time of existing to be further away from the present, or if it had passed away long ago: therefore we shall be affected towards it more intensely. *Q.e.d.*

PROP. XI. The emotion towards a thing which we imagine to be necessary is more intense, *cæteris paribus,* than towards a thing possible, contingent, or not necessary.

Proof.—In so far as we imagine anything to be necessary we affirm its existence, and on the contrary, we deny the existence of a thing in so far as we imagine it not necessary: and accordingly the emotion towards a thing necessary is more intense, *cæteris paribus,* than towards a thing not necessary. *Q.e.d.*

PROP. XII. The emotion towards a thing which we know to be non-existent at the present time, and which we imagine possible, is more intense, *cæteris paribus,* than that towards a thing contingent.

Proof.—In so far as we imagine the thing as contingent, we are affected by no image of another thing which imposes its existence on it; but, on the other hand, we imagine certain things cut off its present existence. But in so far as we imagine the thing to be possible in the future, we imagine certain things which impose existence on it, that is, which foster hope or fear: and therefore emotion towards a thing possible is more intense. *Q.e.d.*

Corollary.—Emotion towards a thing which we know to be non-existent in the present, and which we imagine as contingent, is far more mild than if we imagine the thing to be present with us.

Proof.—Emotion towards a thing which we imagine to exist in the present is more intense than if we imagined it as future, and it is far more intense if we imagine the future time not to be far distant from the present. Therefore the emotion towards a thing whose time of existing we imagine to be far distant from the present is far more mild than if we imagine it as present, and nevertheless is more intense than if we imagined that thing as contingent. Therefore the emotion towards a thing contingent is far more mild than if we imagined the thing to be with us at the present. *Q.e.d.*

PROP. XIII. Emotion towards a thing contingent, which we know does not exist in the present, is far more mild, *cæteris paribus,* than emotion towards a thing past.

Proof.—In so far as we imagine a thing as contingent, we are affected by the image of no other thing which imposes the existence of that thing; but, on the contrary, we imagine certain things which cut off its present existence. But in so far as we imagine it with reference to time past, we are supposed to imagine something which restores it to memory, or which excites the image of the thing, and thus far accordingly it brings it to pass that we regard it as if it were present. And therefore emotion towards a thing contingent, which we know does not exist in the present, is more mild, *cæteris paribus,* than emotion towards a thing past. *Q.e.d.*

PROP. XIV. A true knowledge of good and evil cannot restrain any emotion in so far as the knowledge is true, but only in so far as it is considered as an emotion.

Proof.—An emotion is an idea whereby the mind affirms a greater or less force of existing of its body, and therefore it has nothing positive which can be removed by the presence of what is true; and consequently a true knowledge of good and evil, in so far as it is true, cannot restrain any emotion. But in so far as it is an emotion, if it is stronger for restraining emotion, thus far only it can hinder or restrain an emotion. *Q.e.d.*

PROP. XV. Desire which arises from a true knowledge of good and evil can be destroyed or checked by many other desires which arise from emotions by which we are assailed.

Proof.—From a true knowledge of good and evil, in so far as this is an emotion, there necessarily arises desire, which is the greater according as the emotion from which it arises is greater. But inasmuch as this desire arises from the fact that we truly understand something, it follows also that it is within us in so far as we are active. And therefore it must be understood through our essence alone, and consequently its force and increase must only be defined by human power. Again, the desires which arise from the emotions by which we are assailed are greater according as the emotions are the more intense; and therefore their force and increase must be defined by the power of the external causes, which, if compared with our own power, indefinitely surpasses our power. And therefore the desires which arise from similar emotions can be more intense than that which arises from the knowledge of good and evil; and therefore they will be able to check or destroy it. *Q.e.d.*

PROP. XVI. The desire which arises from the knowledge of good and evil, in so far as this knowledge has reference to the future, can more easily be checked or destroyed than the desire of things which are pleasing in the present.

Proof.—Emotion towards a thing which we imagine to be future is less intense than towards a thing present. But the desire which arises from the knowledge of good and evil, although this knowledge should concern things which are good in the present, can be destroyed or checked by any headstrong desire. Therefore the desire which arises from such knowledge, in so far as it has reference to the future, can be more easily destroyed or checked, etc. *Q.e.d.*

PROP. XVII. Desire which arises from true knowledge of good and evil, in so far as this concerns things contingent, can be far more easily restrained than the desire for things which are present.

Proof.—This proposition is proved in the same manner as the previous one.

PROP. XVIII. Desire which arises from pleasure is stronger, *cæteris paribus,* than the desire which arises from pain.

Proof.—Desire is the very essence of man, that is, the endeavour wherewith man endeavours to persist in his being. Wherefore desire which arises from pleasure is helped or increased by the emotion of pleasure itself; but that desire which arises from sadness or pain is diminished or hindered by the emotion of pain. And therefore the force of desire which arises from pleasure must be defined by human power, and at the same time, by the power of an external cause; but that which arises from pain must only be defined by human power: and therefore the former is stronger than the latter. *Q.e.d.*

PROP. XIX. Each one necessarily desires or turns from, by the laws of his nature, what he thinks to be good or evil.

Proof.—The knowledge of good and evil is the emotion of pleasure or pain in so far as we are conscious of it: and therefore every one necessarily desires what he thinks to be good, and turns from what he thinks to be evil. But this desire is nothing else than the very essence or nature of man. Therefore every one, from the laws of his nature alone, necessarily desires or turns away from, etc. *Q.e.d.*

PROP. XX. The more each one seeks what is useful to him, that is, the more he endeavours and can preserve his being, the more he is endowed with virtue; and, on the contrary, the more one neglects to preserve what is useful, or his being, he is thus far impotent or powerless.

Proof.—Virtue is human power itself, which is defined by the essence of man alone, that is, which is defined by the endeavour alone wherewith the endeavours to persist in his own being. The more, therefore, he endeavours and succeeds in preserving his own essence, the more he is endowed with virtue, and consequently in so far as he neglects to preserve his being he is thus far wanting in power. *Q.e.d.*

PROP. XXI. No one can desire to be blessed, to act well, or live well, who at the same time does not desire to be, to act, and to live, that is, actually to exist.

Proof.—The proof of this proposition, or rather the thing itself, is self-evident, and appears from the definition of desire. For the desire of being blessed, of acting well, and of living well, etc., is the very essence of man, that is, the endeavour wherewith each one endeavours to preserve his own being. Therefore no one can desire, etc. *Q.e.d.*

PROP. XXII. No virtue can be conceived as prior to this virtue of endeavouring to preserve oneself.

Proof.—The endeavour of preserving oneself is the very essence of a thing. If, therefore, any virtue can be conceived as prior to this one, namely, this endeavour, the essence of the thing would therefore be conceived prior to itself, which, as is self-manifest, is absurd. Therefore no virtue, etc. *Q.e.d.*

Corollary.—The endeavour of preserving oneself is the first and only basis of virtue, for prior to this principle nothing else can be conceived, and without it no virtue can be conceived.

PROP. XXIII. Man, in so far as he is determined to do anything, by the fact that he has inadequate ideas cannot absolutely be said to act from virtue, but only in so far as he is determined by the fact that he understands.

Proof.—In so far as a man is determined to do something by the fact that he has inadequate ideas, suffers or is passive, that is, he does something which cannot be perceived through its own essence alone, that is, which does not follow from his virtue. But in so far as he is determined to do something, by the fact that he understands, he is active, that is, he does something which can be perceived through its own essence alone or which follows adequately from his virtue. *Q.e.d.*

PROP. XXIV. To act absolutely according to virtue is nothing else in us than to act under the guidance of reason, to live so, and to preserve one's being on the basis of seeking what is useful to oneself.

Proof.—To act absolutely from virtue is nothing else than to act according to the laws of one's own nature. But we only act so in so far as we understand. Therefore to act according to virtue is nothing else in us than to act, to live, and preserve our being according to the guidance of reason, on the basis of seeking what is useful to oneself. *Q.e.d.*

PROP. XXV. No one endeavours to preserve his being for the sake of anything else.

Proof.—The endeavour wherewith each thing endeavours to persist in its own being is defined by the essence of the thing alone, and from this alone, and not from the essence of any other thing. It necessarily follows that each one endeavours to preserve his own essence. Therefore no one endeavours, etc. *Q.e.d.*

PROP. XXVI. Whatever we endeavour to do under the guidance of reason is nothing else than to understand; nor does the mind, in so far as it uses reason, judge anything useful to itself save what is conducive to understanding.

Proof.—The endeavour to preserve oneself is nothing else than the essence of the thing which, in so far as it exists as such, is conceived to have force for persisting in existing, and for doing those things which necessarily follow from its given nature. But the essence of reason is nothing else than the mind itself in so far as it understands clearly and distinctly. Therefore, whatever we endeavour to do under the guidance of reason is nothing else than to understand. Again, as this endeavour of the mind, in so far as the mind reasons, endeavours to preserve its being, it does nothing else than to understand. Therefore this endeavour to understand is the first and only basis of virtue. Nor do we endeavour to understand for the sake of any end, but, on the contrary, the mind, in so far as it reasons, cannot conceive anything as good to itself save what is conducive to understanding.

PROP. XXVII. We know nothing to be certainly good or evil save what is truly conducive to understanding or what prevents us from understanding.

Proof.—The mind, in so far as it reasons, desires nothing else than to understand, nor does it judge anything useful to itself save what is conducive to understanding. But the mind has no certainty in things save in so far as it has adequate ideas, or, what is the same thing, in so far as it reasons. Therefore we understand nothing to be certainly good save what is conducive to understanding, and, on the contrary, that to be bad which can prevent us from understanding. *Q.e.d.*

PROP. XXVIII. The greatest good of the mind is the knowledge of God, and the greatest virtue of the mind is to know God.

Proof.—The greatest thing that the mind can understand is God, that is, a being absolutely infinite, and without which nothing can either be or be conceived. Therefore the thing of the greatest use or good to the mind is the knowledge of God. Again, the mind, in so far as it understands, thus far only is active, and thus far can it be absolutely said that it acts according to virtue. To understand, therefore, is the absolute virtue of the mind. But the greatest thing that the mind can understand is God. Therefore the greatest virtue of the mind is to understand or know God. *Q.e.d.*

PROP. XXIX. Any individual thing whose nature is altogether different to ours can aid or hinder our power of understanding, and absolutely nothing can be either good or bad save if it have something in common with us.

Proof.—The power of any individual thing, and consequently the power of man, by which he exists and works, is only determined by another individual thing whose nature must be understood through the same attribute through which human nature is conceived. Therefore our power of acting, in whatever way it may be conceived, can be determined, and consequently aided or hindered, by the power of some other thing which has something in common with us, and not by the power of something whose nature is altogether different to ours; and inasmuch as we call that good or bad which is the cause of pleasure or pain, that is, which increases or diminishes, aids or hinders our power of acting, therefore the thing whose nature is entirely different to ours can be neither good nor bad to us. *Q.e.d.*

Prop. XXX. Nothing can be bad through that which it has in common with our nature; but in so far as it is bad, thus far it is contrary to us.

Proof.—We call that bad which is the cause of pain, that is, which increases or diminishes our power of acting. If, therefore, anything through that which it has in common with us were bad to us, it would therefore be able to diminish or hinder what it has in common with us, which is absurd. Therefore nothing through that which it has in common with us can be bad to us; but, on the other hand, in so far as it is bad, that is, in so far as it can diminish or hinder our power of action, thus far it is contrary to us. *Q.e.d.*

Prop. XXXI. In so far as anything agrees with our nature, thus far it is necessarily good.

Proof.—In so far as anything agrees with our nature it cannot be bad. It will therefore be either good or indifferent. If we suppose this, that it is neither good nor bad, then nothing will follow from its nature which can serve for the preservation of our nature, that is, which serves for the preservation of the thing itself. But this is absurd. It will therefore be, in so far as it agrees with our nature, necessarily good. *Q.e.d.*

Corollary.—Hence it follows that the more a thing agrees with our nature, the more useful or good it is to us, and, on the other hand, the more useful anything is to us, the more it agrees with our nature. For in so far as it does not agree with our nature it will necessarily be different to our nature or contrary to it. If it is different, then it can be neither good nor bad; if it is contrary, it will therefore be contrary to that which agrees with our nature, that is, contrary to good or bad. Nothing, therefore, save in so far as it agrees with our nature, can be good; and therefore the more it agrees with our nature, the more useful it is to us, and contrariwise. *Q.e.d.*

Prop. XXXII. In so far as men are liable to passions they cannot thus far be said to agree in nature.

Proof.—Things which are said to agree in nature are understood to agree in power, but not in want of power or negation, and consequently in passion. Wherefore men, in so far as they are liable to passions, cannot be thus far said to agree in nature. *Q.e.d.*

PROP. XXXIII. Men can differ in nature in so far as they are assailed by emotions which are passions, and thus far one and the same man is variable and inconstant.

Proof.—The nature or essence of emotion cannot be explained through our essence or nature alone, but by the power, that is, by the nature of external causes compared with our own, it must be defined. Whence it comes about that there are as many species of each emotion as there are species of objects by which we are affected, and that men are affected by one and the same object in different manners, and thus far disagree in nature, and moreover, that one and the same man is affected in different manners towards the same object, and thus far is variable, etc. *Q.e.d.*

PROP. XXXIV. Men, in so far as they are assailed by emotions which are passions, can be contrary one to the other.

Proof.—A man, e.g., Peter, can be the cause that Paul is saddened, inasmuch as he has something similar to a thing which Paul hates, or inasmuch as Peter possesses alone something which Paul also loves, or on other accounts. And therefore it hence comes to pass that Paul hates Peter, and consequently it may easily happen that Peter hates Paul on the other hand, and therefore that they endeavour to work each other reciprocal harm, that is, that they become contrary one to the other. But the emotion of pain is always a passion: therefore men, in so far as they are assailed by emotions which are passions, can be contrary one to the other. *Q.e.d.*

PROP. XXXV. In so far as men live under the guidance of reason, thus far only they always necessarily agree in nature.

Proof.—In so far as men are assailed by emotions which are passions they can be different in nature and contrary one to the other. But men are said to be active only in so far as they live under the guidance of reason, and therefore whatever follows from human nature, in so far as it is defined by reason, must be understood through human nature alone as its proximate cause. But inasmuch as each one desires according to the laws of his own nature what is good, and endeavours to remove what he thinks to be bad, and inasmuch as that which we judge to be good or bad, according to the dictate of reason, is necessarily good or bad, therefore men, in so far as they live according to the dictates of reason, do those things which are necessarily good to human nature, and consequently to each man, that is, which agree with the nature of each man. And therefore men also necessarily agree one with the other in so far as they live according to the mandate of reason. *Q.e.d.*

Corollary I.—There is no individual thing in nature more useful to man than one who lives under the guidance of reason. For that is most useful to man which mostly agrees with his nature, that is, man. But man is absolutely active according to the laws of his nature when he lives under the guidance of reason, and thus far only can he agree necessarily with the nature of another man. Therefore there is nothing more useful to man than a man, etc. *Q.e.d.*

Corollary II.—As each man seeks that most which is useful to him, so men are most useful one to the other. For the more each man seeks what is useful to him and endeavours to preserve himself, the more he is endowed with virtue, or, what is the same thing, the more power he is endowed with to act according to the laws of his nature, that is, to live under the guidance of reason. But men mostly agree in nature when they live under the guidance of reason. Therefore men are most useful one to the other when each one most seeks out what is useful to himself. *Q.e.d.*

PROP. XXXVI. The greatest good of those who follow virtue is common to all, and all can equally enjoy it.

Proof.—To act from virtue is to act from the instruction of reason, and whatever we endeavour to do from reason is understanding. And therefore the greatest good of those who follow virtue is to know God, that is, the good which is common to all men, and which can be possessed equally by all men, in so far as they are of the same nature. *Q.e.d.*

PROP. XXXVII. The good which each one who follows virtue desires for himself, he also desires for other men, and the more so the more knowledge he has of God.

Proof.—Men, in so far as they live under the guidance of reason, are most useful to men; and therefore we endeavour, under the guidance of reason, to bring it about that men live under the guidance of reason. But the good which each person who lives according to the dictate of reason, that is, who follows virtue, desires for himself, he desires also for other men. Again, desire, in so far as it has reference to the mind, is the very essence of the mind; but the essence of the mind consists of knowledge, which involves knowledge of God, and without which it cannot exist or be conceived. And therefore, according as the essence of the mind involves a greater knowledge of God, so the desire with which he who follows virtue desires the good which he desires for himself for others, will be greater. *Q.e.d.*

PROP. XXXVIII. That is useful to man which so disposes the human body that it can be affected in many modes, or which renders it capable of affecting external bodies in many modes, and the more so according as it renders the body more apt to be affected in many modes or to affect other bodies so; and, on the contrary, that is harmful to man which renders the body less apt for this.

Proof.—The more the body is rendered apt for this, the more the mind is rendered apt for perceiving: and therefore that which disposes the body in that way and renders it apt for this, is necessarily good or useful, and more useful the more apt it renders the body for this, and, on the contrary, that is harmful which renders the body less apt for this. *Q.e.d.*

Prop. XXXIX. Whatever brings it to pass that the proportion of motion and rest which the parts of the human body hold one to the other is preserved, is good; and contrariwise, that is bad which brings it about that the parts of the human body have another proportion mutually of motion and rest.

Proof.—The human body needs for its preservation many other bodies; but that which constitutes the form of the human body consists of this, that its parts convey one to the other their motions mutually in a certain ratio. Therefore that which brings it about that the proportion of motion and rest which the parts of the body have one to the other is preserved, preserves the form of the human body, and consequently brings it to pass that the human body can be affected in many ways, and also that it can affect external bodies in many ways: and therefore it is good. Again, that which brings it to pass that the parts of the human body assume some other proportion of motion and rest, bring it to pass that the human body assumes another form, that is, that the human body is destroyed, and consequently rendered entirely inapt for being affected in many modes: and therefore it is bad. *Q.e.d.*

Prop. XL. Whatever is conducive of the common society of men, or whatever brings it about that men live together in peace and agreement, is useful, and, on the contrary, that is bad which induces discord in the state.

Proof.—Whatever brings it about that men live together in agreement, brings it about at the same time that they live under the guidance of reason, and therefore it is good: and that, on the other hand, is bad which fosters discord. *Q.e.d.*

Prop. XLI. Pleasure clearly is not evil but good; but pain, on the contrary, is clearly evil.

Proof.—Pleasure is an emotion by which the power of acting of the body is increased or aided; but pain contrariwise is an emotion whereby the body's power of acting is diminished or hindered; and therefore pleasure is certainly good, etc. *Q.e.d.*

Prop. XLII. There cannot be too much merriment, but it is always good; but, on the other hand, melancholy is always bad.

Proof.—Merriment is pleasure which, in so far as it has reference to the body, consists of this, that all the parts of the body are equally affected, that is, that the body's power of acting is increased or aided in such a way as all the parts preserve the same proportions of motion and rest one with the other; and therefore merriment is always good, and can have no excess. But melancholy is pain which, in so far as it has reference to the body, consists of this, that the body's power of acting is absolutely diminished or hindered; and therefore it is always bad. *Q.e.d.*

PROP. XLIII. Titillation can be excessive and be bad; but grief may be good in so far as titillation or pleasure is bad.

Proof.—Titillation is pleasure which, in so far as it has reference to the body, consists of this, that one or several parts of the body are affected beyond the rest; the power of this emotion can be so great that it surpasses the remaining actions of the body, and it may become very fixedly adhered to this, and accordingly prevent the body from being ready to be affected by many other modes; and therefore it can be bad. Again, grief which, on the other hand, is pain, considered in itself cannot be good. But inasmuch as its force and increase is defined by the power of an external cause compared with our own, we can therefore conceive infinite degrees and modes of the forces of this emotion; and so we can conceive such a mode or grade which can restrain titillation so that it is not excessive, and thus far bring it about that the body should not be rendered less apt; and thus far it will be good. *Q.e.d.*

PROP. XLIV. Love and desire can be excessive.

Proof.—Love is pleasure accompanied by the idea of an external cause. Therefore titillation accompanied by the idea of an external cause is love; and therefore love can be excessive. Again, desire is the greater according as the emotion from which it arose is greater. Wherefore, as an emotion can surpass all the other actions of man, so also can desire which arises from that emotion surpass other desires, and so it can have the same excess as we proved in the previous proposition titillation to have. *Q.e.d.*

PROP. XLV. Hatred can never be good.

Proof.—We endeavour to destroy the man whom we hate, that is, we endeavour to do something which is bad. Therefore, etc. *Q.e.d.*

Let it be noted that here and in the following propositions I only understand by hatred that towards men.

Corollary I.—Envy, derision, contempt, rage, revenge, and the other emotions which have reference to hatred or arise from it, are bad.

Corollary II.—Whatever we desire owing to the fact that we are affected with hatred is evil and unjust in the state.

PROP. XLVI. He who lives under the guidance of reason endeavours as much as possible to repay his fellow's hatred, rage, contempt, etc., with love and nobleness.

Proof.—All emotions of hatred are bad: and therefore he who lives according to the precepts of reason will endeavour as much as possible to bring it to pass that he is not assailed by emotions of hatred, and consequently he will endeavour to prevent any one else from suffering those emotions. But hatred is increased by reciprocated hatred, and, on the contrary, can be demolished by love in such a way that hatred is transformed into love. Therefore he who lives under the guidance of reason will endeavour to repay another's hatred, etc., with love, that is nobleness. *Q.e.d.*

PROP. XLVII. The emotions of hope and fear cannot be in themselves good.

Proof.—The emotions of hope and fear are not given without pain. For fear is sadness or pain, and hope is not given without fear. And thus these emotions cannot be in themselves good, but only in so far as they can restrain an excess of pleasure. *Q.e.d.*

PROP. XLVIII. The emotions of partiality and disparagement are always bad.

Proof.—Now these emotions are opposed to reason, and therefore they are bad. *Q.e.d.*

PROP. XLIX. Partiality easily renders the man who is over-estimated, proud.

Proof.—If we see any one praises more than justly what is in us through love we are easily exulted, or we are affected with pleasure, and we easily believe whatever good we hear said about us. And therefore we esteem ourselves beyond the limits of justice through self-love, that is, we easily become proud. *Q.e.d.*

PROP. L. Pity in a man who lives under the guidance of reason is in itself bad and useless.

Proof.—Now pity is sadness, and therefore is bad in itself. The good which follows from it, namely, that we endeavour to free the man whom we pity from his misery, we desire to do from the mere command of reason, nor can we do anything which we know to be good save under the guidance of reason. And therefore pity in a man who lives under the guidance of reason is bad and useless in itself. *Q.e.d.*

Corollary.—Hence it follows that a man who lives according to the dictate of reason endeavours as far as possible not to be touched with pity.

PROP. LI. Favour is not opposed to reason, but can agree with it and arise from it.

Proof.—Now favour is love towards him who has benefited another: and therefore it can have reference to the mind in so far as it is said to be active, that is, in so far as it understands; and therefore it agrees with reason, etc. *Q.e.d.*

PROP. LII. Self-complacency can arise from reason, and that self-complacency which arises from reason alone is the greatest.

Proof.—Self-complacency is pleasure arisen from the fact that man regards himself and his power of acting. But the true power of acting of man or his virtue is reason itself, which man clearly and distinctly regards. Therefore self-complacency arises from reason. Again, man while he regards himself perceives nothing clearly and distinctly, save those things which follow from his power of acting, that is, which follow from his power of understanding. Therefore from this self-regarding the greatest self-complacency possible arises. *Q.e.d.*

PROP. LIII. Humility is not a virtue if it does not arise from reason.

Proof.—Humility is pain which arises from the fact that man regards his own want of power. But in so far as man knows himself by true reason, thus far he is supposed to understand his essence, that is, his power. Wherefore if man, while he regards himself, perceives any weakness of his, it arises not from the fact that he understands himself, but from the fact that his power of acting is hindered. But if we suppose that man conceives his weakness from the fact that he understands something more powerful than himself, whose knowledge determines his power of acting, then we conceive nothing else than that man distinctly understands himself, and thereby his power of acting is aided. Wherefore humility or pain, which arises from the fact that man regards his weakness, does not arise from true contemplation or reason, and is not a virtue but a passion. *Q.e.d.*

PROP. LIV. Repentance is not a virtue, or, in other words, it does not arise from reason, but he who repents of an action is twice as unhappy or as weak as before.

Proof.—The first part of this proposition is proved in the same manner as the preceding proposition. The second part is clear merely from the definition of this emotion. For the man allows himself to be overcome first by evil desire and then by pain.

PROP. LV. The greatest pride or dejection is the greatest ignorance of self.

Proof.—This is clear from Definitions of the Emotions 28 and 29 [as follows]:

28. Pride (*superbia*) is over-estimation of oneself by reason of self-love.

Explanation.—Pride is different from partiality, for the latter has reference to the over-estimation of an external object, while the former has reference to self-over-estimation. However, as partiality is the effect or property of love, so pride is that of self-love (*philautia*), which therefore may be defined as love of self, or self-complacency, in so far as it thus affects man so as to over-estimate himself. There is no contrary to this emotion. For no one under-estimates oneself by reason of self-hate, that is, no one under-estimates himself in so far as he imagines that he cannot do this or that. For whatever a man imagines that he cannot do, he imagines it necessarily, and by that very imagination he is so disposed that in truth he cannot do what he imagines he cannot do. For so long as he imagines that he cannot do this or that, so long is he determined not to do it: and consequently, so long it is impossible to him that he should do it. However, if we pay attention to these things, which depend solely on opinion, we shall be able to conceive that it is possible that a man should under-estimate himself. For it can well come to pass that any one, while sadly regarding his weakness, should imagine that he is despised by all, and that while all other men are thinking of nothing less than of despising him. A man, moreover, may under-estimate himself if he deny himself something in the present with relation to future time of which he is uncertain: as, for example, if he should deny that he can conceive anything certain, or desire or do anything save what is wicked and disgraceful, etc. We could, moreover, say that any one under-estimates himself when we see that he dares not do certain things from too great a fear of shame which others who are his equals do without any fear. We can therefore oppose this emotion to pride; I shall call it self-despising or dejection (*abjectio*). For as self-complacency arises from pride, so self-despising arises from humility: and this therefore may thus be defined:

29. Self-despising or dejection (*abjectio*) is under-estimating oneself by reason of pain.

Explanation.—We are wont, nevertheless, to contrast pride with humility, but then more when we regard their effects than their nature. For we are wont to call him proud who praises himself too much, who relates only his own great deeds and only the evil ones of others, who wishes to be before others, and who lives with that gravity and adornment which is natural to those who are far above him in rank. On the other hand, we call him humble who often blushes, who confesses his faults, and relates the virtues and great deeds of others, who yields to all, who walks with a bowed head, and neglects to take upon himself any ornament of dress. But these emotions of humility and self-despising are very rare, for human nature considered in itself strives as much as possible against them; and therefore those who are believed to be most abject and humble are usually most ambitious and envious.

PROP. LVI. The greatest pride or dejection indicates the greatest weakness cf mind.

Proof.—The primary basis of virtue is self-preservation, and that under the guidance of reason. He, therefore, who knows not himself, knows not the basis of all virtues, and consequently is ignorant of all virtues. Again, to act from virtue is nothing else than to act under the guidance of reason, and he who acts under the guidance of reason must necessarily know that he acts under the guidance of reason. He, therefore, who has the greatest ignorance of himself, and consequently of all the virtues, acts the least from virtue, that is, he is most weak in his mind; and therefore the greatest pride or dejection indicates the greatest weakness of mind. *Q.e.d.*

Corollary.—Hence it follows most clearly that proud and dejected people are most liable to emotions.

PROP. LVII. A proud man loves the presence of parasites or flatterers, but the presence of noble people he hates.

Proof.—Pride is pleasure arisen from the fact that man over-estimates himself; this opinion a proud man endeavours as much as possible to foster. And therefore he will love the presence of parasites or flatterers, and as for the company or presence of noble men, he will hate it. *Q.e.d.*

PROP. LVIII. Honour is not opposed to reason, but can arise from it.

Proof.—This is clear from Definition of Emotion 30 [as follows]:

30. Honour or glory (*gloria*) is pleasure accompanied by the idea of some action of ours which we imagine others to praise.

PROP. LIX. For all actions for which we are determined by an emotion which is a passion we can be determined without that emotion by reason alone.

Proof.—To act from reason is nothing else than to do those things which follow from the necessity of our nature considered in itself. But pain is bad in so far as it diminishes or hinders this power of acting. Therefore from this emotion we can be determined for no action which we could not do if we were led by reason. Moreover, pleasure is bad in so far as it prevents man from being ready for action. And therefore we can be determined for no action which we could not do if we were led by reason. Again, in so far as pleasure is good it agrees with reason, nor is it a passion save in so far as it does not increase man's power of acting to the extent that he perceives himself and his actions adequately. Wherefore if a man affected with pleasure is led to such perfection that he conceives himself and his actions adequately, he will be as apt, nay more apt, for those actions for which he was determined by emotions which are passions. But all emotions have reference either to pleasure, pain, or desire, and desire is nothing else than the endeavour to act. Therefore for all actions for which we are determined by an emotion which is a passion we can be determined by reason alone. *Q.e.d.*

PROP. LX. Desire which arises from pleasure or pain which has reference to one or certain parts of the body has no advantage to man as a whole.

Proof.—Let it be supposed that a part, e.g., A, of a body is so aided by the force of some external cause that it overcomes the rest. This part will not endeavour to lose its forces in order that the other parts may perform their functions, or it would then have the force or power of losing its forces, which is absurd. That part will therefore endeavour, and consequently the mind also will endeavour, to preserve its condition; and therefore desire which arises from such an emotion of pleasure will not bring advantage to the body as a whole. Then if, on the other hand, it is supposed that the part A is hindered in such a way that the remaining parts overcome it, it may be proved in the same manner that the desire which arises from pain will not bring advantage to the body as a whole. *Q.e.d.*

PROP. LXI. Desire which arises from reason can have no excess.

Proof.—Desire absolutely considered is the very essence of man in so far as it is conceived as determined in any manner to do anything. Therefore desire which arises from reason, that is, which is engendered in us in so far as we are active, is the very essence or nature of man in so far as it is conceived as determined to do those things which are adequately conceived through the essence of man alone. If, therefore, this desire can have excess, then human nature considered in itself can exceed itself, or could do more than it can do, which is a manifest contradiction. And therefore this desire cannot have excess. *Q.e.d.*

PROP. LXII. In so far as the mind conceives a thing according to the dictate of reason, it will be equally affected whether the idea be of a thing present, past, or future.

Proof.—Whatever the mind conceives under the guidance of reason, it conceives entirely under a certain species of eternity or necessity, and is affected with the same certainty. Wherefore, whether the idea be of a thing future, past, or present, the mind will conceive it by the same necessity and will be affected with the same certainty; and whether the idea be of a thing present, past, or future, it will nevertheless be equally true, that is, it will have, nevertheless, the same properties of an adequate idea. And therefore in so far as the mind conceives a thing according to the dictates of reason it is affected in the same manner, whether the idea be of a thing future, past, or present. *Q.e.d.*

Prop. LXIII. He that is led by fear to do good in order to avoid evil is not led by reason.

Proof.—All emotions which have reference to the mind in so far as it is active, that is, which have reference to reason, are none other than the emotions of pleasure and desire. And therefore he that is led by fear to do good in order to avoid evil is not led by reason. *Q.e.d.*

Corollary.—By reason of the desire which arises from reason we directly follow what is good and indirectly avoid what is evil.

Proof.—The desire which arises from reason can only arise from the emotion of pleasure which is not a passion, that is, from pleasure which cannot be excessive, and not from pain. And accordingly this desire arises from the knowledge of good, and not from that of evil. And therefore under the guidance of reason we directly desire what is good, and thus far only we avoid what is evil. *Q.e.d.*

Prop. LXIV. The knowledge of evil is inadequate knowledge.

Proof.—The knowledge of evil is pain itself in so far as we are conscious of it. But pain is a transition to a lesser state of perfection, which on that account cannot be understood through the essence itself of man. And accordingly it is a passion which depends on inadequate ideas, and consequently the knowledge of evil is inadequate. *Q.e.d.*

Corollary.—Hence it follows that if the human mind had only adequate ideas it would form no notion of evil.

Prop. LXV. Under the guidance of reason we follow the greater of two things which are good and the lesser of two things which are evil.

Proof.—A good thing which prevents us from enjoying a greater good is in truth an evil, for good and bad is said of things in so far as we compare them one with the other, and a lesser evil is in truth a good. Wherefore under the guidance of reason we desire or follow only the greater of two things which are good and the lesser of two which are evil. *Q.e.d.*

Corollary.—We may follow under the guidance of reason the lesser evil as if it were the greater good, and neglect the lesser good as the cause of a greater evil. For the evil which is here called lesser is in truth good, and, on the other hand, the good is evil. Wherefore we desire the former and avoid the latter. *Q.e.d.*

Prop. LXVI. Under the guidance of reason we desire a greater future good before a lesser present one, and a lesser evil in the present "before a greater in the future" (Van Vloten's version).

Proof.—If the mind could have adequate knowledge of a future thing, it would be affected with the same emotion towards a future thing as towards a present one. Wherefore, in so far as we have regard to reason, as we are supposed to do in this proposition, whether the greater good or evil be supposed future or present, the thing is the same. And therefore we desire a greater future good before a lesser present one. *Q.e.d.*

Corollary.—We desire under the guidance of reason a lesser present evil which is the cause of a greater future good, and we avoid a lesser present good which is the cause of a greater future evil.

PROP. LXVII. A free man thinks of nothing less than of death, and his wisdom is a meditation not of death but of life.

Proof.—A free man, that is, one who lives according to the dictate of reason alone, is not led by the fear of death, but directly desires what is good, that is, to act, to live, and preserve his being on the basis of seeking what is useful to him. And therefore he thinks of nothing less than of death, but his wisdom is a meditation of life. *Q.e.d.*

PROP. LXVIII. If men were born free they would form no conception of good and evil as long as they were free.

Proof.—I said that he was free who is led by reason alone. He, therefore, who is born free and remains free has only adequate ideas, and accordingly has no conception of evil, and consequently none of good. *Q.e.d.*

PROP. LXIX. The virtue of a free man appears equally great in refusing to face difficulties as in overcoming them.

Proof.—An emotion cannot be hindered or taken away save by a contrary emotion stronger in restraining. But blind daring and fear are emotions which can be conceived equally great. Therefore an equally great virtue or fortitude of mind is required to restrain daring as to restrain fear, that is, a free man declines dangers with the same mental virtue as that with which he attempts to overcome them. *Q.e.d.*

Corollary.—Therefore a free man is led by the same fortitude of mind to take flight in time as to fight; or a free man chooses from the same courage or presence of mind to fight or to take flight.

PROP. LXX. A free man, who lives among ignorant people, tries as much as he can to refuse their benefits.

Proof.—Every one judges according to his own disposition what is good. Therefore an ignorant man who has conferred a benefit on any one will estimate it according to his own disposition, and if he sees it to be estimated less by him to whom he gave it, he will be pained. But the free man desires to join other men to him in friendship, and not to repay men with similar gifts according to their emotion towards him: he tries to lead himself and others according to the free judgment of reason, and to do those things only which he knows to be of primary importance. Therefore a free man, lest he should become hateful to the ignorant, and lest he should be governed not by their desire or appetite, but by reason alone, endeavours as far as possible to refuse their benefits. *Q.e.d.*

PROP. LXXI. Only free men are truly grateful one to the other.

Proof.—Only free men are truly useful one to the other, and are united by the closest bond of friendship, and endeavour to benefit each other with an equal impulse of love. And therefore only free men are truly grateful one to the other. *Q.e.d.*

PROP. LXXII. A free man never acts by fraud, but always with good faith.

Proof.—If a free man were to do something by fraud in so far as he is free, he would act according to the dictate of reason; and therefore to act fraudulently would be a virtue, and consequently it would be most advantageous to each one to act fraudulently, that is, it would be most advantageous for men to agree only in what they say, but to be contrary one to the other in what they do, which is absurd. Therefore a free man, etc. *Q.e.d.*

PROP. LXXIII. A man who is guided by reason is more free in a state where he lives according to common law than in solitude where he is subject to no law.

Proof.—A man who is guided by reason is not held in subjection by fear, but in so far as he endeavours to preserve his being according to the dictates of reason, that is, in so far as he endeavours to live freely, he desires to have regard for common life and advantage, and consequently he desires to live according to the ordinary decrees of the state. Therefore a man who is guided desires, in order to live with more freedom, to regard the ordinary laws of the state. *Q.e.d.*

FIFTH PART: CONCERNING THE POWER OF THE INTELLECT OR HUMAN FREEDOM

AXIOMS

I. IF in the same subject two contrary actions are excited, a change must take place in both or in one of them until they cease to be contrary.

II. The power of emotion is defined by the power of its cause in so far as its essence is explained or defined through the essence of its cause. This axiom is clear from Prop. 7, Part III.

PROPOSITIONS

Prop. I. Just as thoughts and the ideas of the mind are arranged and connected in the mind, so in the body its modifications or the modifications of things are arranged and connected according to their order.

Proof.—The order and connection of ideas is the same as the order and connection of things, and vice versa, the order and connection of things is the same as the order and connection of ideas. Wherefore just as the order and connection of ideas in the mind is made according to the order and connection of the modifications of the body, so, vice versa, the order and connection of the modifications of the body is made according as thoughts and the ideas of things are arranged and connected in the mind. *Q.e.d.*

Prop. II. If we remove disturbance of the mind or emotion from the thought of an external cause and unite it to other thoughts, then love or hatred towards the external cause, as well as waverings of the mind which arise from these emotions, are destroyed.

Proof.—Now that which constitutes the form of love or hatred is pleasure or pain accompanied by the idea of an external cause. When this then is removed, the form of love or hatred is also removed: and therefore these emotions and those which arise from them are destroyed. *Q.e.d.*

Prop. III. An emotion which is a passion ceases to be a passion as soon as we form a clear and distinct idea of it.

Proof.—An emotion which is a passion is a confused idea. If, therefore, we form a clear and distinct idea of this emotion, this idea will be distinguished from the emotion in so far as it has reference to the mind alone by reason alone: and therefore the emotion will cease to be a passion. *Q.e.d.*

Corollary.—Therefore the more an emotion becomes known to us, the more it is within our power and the less the mind is passive to it.

Prop. IV. There is no modification of the body of which we cannot form some clear and distinct conception.

Proof.—Things which are common to all can only be adequately conceived: and therefore there is no modification of the body of which we cannot form some clear and distinct conception. *Q.e.d.*

Corollary.—Hence it follows that there is no emotion of which we cannot form some clear and distinct conception. For an emotion is the idea of a modification of the body, which on that account must involve some clear and distinct conception.

PROP. V. Emotion towards a thing which we imagine simply and not as necessary nor possible nor contingent, is, *cæteris paribus,* the greatest of all.

Proof.—Emotion towards a thing which we imagine to be free is greater than that towards one which is necessary, and consequently still greater than that towards a thing which we imagine as possible or contingent. But to imagine a thing as free is nothing else than that we imagined it simply while we were ignorant of the causes by which it was determined for acting. Therefore emotion towards a thing which we imagine simply is greater, *cæteris paribus,* than towards a thing necessary, possible, or contingent, and consequently the greatest. *Q.e.d.*

PROP. VI. In so far as the mind understands all things as necessary it has more power over the emotions or is less passive to them.

Proof.—The mind understands all things as necessary, and to be determined for existing and acting by the infinite connection of causes: and therefore it brings it about that it is less passive to the emotions which arise from them and it will be affected less towards them. *Q.e.d.*

PROP. VII. Emotions which arise or are excited by reason, if we regard time, are greater than those which are referred to individual things which we regard as absent.

Proof.—We do not regard a thing as absent by reason of the emotion with which we imagine it, but by reason of the fact that the body is affected by another emotion which cuts off the existence of that thing. Wherefore an emotion which is referred to a thing which we regard as absent is not of such a nature that surpasses and overcomes the other actions and power of man, but contrariwise is of such a nature that it can be hindered in some manner by those modifications which cut off the existence of its external cause. But emotion which arises from reason has reference necessarily to the common properties of things which we always regard as present, and which we always imagine in the same manner. Wherefore such an emotion remains the same always, and consequently emotions which are contrary to it, and which are not aided by their external causes, must more and more accommodate themselves with it until they are no longer contrary, and thus far emotion which arises from reason is the stronger. *Q.e.d.*

PROP. VIII. The more an emotion is excited by many emotions concurring at the same time, the greater it will be.

Proof.—Many causes can do more at the same time than if they were fewer. And therefore the more an emotion is excited by many causes at the same time, the stronger it is. *Q.e.d.*

PROP. IX. Emotion which has reference to many different causes which the mind regards at the same time as the emotion itself is less harmful, and we are less passive to it and less affected toward each cause than another emotion equally great which has reference to one alone or fewer causes.

Proof.—An emotion is bad or harmful only in so far as the mind is prevented by it from thinking as much as before. And therefore that emotion by which the mind is determined for regarding many objects at the same time is less harmful than another equally great which detains the mind in the contemplation of one alone or fewer objects in such a manner that it cannot think of the others: which was the first point. Again, inasmuch as the essence of the mind, that is, its power, consists of thought alone, therefore the mind is less passive to an emotion by which it is determined for the regarding of many things than to an emotion equally great which holds the mind occupied in regarding one alone or fewer objects: which is the second point. Finally, this emotion, in so far as it has reference to many external causes, is less towards each one of them. *Q.e.d.*

PROP. X. As long as we are not assailed by emotions which are contrary to our nature we are able to arrange and connect the modifications of the body according to their intellectual order.

Proof.—The emotions which are contrary to our nature, that is, which are evil, are evil in so far as they prevent the mind from understanding. As long, therefore, as we are assailed by emotions which are contrary to our nature, so long the mind's power by which it endeavours to understand things is not hindered; and therefore so long it has the power of forming clear and distinct ideas and of deducing certain ones from others: and consequently so long we have the power of arranging and connecting the modifications of the body according to their intellectual order. *Q.e.d.*

PROP. XI. The more any image has reference to many things, the more frequent it is, the more often it flourishes, and the more it occupies the mind.

Proof.—The more an image or emotion has reference to many things, the more causes there are by which it can be excited and cherished, all of which the mind regards at the same time with the emotion. And therefore the emotion is more frequent or more often flourishes, and it occupies the mind more. *Q.e.d.*

PROP. XII. The images of things are more easily joined to images which have reference to things which we understand clearly and distinctly than to others.

Proof.—Things which we clearly and distinctly understand are either the common properties of things or what we deduce from them, and consequently they are more often excited in us. And therefore it can more easily happen that we should regard things at the same time with these than with other things, and consequently that they are associated with these more easily than with other things. *Q.e.d.*

PROP. XIII. The more an image is associated with many other things, the more often it flourishes.

Proof.—The more an image is associated with many other things, the more causes there are by which it can be excited. *Q.e.d.*

PROP. XIV. The mind can bring it to pass that all the modifications of the body or images of things have reference to the idea of God.

Proof.—There is no modification of the body of which the mind cannot form a clear and distinct conception. And therefore it can bring it to pass that all the images have reference to the idea of God. *Q.e.d.*

PROP. XV. He who understands himself and his emotions loves God, and the more so the more he understands himself and his emotions.

Proof.—He who clearly and distinctly understands himself and his emotions, rejoices accompanied with the idea of God. And therefore he loves God, and the more so the more he understands himself and his emotions. *Q.e.d.*

PROP. XVI. This love towards God must occupy the mind chiefly.

Proof.—This love is associated with all the modifications of the mind, by all of which it is cherished. And therefore it must chiefly occupy the mind. *Q.e.d.*

PROP. XVII. God is free from passions, nor is he affected with any emotion of pleasure or pain.

Proof.—All ideas, in so far as they have reference to God, are true, that is, they are adequate: and therefore God is without passions. Again, God cannot pass to a higher or a lower perfection: and therefore he is affected with no emotion of pleasure or pain. *Q.e.d.*

Corollary.—God, to speak strictly, loves no one nor hates any one. For God is affected with no emotion of pleasure or pain, and consequently loves no one nor hates any one.

PROP. XVIII. No one can hate God.

Proof.—The idea of God in us is adequate and perfect. And therefore in so far as we regard God we are active, and consequently there can be no pain accompanied by the idea of God, that is, none can hate God. *Q.e.d.*

Corollary.—Love towards God cannot be changed into hatred.

PROP. XIX. He who loves God cannot endeavour to bring it about that God should love him in return.

Proof.—If man desired this, he would therefore desire that the God whom he loves should not be God, and consequently he would desire to be pained, which is absurd. Therefore he who loves God, etc. *Q.e.d.*

PROP. XX. This love towards God cannot be polluted by an emotion either of envy or jealousy, but it is cherished the more, the more we imagine men to be bound to God by this bond of love.

Proof.—This love towards God is the greatest good which we can desire according to the dictate of reason, and it is common to all men, and we desire that all should enjoy it. And therefore it cannot be stained by the emotion of envy, nor again by the emotion of jealousy; but, on the other hand, it must be cherished the more, the more men we imagine to enjoy it. *Q.e.d.*

PROP. XXI. The mind can imagine nothing nor recollect past things save while in the body.

Proof.—The mind does not express the actual existence of its body nor conceives the modifications of the body to be actual save while in the body, and consequently it conceives no body as actually existing save while its own body exists. And thus it can imagine nothing nor recollect past things save while in the body. *Q.e.d.*

PROP. XXII. In God, however, there is necessarily granted the idea which expresses the essence of this or that human body under the species of eternity.

Proof.—God is not only the cause of this or that human body's existence, but also their essence, which therefore must necessarily be conceived through the essence of God, and that under a certain eternal necessity: and this conception must necessarily be granted in God. *Q.e.d.*

PROP. XXIII. The human mind cannot be absolutely destroyed with the human body, but there is some part of it that remains eternal.

Proof.—There is necessarily in God the conception or idea which expresses the essence of the human body, which therefore is something necessarily which appertains to the essence of the human mind. But we attribute to the human mind no duration which can be defined by time, save in so far as it expresses the actual essence of the human body, which is explained by means of duration and is defined by time, that is, we do not attribute duration save as long as the body lasts. But as there is nevertheless something else which is conceived under a certain eternal necessity through the essence of God, this something will be necessarily the eternal part which appertains to the essence of the mind. *Q.e.d.*

PROP. XXIV. The more we understand individual things, the more we understand God.

Proof.—This is clear from Prop. 25, Part I.

PROP. XXV. The greatest endeavour of the mind and its greatest virtue is to understand things by the third class of knowledge.

Proof.—The third class of knowledge proceeds from the adequate idea of certain attributes of God to the adequate knowledge of the essence of things, and the more we understand things in this manner, the more we understand God. And therefore the greatest virtue of the mind, that is, the mind's power or nature, or its greatest endeavour, is to understand things according to the third class of knowledge. *Q.e.d.*

PROP. XXVI. The more apt the mind is to understand things by the third class of knowledge, the more it desires to understand things by this class of knowledge.

Proof.—This is clear. For in so far as we conceive the mind to be apt to understand things by this kind of knowledge, thus far we conceive it as determined to understand things by the same kind of knowledge, and consequently the more apt the mind is for this, the more it desires it. *Q.e.d.*

PROP. XXVII. From this third class of knowledge the greatest possible mental satisfaction arises.

Proof.—The greatest virtue of the mind is to know God, or to understand according to the third class of knowledge: and this virtue is the greater according as the mind knows more things by this class of knowledge. And therefore he who knows things according to this class of knowledge, passes to the greatest state of perfection, and consequently he is affected with the greatest pleasure, and that accompanied by the idea of himself and his virtue: and therefore from this kind of knowledge the greatest satisfaction possible arises. *Q.e.d.*

PROP. XXVIII. The endeavour or desire of knowing things according to the third class of knowledge cannot arise from the first but the second class of knowledge.

Proof.—This proposition is self-evident. For whatever we understand clearly and distinctly, we understand either through itself or through something else that is conceived through itself: that is, the ideas which are distinct and clear in us, or which have reference to the third class of knowledge, cannot follow from ideas mutilated and confused which have reference to the first class of knowledge, but from adequate ideas or from the second and third class of knowledge. And therefore the desire of knowing things by the third class of knowledge cannot arise from knowledge of the first class, but only of the second. *Q.e.d.*

Prop. XXIX. Whatever the mind understands under the species of eternity, it does not understand owing to the fact that it conceives the actual present existence of the body, but owing to the fact that it conceives the essence of the body under the species of eternity.

Proof.—In so far as the mind conceives the present existence of its body, thus far it conceives duration which can be determined by time, and thus far only it has the power of conceiving things with relation to time. But eternity cannot be explained through time. Therefore the mind thus far has not the power of conceiving things under the species of eternity, but inasmuch as it is the nature of reason to conceive things under the species of eternity, and it appertains to the nature of the mind to conceive the essence of the body under the species of eternity, and save these two nothing else appertains to the essence of the mind. Therefore this power of conceiving things under the species of eternity does not appertain to the mind save in so far as it conceives the essence of the body under the species of eternity. *Q.e.d.*

Prop. XXX. The human mind in so far as it knows itself and its body under the species of eternity, thus far it necessarily has knowledge of God, and knows that it exists in God and is conceived through God.

Proof.—Eternity is the essence of God in so far as this necessarily involves existence. Therefore to conceive things under the species of eternity is to conceive them in so far as they are conceived through the essence of God as real entities, or in so far as they involve existence through the essence of God. And therefore our mind, in so far as it conceives itself and its body under a species of eternity, has thus far necessarily a knowledge of God, and knows, etc. *Q.e.d.*

Prop. XXXI. The third kind of knowledge depends on the mind as its formal cause in so far as the mind is eternal.

Proof.—The mind conceives nothing under the species of eternity save in so far as it conceives the essence of its body under the species of eternity, that is, save in so far as it is eternal. And therefore in so far as it is eternal it has knowledge of God, and this is necessarily adequate: and therefore the mind, in so far as it is eternal, is apt for understanding all those things which can follow from a given knowledge of God, that is, for understanding things by the third class of knowledge: and therefore the mind, in so far as it is eternal, is the adequate or formal cause of this. *Q.e.d.*

Prop. XXXII. Whatever we understand according to the third class of knowledge we are pleased with, and that accompanied with the idea of God as the cause.

Proof.—From this knowledge follows the greatest possible satisfaction of mind, that is, pleasure arises, and that accompanied by the idea of the mind, and consequently accompanied also by the idea of God as the cause. *Q.e.d.*

Corollary.—From the third kind of knowledge arises necessarily the intellectual love of God. For from this kind of knowledge arises pleasure accompanied by the idea of God as the cause, that is, the love of God, not in so far as we imagine him present, but in so far as we understand God to be eternal: this is what I call intellectual love towards God.

PROP. XXXIII. The intellectual love towards God which arises from the third kind of knowledge is eternal.

Proof.—The third kind of knowledge is eternal: and therefore love which arises from it is also necessarily eternal. *Q.e.d.*

PROP. XXXIV. The mind is only liable to emotions which are referred to passions while the body lasts.

Proof.—Imagination is the idea with which the mind regards anything as present, which nevertheless indicates rather the present disposition of the human body than the nature of the eternal body. Therefore emotion is imagination in so far as it indicates the present disposition of the body: and therefore the mind is only liable to emotions which are referred to passions while the body lasts. *Q.e.d.*

Corollary.—Hence it follows that no love save intellectual love is eternal.

PROP. XXXV. God loves himself with infinite intellectual love.

Proof.—God is absolutely infinite, that is, the nature of God enjoys infinite perfection, and that accompanied by the idea of himself, that is, by the idea of his cause, and this is what we said to be intellectual love.

PROP. XXXVI. The mental intellectual love towards God is the very love of God with which God loves himself, not in so far as he is infinite, but in so far as he can be expressed through the essence of the human mind considered under the species of eternity, that is, mental intellectual love towards God is part of the infinite love with which God loves himself.

Proof.—This mental love must be referred to the actions of the mind, which therefore is an action with which the mind regards itself accompanied by the idea of God as a cause, that is, an action by which God, in so far as he may be expressed through the human mind, regards himself accompanied by the idea of himself. And therefore this mental love is part of the infinite love with which God loves himself. *Q.e.d.*

Corollary.—Hence it follows that God, in so far as he loves himself, loves men, and consequently that the love of God for men and the mind's intellectual love towards God is one and the same thing.

PROP. XXXVII. There is nothing in nature which is contrary to this intellectual love or which can remove it.

Proof.—This intellectual love follows necessarily from the nature of the mind in so far as it is considered as an eternal truth through the nature of God. If, therefore, there be anything contrary to this, it must be contrary to what is true, and consequently whatever could remove this love would bring it about that what is true should be made false, which (as is self-evident) is absurd. Therefore there is nothing in nature, etc. *Q.e.d.*

PROP. XXXVIII. The more the mind understands things by the second and third kinds of knowledge, the less it will be passive to emotions which are evil, and the less it will fear death.

Proof.—The essence of the mind consists of knowledge. The more things then the mind understands by the second and third kinds of knowledge, the greater will be that part of it that remains, and consequently the greater will be the part of it that is not touched by emotions which are contrary to our nature, that is, which are evil. The more then the mind understands things by the second and third kinds of knowledge, the greater will be that part of it which remains unhurt, and consequently it will be less subject to emotions, etc. *Q.e.d.*

PROP. XXXIX. He who has a body capable of many things, has a mind of which the greater part is eternal.

Proof.—He who has a body apt for doing many things is less assailed by emotions which are evil, that is, by emotions which are contrary to our nature. And therefore he has the power of arranging and connecting the modifications of the body according to intellectual order, and consequently of bringing it to pass that all the modifications of the body have reference to the idea of God, from which it follows that he is affected with love towards God, and this love must occupy or constitute the greatest part of his mind: and therefore he has a mind of which the greatest part is eternal. *Q.e.d.*

PROP. XL. The more perfection anything has, the more active and the less passive it is; and contrariwise, the more active it is, the more perfect it becomes.

Proof.—The more perfect anything is, the more reality it has, and consequently it is more active and less passive: which proof can proceed in an inverted order; from which it may follow that a thing is more perfect the more active it is. *Q.e.d.*

Corollary.—Hence it follows that the part of the mind which remains, of whatever size it is, is more perfect than the rest. For the eternal part of the mind is the intellect, through which alone we are said to act; but that part which we see to perish is the imagination, through which alone we are said to be passive. And therefore the first part, of whatever size it may be, is more perfect than the other. *Q.e.d.*

PROP. XLI. Although we did not know that our mind is eternal, we would hold before all things piety and religion, and absolutely all things which we have shown in Part IV, to have reference to courage and nobility.

Proof.—The first and only basis of virtue or a system of right living is the seeking of what is useful to oneself. But to determine these things which reason dictates to be useful to us, we had no regard for the eternity of the mind, which we have only considered in this fifth part. Therefore, although we were ignorant at that time that the mind is eternal, yet we held those things first which we showed to have reference to courage and nobleness. And therefore, though we were ignorant of it now, we should hold first these precepts of reason. *Q.e.d.*

PROP. XLII. Blessedness is not the reward of virtue, but virtue itself: nor should we rejoice in it for that we restrain our lusts, but, on the contrary, because we rejoice therein we can restrain our lusts.

Proof.—Blessedness consists of love towards God, and this love arises from the third kind of knowledge. And therefore this love must be referred to the mind in so far as it is active, and therefore it is virtue itself: which is the first point. Again, the more the mind rejoices in this divine love or blessedness, the more it understands, that is, the more power it has over the emotions, and the less passive it is to emotions which are evil. And therefore, by the very fact that the mind rejoices in this divine love or blessedness, it has the power of restraining lusts, inasmuch as human power to restrain lusts consists of intellect alone. Therefore no one rejoices in blessedness because he restrained lusts, but, on the contrary, the power of restraining lusts arises from blessedness itself. *Q.e.d.*

AN ESSAY CONCERNING
HUMAN UNDERSTANDING

by

JOHN LOCKE

CONTENTS

An Essay Concerning Human Understanding

JOHN LOCKE

1632–1704

SIX YEARS after the death of Francis Bacon and three months before the birth of Baruch Spinoza, on the 29th of August 1632, there was born at Wrington in Somersetshire, England, one of the great philosophical geniuses of modern times— John Locke. At thirty-eight he was to begin a work, the *Essay Concerning Human Understanding,* which, when published eighteen years later, 1688, was to challenge the philosophic world of his day.

Locke's father was a genial Puritan whose time was taken up largely with supervising a small estate, practicing law, and educating his son in the classical tradition and in the tenets of English Puritanism. For a time he was engaged in military service with the parliamentary party.

In 1646 young Locke entered Westminster School, where he continued his education for six years. Here he was unhappy and developed a prejudice against public schools. This prejudice is clearly evident in his treatise *Some Thoughts Concerning Education.*

At twenty Locke entered the College of Christ Church, Oxford. Here began a period of study and activity which to a great extent determined his later point of view. Christ Church, at that time, was dominated by John Owen, the Puritan dean and vice-chancellor of the university. Under Owen's influence the Independents, who at first advocated religious toleration, ruled Oxford. But the subsequent fanaticism of the Independents, who made of religious toleration a dogma, coupled with the intolerance of the Presbyterians, turned Locke away from Puritanism to an independence which was his own. This leaning is evidenced in his famous *Letter on Toleration* and in the intellectual battles which developed after the publication of the Essay.

In 1656 Locke won his bachelor's degree and two years later received his master's degree at Oxford. In 1660 he served as tutor at Christ Church, lecturing on Greek, rhetoric, and philosophy.

But Locke was more interested in the sciences and was devoting much time to experiments in the field of chemistry. For a few years he was restless, chafing under the restraint of his professional career and yearning for something which would permit him greater freedom. At one time he contemplated taking orders in the Church of England, but his dread of ecclesiastical bondage induced him to give up this idea.

Then he turned to medicine and, by 1666, he became a practicing physician in Oxford. Though known to his friends as Doctor Locke, he never received a medical degree. Indeed, owing to his chronic tuberculosis and asthma, he gave up medicine as a career.

In 1666 an incident occurred which determined much of Locke's later life. Through his physician, Dr. Thomas, he was introduced to Lord Ashley, who later became the first Earl of Shaftesbury. Lord Ashley had come to Oxford for his health and found great attraction in the young physician and scholar. The two men had much in common, and almost immediately there developed a friendship which was to last for many years.

In 1667 Locke moved into Ashley's London home, Exeter House, as the confidential secretary and companion of his new-found friend. This appointment removed Locke from the confines of the study into the world of men and events. At Exeter House it was the custom for important personages to gather and to discuss matters of many interests. At one of these discussions, in 1670, the participants became so involved that there seemed no way out. Locke observed that before they proceeded further, it might be wise to define the "limits of human understanding." This observation appealed to the group. They suggested that he expand his remarks for their benefit. He believed he could do this immediately and on "one sheet of paper." But it took him eighteen years to release his speculations in a volume of many hundreds of pages. This volume was his *Essay Concerning Human Understanding.*

The rest of Locke's life was largely determined by the fortunes of Ashley—now raised to the peerage and known as the Earl of Shaftesbury. In 1675, when Shaftesbury fell into disgrace, Locke was compelled to flee to France, where he remained until Shaftesbury was restored to power in 1679. But Locke was under suspicion, and his life was far from pleasant. In 1683 he retired to Holland and lived under the assumed name of Dr. Van der Linden. The English Government sought to arrest him, but he managed to escape and was able to live in some comfort.

In Holland, Locke began his great period of publication. His *Essay* came out in 1688. He continued his work when he returned to England, after the landing of William of Orange, in 1689. In that same year, when he issued his *Letter on Toleration,* the clergy attacked him fiercely and continued their attacks from then on until October 28, 1704, when he died "in perfect charity with all men, and in sincere communion with the whole church of Christ, by whatever name Christ's followers call themselves."

Today we accept much of Locke's controversial writing as a matter of fact. But in his own day he lived the life of an intellectual pioneer. He initiated the criticism of human knowledge and fought for the privilege of careful observation. He worked in season and out of season for free inquiry and universal toleration, and he was the sworn enemy of all loose thinking, fanaticism, and intolerance wherever found. He helped make possible the modern world of thought.

What is the *actual* truth, Locke asked himself, as compared with the so-called *accepted* truths of mankind? In order to answer this question, he said, "Let us put the ideas of our mind, just as we put the things of the laboratory, to the test of experience."

We find that the so-called simple ideas—the ideas of heat and of cold, for example—come to us directly from our experience. But what about the complex ideas—the ideas of beauty, of justice, of love? These, too, declares Locke, come from our experience. A complex idea is a combination of simple ideas. We experience a number of beautiful things, and we combine these concrete beautiful objects into an abstract concept of beauty. Our idea of eternity is a combination of our ideas of time—seconds, minutes, hours, days, years, centuries. The same is true of our ideas of space. Our mind has a way of combining *concrete units of experience* into *abstract conceptions.*

All knowledge, therefore, is based upon our experience. Our knowledge of God is based upon our experience of ourselves. Each man has his own experiences, and consequently his own conception of God. There is no such thing as an absolute God, absolute truth, absolute justice, absolute love. Let each man square himself with the world in accordance with his own lights. Let not society impose arbitrary standards upon the individual. Leave every man to his own conscience and his own religion. Let there be freedom of religion, of speech, and of thought. For in the freedom of each is the happiness of all.

AN ESSAY CONCERNING HUMAN UNDERSTANDING

Book One

I. INTRODUCTION

An inquiry into the understanding, pleasant and useful.—Since it is the understanding that sets man above the rest of sensible beings, and gives him all the advantage and dominion which he has over them, it is certainly a subject, even for its nobleness, worth our labour to inquire into. The understanding, like the eye, whilst it makes us see and perceive all other things, takes no notice of itself; and it requires art and pains to set it at a distance, and make it its own object.

It shall suffice to my present purpose, to consider the discerning faculties of a man as they are employed about the objects which they have to do with; and I shall imagine I have not wholly misemployed myself in the thoughts I shall have on this occasion, if, in this historical, plain method, I can give any account of the ways whereby our understandings come to attain those notions of things we have, and can set down any measures of the certainty of our knowledge, or the grounds of those persuasions which are to be found amongst men, so various, different, and wholly contradictory; and yet asserted somewhere or other with such assurance, and confidence, that he that shall take a view of the opinions of mankind, observe their opposition, and at the same time consider the fondness and devotion wherewith they are embraced, the resolution and eagerness wherewith they are maintained, may perhaps have reason to suspect that either there is no such thing as truth at all, or that mankind hath no sufficient means to attain a certain knowledge of it.

Useful to know the extent of our comprehension.—If by this inquiry into the nature of the understanding, I can discover the powers thereof, how far they reach, to what things they are in any degree proportionate, and where they fail us, I suppose it may be of use to prevail with the busy mind of man to be more cautious in meddling with things exceeding its comprehension, to stop when it is at the utmost extent of its tether, and to sit down in a quiet ignorance of those things which, upon examination, are found to be beyond the reach of our capacities.

Knowledge of our capacity a cure of scepticism and idleness.—When we know our own strength, we shall the better know what to undertake with hopes of success; and when we have well surveyed the powers of our own minds, and made some estimate what we may expect from them, we shall not be inclined either to sit still, and not set our thoughts on work at all, in despair of knowing anything; nor, on the other side, question everything, and disclaim all knowledge, because some things are not to be understood. Our business here is not to know all things, but those which concern our conduct. If we can find out those measures whereby a rational creature, put in that state which man is in in this world, may and ought to govern his opinions and actions depending thereon, we need not be troubled that some other things escape our knowledge.

Occasion of this Essay.—This was that which gave the first rise to this Essay concerning the Understanding. For I thought that the first step towards satisfying several inquiries the mind of man was very apt to run into, was, to take a survey of our own understandings, examine our own powers, and see to what things they were adapted. Till that was done, I suspected we began at the wrong end, and in vain sought for satisfaction in a quiet and sure possession of truths that most concerned us, whilst we let loose our thoughts into the vast ocean of being; as if all that boundless extent were the natural and undoubted possession of our understandings, wherein there was nothing exempt from its decisions, or that escaped its comprehension.

What "idea" stands for.—Thus much I thought necessary to say concerning the occasion of this inquiry into human understanding. But, before I proceed on to what I have thought on this subject, I must here, in the entrance, beg pardon of my reader for the frequent use of the word "idea" which he will find in the following treatise. It being that term which, I think, serves best to stand for whatsoever is the object of the understanding when a man thinks, I have used it to express whatever is meant by phantasm, notion, species, or whatever it is which the mind can be employed about in thinking; and I could not avoid frequently using it.

I presume it will be easily granted me, that there are such *ideas* in men's minds. Everyone is conscious of them in himself; and men's words and actions will satisfy him that they are in others.

II. NO INNATE PRINCIPLES IN THE MIND

The way shown how we come by any knowledge, sufficient to prove it not innate.—It is an established opinion among some men, that there are in the understanding certain innate principles; some primary notions, characters, as it were, stamped upon the mind of man, which the soul receives in its very first being, and brings into the world with it. It would be sufficient to convince unprejudiced readers of the falseness of this supposition, if I should only show how men, barely by the use of their natural faculties, may attain to all the knowledge they have, without the help of any innate impressions, and may arrive at certainty without any such original notions or principles.

General assent the great argument.—There is nothing more commonly taken for granted, than that there are certain principles, both speculative and practical, universally agreed upon by all mankind; which therefore, they argue, must needs be constant impressions which the souls of men receive in their first beings, and which they bring into the world with them, as necessarily and really as they do any of their inherent faculties.

Universal consent proves nothing innate.—This argument, drawn from universal consent, has this misfortune in it, that if it were true in matter of fact, that there were certain truths wherein all mankind agreed, it would not prove them innate, if there can be any other way shown, how men may come to that universal agreement in the things they do consent in; which I presume may be done.

"What is, is"; and, "It is impossible for the same thing to be, and not to be," not universally assented to.—But, which is worse, this argument of universal consent, which is made use of to prove innate principles, seems to me a demonstration that there are none such; because there are none to which all mankind give an universal assent. I shall begin with the speculative, and instance in those magnified principles of demonstration: "Whatsoever is, is"; and, "It is impossible for the same thing to be, and not to be," which, of all others, I think, have the most allowed title to innate. These have so settled a reputation of maxims universally received, that it will, no doubt, be thought strange if anyone should seem to question it. But yet I take liberty to say, that these propositions are so far from having an universal assent, that there are a great part of mankind to whom they are not so much as known.

The steps by which the mind attains several truths.—The senses at first let in particular ideas, and furnish the yet empty cabinet: and the mind by degrees growing familiar with some of them, they are lodged in the memory, and names got to them. Afterwards the mind, proceeding farther, abstracts them, and by degrees learns the use of general names. In this manner the mind comes to be furnished with ideas and language, the materials about which to exercise its discursive faculty; and the use of reason becomes daily more visible, as these materials, that give it employment, increase. But though the having of general ideas, and the use of general words and reason, usually grow together, yet I see not how this any way proves them innate. The knowledge of some truths, I confess, is very early in the mind; but in a way that shows them not to be innate. For, if we will observe, we shall find it still to be about ideas not innate, but acquired; it being about those first, which are imprinted by external things, with which infants have earliest to do, which make the most frequent impressions on their senses. In ideas thus got, the mind discovers that some agree, and others differ, probably as soon as it has any use of memory, as soon as it is able to retain and receive distinct ideas. But whether it be then or no, this is certain, it does so long before it has the use of words, or comes to that which we commonly call "the use of reason." For a child knows as certainly, before it can speak, the difference between the ideas of sweet and bitter, as it knows afterwards, when it comes to speak, that wormwood and sugarplums are not the same thing.

III. NO INNATE PRACTICAL PRINCIPLES

No moral principles so clear and so generally received as the fore-mentioned speculative maxims.—If speculative maxims have not an actual universal assent from all mankind, it is much more visible concerning practical principles, that they come short of an universal reception; and I think it will be hard to instance any one moral rule which can pretend to so general and ready an assent as, "What is, is," or to be so manifest a truth as this, "That it is impossible for the same thing to be, and not to be." Whereby it is evident that they are farther removed from a title to be innate; and the doubt of their being native impressions on the mind is stronger against these moral principles than the other. Not that it brings their truth at all in question. They are equally true, though not equally evident. Those speculative maxims carry their own evidence with them; but moral principles require reasoning and discourse, and some exercise of the mind, to discover the certainty of their truth. They lie not open as natural characters engraven on the mind; which if any such were, they must needs be visible by themselves, and by their own light be certain and known to everybody. But this is no derogation to their truth and certainty; no more than it is to the truth or certainty of the three angles of a triangle being equal to two right ones, because it is not so evident as, "The whole is bigger than a part," nor so apt to be assented to at first hearing. It may suffice that these moral rules are capable of demonstration; and therefore it is our own fault if we come not to a certain knowledge of them. But the ignorance wherein many men are of them, and the slowness of assent wherewith others receive them, are manifest proofs that they are not innate, and such as offer themselves to their view without searching.

Virtue generally approved, not because innate, but because profitable.

—Hence naturally flows the great variety of opinions concerning the moral rules, which are to be found among men according to the different sorts of happiness they have a prospect of, or propose to themselves; which could not be, if practical principles were innate, and imprinted in our minds immediately by the hand of God. I grant the existence of God is so many ways manifest, and the obedience we owe him so congruous to the light of reason, that a great part of mankind give testimony to the law of nature; but yet I think it must be allowed, that several moral rules may receive from mankind a very general approbation, without either knowing or admitting the true ground of morality; which can only be the will and law of a God, who sees men in the dark, has in his hand rewards and punishments, and power enough to call to account the proudest offender.

Men's actions convince us, that the rule of virtue is not their internal principle.—For, if we will not in civility allow too much sincerity to the professions of most men, but think their actions to be the interpreters of their thoughts, we shall find that they have no such internal veneration for these rules, nor so full a persuasion of their certainty and obligation. The great principle of morality, "To do as one would be done to," is more commended than practised.

Men have contrary practical principles.—He that will carefully peruse the history of mankind, and look abroad into the several tribes of men, and with indifference survey their actions, will be able to satisfy himself that there is scarce that principle of morality to be named, or rule of virtue to be thought on (those only excepted that are absolutely necessary to hold society together, which commonly, too, are neglected betwixt distinct societies), which is not, somewhere or other, slighted and condemned by the general fashion of whole societies of men, governed by practical opinions and rules of living quite opposite to others.

Those who maintain innate practical principles, tell us not what they are.—The difference there is amongst men, in their practical principles, is so evident, that, I think, I need say no more to evince that it will be impossible to find any innate moral rules by this mark of general assent. And it is enough to make one suspect, that the supposition of such innate principles is but an opinion taken up at pleasure; since those who talk so confidently of them are so sparing to tell us which they are. This might with justice be expected from those men who lay stress upon this opinion; and it gives occasion to distrust either their knowledge or charity, who, declaring that God has imprinted on the minds of men the foundations of knowledge and the rules of living, are yet so little favourable to the information of their neighbours, or the quiet of mankind, as not to point out to them which they are, in the variety men are distracted with. But, in truth, were there any such innate principles, there would be no need to teach them.

Contrary principles in the world.—I easily grant that there are great numbers of opinions which, by men of different countries, educations, and tempers, are received and embraced as first and unquestionable principles; many whereof, both for their absurdity as well as opposition one to another, it is impossible should be true. But yet all those propositions, how remote soever from reason, are so sacred somewhere or other, that men even of good understanding in other matters will sooner part with their lives, and whatever is dearest to them, than suffer themselves to doubt, or others to question, the truth of them.

How men commonly come by their principles.—This, however strange it may seem, is that which every day's experience confirms: and will not, perhaps, appear so wonderful if we consider the ways and steps by which it is brought about, and how really it may come to pass, that doctrines that have been derived from no better original than the superstition of a nurse, or the authority of an old woman, may, by length of time and consent of neighbours, grow up to the dignity of principles in religion or morality. For such who are careful (as they call it) to principle children well (and few there be who have not a set of those principles for them which they believe in), instil into the unwary, and as yet unprejudiced, understanding (for white paper receives any characters) those doctrines they would have them retain and profess. These—being taught them as soon as they have any apprehension, and still as they grow up confirmed to them, either by the open profession or tacit consent of all they have to do with; or at least by those of whose wisdom, knowledge, and piety they have an opinion, who never suffer those propositions to be otherwise mentioned but as the basis and foundation on which they build their religion or manners—come, by these means, to have the reputation of unquestionable, self-evident, and innate truths.

Principles must be examined.—By this progress how many there are who arrive at principles which they believe innate, may be easily observed in the variety of opposite principles held and contended for by all sorts and degrees of men. And he that shall deny this to be the method wherein most men proceed to the assurance they have of the truth and evidence of their principles, will, perhaps, find it a hard matter any other way to account for the contrary tenets, which are firmly believed, confidently asserted, and which great numbers are ready at any time to seal with their blood. And, indeed, if it be the privilege of innate principles to be received upon their own authority, without examination, I know not what may not be believed, or how anyone's principles can be questioned. If they may and ought to be examined and tried, I desire to know how first and innate principles can be tried; or at least it is reasonable to demand the marks and characters whereby the genuine innate principles may be distinguished from others; that so, amidst the great variety of pretenders, I may be kept from mistakes in so material a point as this. When this is done, I shall be ready to embrace such welcome and useful propositions; and till then I may with modesty doubt, since I fear universal consent (which is the only one produced) will scarce prove a sufficient mark to direct my choice, and assure me of any innate principles. From what has been said, I think it past doubt, that there are no practical principles wherein all men agree, and therefore none innate.

IV. OTHER CONSIDERATIONS CONCERNING INNATE PRIN-CIPLES BOTH SPECULATIVE AND PRACTICAL

Principles not innate, unless their ideas be innate.—Had those who would persuade us that there are innate principles, not taken them together in gross, but considered separately the parts out of which those propositions are made, they would not, perhaps, have been so forward to believe they were innate; since, if the ideas which made up those truths were not, it was impossible that the propositions made up of them should be, innate, or our knowledge of them be born with us. For if the ideas be not innate, there was a time when the mind was without those principles; and then they will not be innate, but be derived from some other original: for where the ideas themselves are not, there can be no knowledge, no assent, no mental or verbal propositions about them.

Ideas, especially those belonging to principles, not born with children. —If we will attentively consider new-born children, we shall have little reason to think that they bring many ideas into the world with them: for, bating, perhaps, some faint ideas of hunger, and thirst, and warmth, and some pains which they may have felt in the womb, there is not the least appearance of any settled ideas at all in them; especially of ideas answering the terms which make up those universal propositions that are esteemed innate principles. One may perceive how, by degrees, afterwards, ideas come into their minds; and that they get no more, nor no other, than what experience, and the observation of things that come in their way, furnish them with; which might be enough to satisfy us that they are not original characters stamped on the mind.

Idea of God not innate.—If any idea can be imagined innate, the idea of God may, of all others, for many reasons, be thought so; since it is hard to conceive how there should be innate moral principles without an innate idea of a Deity: without a notion of a law-maker, it is impossible to have a notion of a law, and an obligation to observe it. But had all mankind everywhere a notion of a God (whereof yet history tells us the contrary), it would not from thence follow that the idea of him was innate. For though no nation were to be found without a name and some few dark notions of him, yet that would not prove them to be natural impressions on the mind, no more than the names of "fire," or the "sun," "heat," or "number," do prove the ideas they stand for to be innate, because the names of those things, and the ideas of them, are so universally received and known amongst mankind.

Nor, on the contrary, is the want of such a name, or the absence of •such a notion out of men's minds, any argument against the being of a God, any more than it would be a proof that there was no loadstone in the world, because a great part of mankind had neither a notion of any such thing, nor a name for it; or be any show of argument to prove, that there are no distinct and various species of angels, or intelligent beings above us, because we have no ideas of such distinct species or names for them. For men, being furnished with words by the common language of their own countries, can scarce avoid having some kind of ideas of those things whose names those they converse with have occasion frequently to mention to them: and if it carry with it the notion of excellency, greatness, or something extraordinary; if apprehension and concernment accompany it; if the fear of absolute and irresistible power set it on upon the mind; the idea is likely to sink the deeper and spread the farther; especially if it be such an idea as is agreeable to the common light of reason, and naturally deducible from every part of our knowledge, as that of a God is. For the visible marks of extraordinary wisdom and power appear so plainly in all the works of the creation, that a rational creature who will but seriously reflect on them, cannot miss the discovery of a Deity; and the influence that the discovery of such a Being must necessarily have on the minds of all that have but once heard of it is so great, and carries such a weight of thought and communication with it, that it seems stranger to me that a whole nation of men should be anywhere found so brutish as to want the notion of a God, than that they should be without any notion of numbers, or fire.

Ideas of God various in different men.—I grant, that if there were any ideas to be found imprinted on the minds of men, we have reason to expect it should be the notion of his Maker, as a mark God set on his own workmanship, to mind man of his dependence and duty; and that herein should appear the first instances of human knowledge. But how late is it before any such notion is discoverable in children! and when we find it there, how much more does it resemble the opinion and notion of the teacher, than represent the true God! He that shall observe in children the progress whereby their minds attain the knowledge they have, will think that the objects they do first and most familiarly converse with, are those that make the first impressions on their understandings; nor will he find the least footsteps of any other. It is easy to take notice how their thoughts enlarge themselves only as they come to be acquainted with a greater variety of sensible objects, to retain the ideas of them in their memories, and to get the skill to compound and enlarge them, and several ways put them together.

If the idea of God be not innate, no other can be supposed innate.— Since, then, though the knowledge of a God be the most natural discovery of human reason, yet the idea of him is not innate, as, I think, is evident from what has been said; I imagine there will be scarce any other idea found that can pretend to it; since, if God had set any impression, any character, on the understanding of men, it is most reasonable to expect it should have been some clear and uniform idea of himself, as far as our weak capacities were capable to receive so incomprehensible and infinite an object. But our minds being at first void of that idea which we are most concerned to have, it is a strong presumption against all other innate characters. I must own, as far as I can observe, I can find none, and would be glad to be informed by any other.

No propositions can be innate since no ideas are innate.—Whatever, then, we talk of innate, either speculative or practical, principles, it may with as much probability be said, that a man hath £100 sterling in his pocket, and yet denied that he hath either penny, shilling, crown, or any other coin out of which the sum is to be made up; as to think, that certain propositions are innate, when the ideas about which they are can by no means be supposed to be so. The general reception and assent that is given doth not at all prove that the ideas expressed in them are innate; for in many cases, however the ideas came there, the assent to words expressing the agreement or disagreement of such ideas will necessarily follow.

Everyone that hath a true idea of God and worship, will assent to this proposition, that "God is to be worshipped," when expressed in a language he understands; and every rational man that hath not thought on it to-day, may be ready to assent to this proposition to-morrow; and yet millions of men may be well supposed to want one or both of those ideas to-day. For if we will allow savages and most country people to have ideas of God and worship (which conversation with them will not make one forward to believe), yet, I think, few children can be supposed to have those ideas, which therefore they must begin to have some time or other; and then they will also begin to assent to that proposition, and make very little question of it ever after. But such an assent upon hearing no more proves the ideas to be innate, than it does that one born blind (with cataracts which will be couched to-morrow) had the innate ideas of the sun or light, or saffron or yellow, because, when his sight is cleared, he will certainly assent to this proposition, that "the sun is lucid," or that "saffron is yellow"; and therefore if such an assent upon hearing cannot prove the ideas innate, it can much less the propositions made up of those ideas. If they have any innate ideas, I would be glad to be told what and how many they are.

Book Two

1. OF IDEAS IN GENERAL, AND THEIR ORIGINAL

Idea is the object of thinking.—Every man being conscious to himself, that he thinks, and that which his mind is applied about, whilst thinking, being the ideas that are there, it is past doubt that men have in their mind several ideas, such as are those expressed by the words, "whiteness, hardness, sweetness, thinking, motion, man, elephant, army, drunkenness," and others. It is in the first place then to be inquired, How he comes by them? I know it is a received doctrine, that men have native ideas and original characters stamped upon their minds in their very first being. This opinion I have at large examined already; and, I suppose, what I have said in the foregoing book will be much more easily admitted, when I have shown whence the understanding may get all the ideas it has, and by what ways and degrees they may come into the mind; for which I shall appeal to everyone's own observation and experience.

All ideas come from sensation or reflection.—Let us then suppose the mind to be, as we say, white paper, void of all characters, without any ideas; how comes it to be furnished? Whence comes it by that vast store, which the busy and boundless fancy of man has painted on it with an almost endless variety? Whence has it all the materials of reason and knowledge? To this I answer, in one word, from experience: in that all our knowledge is founded, and from that it ultimately derives itself. Our observation, employed either about external sensible objects, or about the internal operations of our minds, perceived and reflected on by ourselves, is that which supplies our understandings with all the materials of thinking. These two are the fountains of knowledge, from whence all the ideas we have, or can naturally have, do spring.

The object of sensation one source of ideas.—First. Our senses, conversant about particular sensible objects, do convey into the mind several distinct perceptions of things, according to those various ways wherein those objects do affect them; and thus we come by those ideas we have of yellow, white, heat, cold, soft, hard, bitter, sweet, and all those which we call sensible qualities; which when I say the senses convey into the mind, I mean, they from external objects convey into the mind what produces there those perceptions. This great source of most of the ideas we have, depending wholly upon our senses, and derived by them to the understanding, I call "sensation."

The operations of our minds the other source of them.—Secondly. The other fountain, from which experience furnisheth the understanding with ideas, is the perception of the operations of our own minds within us, as it is employed about the ideas it has got; which operations, when the soul comes to reflect on and consider, do furnish the understanding with another set of ideas which could not be had from things without; and such are perception, thinking, doubting, believing, reasoning, knowing, willing, and all the different actings of our own minds; which we, being conscious of, and observing in ourselves, do from these receive into our understanding as distinct ideas, as we do from bodies affecting our senses. This source of ideas every man has wholly in himself; and though it be not sense as having nothing to do with external objects, yet it is very like it, and might properly enough be called "internal sense." But as I call the other "sensation," so I call this "reflection," the ideas it affords being such only as the mind gets by reflecting on its own operations within itself.

By reflection, then, in the following part of this discourse, I would be understood to mean that notice which the mind takes of its own operations, and the manner of them, by reason whereof there come to be ideas of these operations in the understanding. These two, I say, viz., external material things as the objects of sensation, and the operations of our own minds within as the objects of reflection, are, to me, the only originals from whence all our ideas take their beginnings. The term "operations" here, I use in a large sense, as comprehending not barely the actions of the mind about its ideas, but some sort of passions arising sometimes from them, such as is the satisfaction or uneasiness arising from any thought.

All our ideas are of the one or the other of these.—The understanding seems to me not to have the least glimmering of any ideas which it doth not receive from one of these two. External objects furnish the mind with the ideas of sensible qualities, which are all those different perceptions they produce in us; and the mind furnishes the understanding with ideas of its own operations.

These, when we have taken a full survey of them, and their several modes, combinations, and relations, we shall find to contain all our whole stock of ideas; and that we have nothing in our minds which did not come in one of these two ways. Let anyone examine his own thoughts, and thoroughly search into his understanding, and then let him tell me, whether all the original ideas he has there, are any other than of the objects of his senses, or of the operations of his mind considered as objects of his reflection; and how great a mass of knowledge soever he imagines to be lodged there, he will, upon taking a strict view, see that he has not any idea in his mind but what one of these two hath imprinted, though perhaps with infinite variety compounded and enlarged by the understanding, as we shall see hereafter.

The original of all our knowledge.—In time the mind comes to reflect on its own operations about the ideas got by sensation, and thereby stores itself with a new set of ideas, which I call "ideas of reflection." These are the impressions that are made on our senses by outward objects, that are extrinsical to the mind; and its own operations, proceeding from powers intrinsical and proper to itself, which, when reflected on by itself, become also objects of its contemplation, are, as I have said, the original of all knowledge. Thus the first capacity of human intellect is, that the mind is fitted to receive the impressions made on it, either through the senses by outward objects, or by its own operations when it reflects on them. This is the first step a man makes towards the discovery of anything, and the ground-work whereon to build all those notions which ever he shall have naturally in this world. All those sublime thoughts which tower above the clouds, and reach as high as heaven itself, take their rise and footing here: in all that great extent wherein the mind wanders in those remote speculations it may seem to be elevated with, it stirs not one jot beyond those ideas which sense or reflection have offered for its contemplation.

II. OF SIMPLE IDEAS

Uncompounded appearances.—The better to understand the nature, manner, and extent of our knowledge, one thing is carefully to be observed concerning the ideas we have; and that is, that some of them are simple, and some complex.

Though the qualities that affect our senses are, in the things themselves, so united and blended that there is no separation, no distance between them; yet it is plain the ideas they produce in the mind enter by the senses simple and unmixed. For though the sight and touch often take in from the same object at the same time different ideas—as a man sees at once motion and colour, the hand feels softness and warmth in the same piece of wax—yet the simple ideas thus united in the same subject are as perfectly distinct as those that come in by different senses; the coldness and hardness which a man feels in a piece of ice being as distinct ideas in the mind as the smell and whiteness of a lily, or as the taste of sugar and smell of a rose: and there is nothing can be plainer to a man than the clear and distinct perception he has of those simple ideas; which, being each in itself uncompounded, contains in it nothing but one uniform appearance or conception in the mind, and is not distinguishable into different ideas.

The mind can neither make nor destroy them.—These simple ideas, the materials of all our knowledge, are suggested and furnished to the mind only by those two ways above mentioned, viz., sensation and reflection. When the understanding is once stored with these simple ideas, it has the power to repeat, compare, and unite them, even to an almost infinite variety, and so can make at pleasure new complex ideas. But it is not in the power of the most exalted wit or enlarged understanding, by any quickness or variety of thoughts, to invent or frame one new simple idea in the mind, not taken in by the ways before mentioned; nor can any force of the understanding destroy those that are there: the dominion of man in this little world of his own understanding, being much-what the same as it is in the great world of visible things, wherein his power, however managed by art and skill, reaches no farther than to compound and divide the materials that are made to his hand but can do nothing towards the making the least particle of new matter, or destroying one atom of what is already in being. The same inability will everyone find in himself, who shall go about to fashion in his understanding any simple idea not received in by his senses from external objects, or by reflection from the operations of his own mind about them. I would have anyone try to fancy any taste which had never affected his palate, or frame the idea of a scent he had never smelt; and when he can do this, I will also conclude, that a blind man hath *ideas* of colours, and a deaf man true, distinct notions of sounds.

III. OF IDEAS OF ONE SENSE

Division of simple ideas.—The better to conceive the ideas we receive from sensation, it may not be amiss for us to consider them in reference to the different ways whereby they make their approaches to our minds, and make themselves perceivable by us.

First, then, there are some which come into our minds by one sense only.

Secondly. There are others that convey themselves into the mind by more senses than one.

Thirdly. Others that are had from reflection only.

Fourthly. There are some that make themselves way, and are suggested to the mind, by all the ways of sensation and reflection.

We shall consider them apart under these several heads.

There are some ideas which have admittance only through one sense, which is peculiarly adapted to receive them. I think it will be needless to enumerate all the particular simple ideas belonging to each sense. Nor indeed is it possible if we would, there being a great many more of them belonging to most of the senses than we have names for. The variety of smells, which are as many almost, if not more, than species of bodies in the world, do most of them want names.

IV. OF SOLIDITY

We receive this idea from touch.—The idea of solidity we receive by our touch; and it arises from the resistance which we find in body to the entrance of any other body into the place it possesses, till it has left it. There is no idea which we receive more constantly from sensation than solidity. Whether we move or rest, in what posture soever we are, we always feel something under us that supports us, and hinders our farther sinking downwards; and the bodies which we daily handle make us perceive that whilst they remain between them, they do, by an insurmountable force, hinder the approach of the parts of our hands that press them. That which thus hinders the approach of two bodies, when they are moving one towards another, I call "solidity."

Solidity fills space.—This is the idea belongs to body, whereby we conceive it to fill space. The idea of which filling of space is, that where we imagine any space taken up by a solid substance, we conceive it so to possess it that it excludes all other solid substances, and will for ever hinder any two other bodies, that move towards one another in a straight line, from coming to touch one another, unless it removes from between them in a line not parallel to that which they move in. This idea of it, the bodies which we ordinarily handle sufficiently furnish us with.

Distinct from space.—This resistance, whereby it keeps other bodies out of the space which it possesses, is so great that no force, how great soever, can surmount it. All the bodies in the world, pressing a drop of water on all sides, will never be able to overcome the resistance which it will make, as soft as it is, to their approaching one another, till it be removed out of their way: whereby our idea of solidity is distinguished both from pure space, which is capable neither of resistance nor motion, and from the ordinary idea of hardness. For a man may conceive two bodies at a distance so as they may approach one another without touching or displacing any solid thing till their superficies come to meet; whereby, I think, we have the clear idea of space without solidity.

On solidity depend impulse, resistance, and protrusion.—By this idea of solidity is the extension of body distinguished from the extension of space: the extension of body being nothing but the cohesion or continuity of solid, separable, movable parts; and the extension of space, the continuity of unsolid, inseparable, and immovable parts. Upon the solidity of bodies also depend their mutual impulse, resistance, and protrusion. Of pure space, then, and solidity, there are several (amongst which I confess myself one) who persuade themselves they have clear and distinct ideas: and that they can think on space without anything in it that resists or is protruded by body. This is the idea of pure space, which they think they have as clear as any idea they can have of the extension of body; the idea of the distance between the opposite parts of a concave superficies being equally as clear without as with the idea of any solid parts between; and on the other side they persuade themselves that they have, distinct from that of pure space, the idea of something that fills space, that can be protruded by the impulse of other bodies, or resist their motion. If there be others that have not these two ideas distinct, but confound them, and make but one of them, I know not how men who have the same idea under different names, or different ideas under the same name, can in that case talk with one another, any more than a man who, not being blind or deaf, has distinct ideas of the colour of scarlet and the sound of a trumpet, would discourse concerning scarlet-colour with the blind man who fancied that the idea of scarlet was like the sound of a trumpet.

What it is.—If anyone asks me, what this solidity is, I send him to his senses to inform him: let him put a flint or a football between his hands, and then endeavour to join them, and he will know. If he thinks this not a sufficient explanation of solidity, what it is, and wherein it consists, I promise to tell him what it is, and wherein it consists, when he tells me what thinking is, or wherein it consists; or explains to me what extension or motion is, which perhaps seems much easier. The simple ideas we have are such as experience teaches them us; but if, beyond that, we endeavour by words to make them clearer in the mind, we shall succeed no better than if we went about to clear up the darkness of a blind man's mind by talking, and to discourse into him the ideas of light and colour. The reason of this I shall show in another place.

V. OF SIMPLE IDEAS OF DIVERS SENSES

THE IDEAS we get by more than one sense are of space or extension, figure, rest and motion: for these make perceivable impressions both on the eyes and touch; and we can receive and convey into our minds the ideas of our extension, figure, motion, and rest of bodies, both by seeing and feeling. But having occasion to speak more at large of these in another place, I here only enumerate them.

VI. OF SIMPLE IDEAS OF REFLECTION

Simple ideas of reflection are the operations of the mind about its other ideas.—The mind, receiving the ideas mentioned in the foregoing chapters from without, when it turns its view inward upon itself, and observes its own actions about those ideas it has, takes from thence other ideas, which are as capable to be the objects of its contemplation as any of those it received from foreign things.

The idea of perception, and idea of willing, we have from reflection.— The two great and principal actions of the mind, which are most frequently considered, and which are so frequent that everyone that pleases may take notice of them in himself, are these two: perception or thinking, and volition or willing. The power of thinking is called "the understanding," and the power of volition is called "the will"; and these two powers or abilities in the mind are denominated "faculties."

VII. OF SIMPLE IDEAS OF BOTH SENSATION AND REFLECTION

Pleasure and pain.—There be other simple ideas which convey themselves into the mind by all the ways of sensation and reflection; viz., pleasure or delight, and its opposite, pain or uneasiness; power, existence, unity.

Delight or uneasiness, one or other of them, join themselves to almost all our ideas both of sensation and reflection; and there is scarce any affection of our senses from without, any retired thought of our mind within, which is not able to produce in us pleasure or pain. By "pleasure" and "pain," I would be understood to signify whatsoever delights or molests us; whether it arises from the thoughts of our minds, or anything operating on our bodies. For whether we call it "satisfaction, delight, pleasure, happiness," &c., on the one side; or "uneasiness, trouble, pain, torment, anguish, misery," &c., on the other; they are still but different degrees of the same thing, and belong to the ideas of pleasure and pain, delight or uneasiness; which are the names I shall most commonly use for those two sorts of ideas.

Pain has the same efficacy and use to set us on work that pleasure has, we being as ready to employ our faculties to avoid that, as to pursue this: only this is worth our consideration—that pain is often produced by the same objects and ideas that produce pleasure in us. This their near conjunction, which makes us often feel pain in the sensations where we expected pleasure, gives us new occasion of admiring the wisdom and goodness of our Maker, who, designing the preservation of our being, has annexed pain to the application of many things to our bodies, to warn us of the harm that they will do, and as advices to withdraw from them. But He, not designing our preservation barely, but the preservation of every part and organ in its perfection, hath in many cases annexed pain to those very ideas which delight us. Thus heat, that is very agreeable to us in one degree, by a little greater increase of it proves no ordinary torment; and the most pleasant of all sensible objects, light itself, if there be too much of it, if increased beyond a due proportion to our eyes, causes a very painful sensation: which is wisely and favourably so ordered by nature, that when any object does by the vehemency of its operation dis-order the instruments of sensation, whose structures cannot but be very nice and delicate, we might by the pain be warned to withdraw before the organ be quite put out of order, and so be unfitted for its proper functions for the future. The consideration of those objects that produce it may well persuade us, that this is the end or use of pain; for though great light be insufferable to our eyes, yet the highest degree of darkness does not at all disease them, because the causing no disorderly motion in it leaves that curious organ unharmed in its natural state. But yet excess of cold as well as heat pains us because it is equally destructive to that temper which is necessary to the preservation of life, and the exercise of the several functions of the body, and which consists in a moderate degree of warmth, or, if you please, a motion of the insensible parts of our bodies confined within certain bounds.

Pleasure and pain.—Though what I have here said may not perhaps make the ideas of pleasure and pain clearer to us than our own experience does, which is the only way that we are capable of having them; yet the consideration of the reason why they are annexed to so many other ideas, serving to give us due sentiments of the wisdom and goodness of the Sovereign Disposer of all things, may not be unsuitable to the main end of these inquiries: the knowledge and veneration of Him being the chief end of all our thoughts, and the proper business of all our understandings.

Existence and unity.—Existence and unity are two other ideas that are suggested to the understanding by every object without, and every idea within. When ideas are in our minds, we consider them as being actually there, as well as we consider things to be actually without us: which is, that they exist, or have existence: and whatever we can consider as one thing, whether a real being or idea, suggests to the understanding the idea of unity.

Power.—Power also is another of those simple ideas which we receive from sensation and reflection. For, observing in ourselves that we can at pleasure move several parts of our bodies which were at rest, the effects also that natural bodies are able to produce in one another occurring every moment to our senses, we both these ways get the idea of power.

Succession.—Besides these there is another idea, which though sug-gested by our senses yet is more constantly offered us by what passes in our own minds; and that is the idea of succession. For if we look immedi-ately into ourselves, and reflect on what is observable there, we shall find our ideas always, whilst we are awake or have any thought, passing in train, one going and another coming without intermission.

Simple ideas the materials of all our knowledge.—These, if they are

not all, are at least (as I think) the most considerate of those simple ideas
which the mind has, and out of which is made all its other knowledge: all
of which it receives only by the two fore-mentioned ways of sensation and
reflection.

VIII. SOME FARTHER CONSIDERATIONS CONCERNING OUR SIMPLE IDEAS

Positive ideas from privative causes.—Concerning the simple ideas of
sensation it is to be considered, that whatsoever is so constituted in
nature as to be able by affecting our senses to cause any perception in the
mind, doth thereby produce in the understanding a simple idea; which,
whatever be the external cause of it, when it comes to be taken notice
of by our discerning faculty, it is by the mind looked on and considered
there to be a real positive idea in the understanding, as much as any other
whatsoever; though perhaps the cause of it be but a privation in the
subject.

Ideas in the mind, qualities in bodies.—To discover the nature of our
ideas the better, and to discourse of them intelligibly, it will be convenient to distinguish them, as they are ideas or perceptions in our minds,
and as they are modifications of matter in the bodies that cause such perceptions in us; that so we may not think (as perhaps usually is done) that
they are exactly the images and resemblances of something inherent in
the subject; most of those of sensation being in the mind no more the
likeness of something existing without us than the names that stand for
them are the likeness of our ideas, which yet upon hearing they are apt
to excite in us.

Whatsoever the mind perceives in itself, or is the immediate object
of perception, thought, or understanding, that I call "idea"; and the power
to produce any idea in our mind, I call "quality" of the subject wherein
that power is. Thus a snowball having the power to produce in us the
ideas of white, cold, and round, the powers to produce those ideas in us
as they are in the snowball, I call "qualities"; and as they are sensations or
perceptions in our understandings, I call them "ideas"; which ideas, if I
speak of them sometimes as in the things themselves, I would be understood to mean those qualities in the objects which produce them in us.

Primary qualities.—Qualities thus considered in bodies are, first, such
as are utterly inseparable from the body, in what estate soever it be; such
as, in all the alterations and changes it suffers, all the force can be used
upon it, it constantly keeps; and such as sense constantly finds in every
particle of matter which has bulk enough to be perceived, and the mind
finds inseparable from every particle of matter, though less than to make

itself singly be perceived by our senses; v.g., take a grain of wheat, divide it into two parts, each part has still solidity, extension, figure, and mobility; divide it again, and it retains still the same qualities: and so divide it on till the parts become insensible, they must retain still each of them all those qualities. For, division (which is all that a mill or pestle or any other body does upon another, in reducing it to insensible parts) can never take away either solidity, extension, figure, or mobility from any body, but only makes two or more distinct separate masses of matter of that which was but one before; all which distinct masses, reckoned as so many distinct bodies, after division, make a certain number. These I call *original* or *primary* qualities of body, which I think we may observe to produce simple ideas in us, viz., solidity, extension, figure, motion or rest, and number.

Secondary qualities. Secondly. Such qualities, which in truth are nothing in the objects themselves, but powers to produce various sensations in us by their primary qualities, i.e., by the bulk, figure, texture, and motion of their insensible parts, as colours, sounds, tastes, &c., these I call *secondary* qualities. To these might be added a third sort, which are allowed to be barely powers, though they are as much real qualities in the subject as those which I, to comply with the common way of speaking, call qualities, but, for distinction, *secondary* qualities. For, the power in fire to produce a new colour or consistence in wax or clay by its primary qualities, is as much a quality in fire as the power it has to produce in me a new idea or sensation of warmth or burning, which I felt not before, by the same primary qualities, viz., the bulk, texture, and motion of its insensible parts.

How primary qualities produce their ideas.—The next thing to be considered is, how bodies produce ideas in us; and that is manifestly by impulse, the only way which we can conceive bodies operate in.

If, then, external objects be not united to our minds when they produce ideas in it, and yet we perceive these original qualities in such of them as singly fall under our senses, it is evident that some motion must be thence continued by our nerves or animal spirits, by some parts of our bodies, to the brain or the seat of sensation, there to produce in our minds the particular ideas we have of them. And since the extension, figure, number, and motion of bodies of an observable bigness, may be perceived at a distance by the sight, it is evident some singly imperceptible bodies must come from them to the eyes, and thereby convey to the brain some motion which produces these ideas which we have of them in us.

How secondary.—After the same manner that the ideas of these original qualities are produced in us, we may conceive that the ideas of secondary qualities are also produced, viz., by the operation of insensible particles on our senses. For it being manifest that there are bodies, and good store of bodies, each whereof are so small that we cannot by any of our senses discover either their bulk, figure, or motion (as is evident in the particles of the air and water, and other extremely smaller than those, perhaps as much smaller than the particles of air or water as the particles of air or water are smaller than pease or hailstones): let us suppose at present that the different motions and figures, bulk and number, of such particles, affecting the several organs of our senses, produce in us those different sensations which we have from the colours and smells of bodies, v.g., that a violet, by the impulse of such insensible particles of matter of peculiar figures and bulks, and in different degrees and modifications of their motions, causes the ideas of the blue colour and sweet scent of that flower to be produced in our minds; it being no more impossible to conceive that God should annex such ideas to such motions with which they have no similitude, than that he should annex the idea of pain to the motion of a piece of steel dividing our flesh, with which that idea hath no resemblance.

What I have said concerning colours and smells may be understood also of tastes and sounds, and other the like sensible qualities; which, whatever reality we by mistake attribute to them, are in truth nothing in the objects themselves, but powers to produce various sensations in us, and depend on those primary qualities, viz., bulk, figure, texture, and motion of parts, as I have said.

Three sorts of qualities in bodies.—The qualities then that are in bodies, rightly considered, are of three sorts:

First. The bulk, figure, number, situation, and motion or rest of their solid parts; those are in them, whether we perceive them or no; and when they are of that size that we can discover them, we have by these an idea of the thing as it is in itself, as is plain in artificial things. These I call *primary* qualities.

Secondly. The power that is in any body by reason of its insensible primary qualities, to operate after a peculiar manner on any of our senses, and thereby produce in us the different ideas of several colours, sounds, smells, tastes, &c. These are usually called *sensible* qualities.

Thirdly. The power that is in any body, by reason of the particular constitution of its primary qualities, to make such a change in the bulk, figure, texture, and motion of another body, as to make it operate on our senses differently from what it did before. Thus the sun has a power to make wax white, and fire, to make lead fluid. These are usually called "powers."

The first of these, as has been said, I think may be properly called real, original, or primary qualities, because they are in the things themselves, whether they are perceived or no; and upon their different modifications it is that the secondary qualities depend.

The other two are only powers to act differently upon other things, which powers result from the different modifications of those primary qualities.

IX. OF PERCEPTION

Perception the first simple idea of reflection.—Perception, as it is the first faculty of the mind exercised about our ideas, so it is the first and simplest idea we have from reflection, and is by some called "thinking" in general. Though thinking, in the propriety of the English tongue, signifies that sort of operation of the mind about its ideas wherein the mind is active; where it, with some degree of voluntary attention, considers anything: for in bare, naked perception, the mind is, for the most part, only passive, and what it perceives it cannot avoid perceiving.

Is only when the mind receives the impression.—What perception is, everyone will know better by reflecting on what he does himself, when he sees, hears, feels, &c., or thinks, than by any discourse of mine. Whoever reflects on what passes in his own mind, cannot miss it; and if he does not reflect, all the words in the world cannot make him have any notion of it.

Which ideas first, is not evident.—As there are some ideas which we may reasonably suppose may be introduced into the minds of children in the womb, subservient to the necessities of their life and being there; so after they are born those ideas are the earliest imprinted which happen to be the sensible qualities which first occur to them: amongst which, light is not the least considerable, nor of the weakest efficacy. And how covetous the mind is to be furnished with all such ideas as have no pain accompanying them, may be a little guessed by what is observable in children new born, who always turn their eyes to that part from whence the light comes, lay them how you please. But the ideas that are most familiar at first being various, according to the divers circumstances of children's first entertainment in the world, the order wherein the several ideas come at first into the mind is very various and uncertain also, neither is it much material to know it.

Perception the inlet of knowledge.—Perception, then, being the first step and degree towards knowledge, and the inlet of all the materials of it, the fewer senses any man as well as any other creature hath, and the fewer and duller the impressions are that are made by them, and the duller the faculties are that are employed about them, the more remote are they from that knowledge which is to be found in some men. But this, being in great variety of degrees (as may be perceived amongst men), cannot certainly be discovered in the several species of animals, much less in their particular individuals. It suffices me only to have remarked here, that perception is the first operation of all our intellectual faculties, and the inlet of all knowledge into our minds. And I am apt, too, to imagine that it is perception in the lowest degree of it which puts the boundaries between animals and the inferior ranks of creatures. But this I mention only as my conjecture by the by, it being indifferent to the matter in hand which way the learned shall determine of it.

X. OF RETENTION

Contemplation.—The next faculty of the mind, whereby it makes a farther progress towards knowledge, is that which I call retention or the keeping of those simple ideas which from sensation or reflection it hath received. This is done two ways. First, by keeping the idea which is brought into it for some time actually in view, which is called contemplation.

Memory.—The other way of retention is the power to revive again in our minds those ideas which after imprinting have disappeared, or have been as it were laid aside out of sight; and thus we do, when we conceive heat or light, yellow or sweet, the object being removed. This is memory, which is, as it were, the storehouse of our ideas. For the narrow mind of man, not being capable of having many ideas under view and consideration at once, it was necessary to have a repository to lay up those ideas, which at another time it might have use of. But our ideas being nothing but actual perceptions in the mind, which cease to be anything when there is no perception of them, this laying up of our ideas in the repository of the memory signifies no more but this,—that the mind has a power, in many cases, to revive perceptions which it has once had, with this additional perception annexed to them,—that it has had them before.

In remembering, the mind is often active.—In this secondary perception, as I may so call it, or viewing again the ideas that are lodged in the memory, the mind is oftentimes more than barely passive; the appearances of those dormant pictures depending sometimes on the will. The mind very often sets itself on work in search of some hidden idea, and turns, as it were, the eye of the soul upon it; though sometimes too they start up in our minds of their own accord, and offer themselves to the understanding, and very often are roused and tumbled out of their dark cells into open daylight by some turbulent and tempestuous passion; our affections bringing ideas to our memory which had otherwise lain quiet and unregarded. This farther is to be observed concerning ideas lodged in the memory, and upon occasion revived by the mind,—that they are not only (as the word "revive" imports) none of them new ones, but also that the mind takes notice of them as of a former impression, and renews its acquaintance with them as with ideas it had known before. So that though ideas formerly imprinted are not all constantly in view, yet in remembrance they are constantly known to be such as have been formerly imprinted, i.e., in view, and taken notice of before by the understanding.

XI. OF DISCERNING, AND OTHER OPERATIONS OF THE MIND

No knowledge without discerning.—Another faculty we may take notice of in our minds, is that of discerning and distinguishing between the several ideas it has. It is not enough to have a confused perception of something in general: unless the mind had a distinct perception of different objects and their qualities, it would be capable of very little knowledge; though the bodies that affect us were as busy about us as they are now, and the mind were continually employed in thinking. On this faculty of distinguishing one thing from another, depends the evidence and certainty of several even very general propositions, which have passed for innate truths; because men, overlooking the true cause why those propositions find universal assent, impute it wholly to native uniform impressions: whereas it in truth depends upon this clear discerning faculty of the mind. whereby it perceives two ideas to be the same or different.

Clearness alone hinders confusion.—To the well distinguishing our ideas, it chiefly contributes that they be clear and determinate; and when they are so, it will not breed any confusion or mistake about them, though the senses should (as sometimes they do) convey them from the same object differently on different occasions, and so seem to err. For though a man in a fever should from sugar have a bitter taste, which at another time would produce a sweet one, yet the idea of bitter in that man's mind would be as clear and distinct from the idea of sweet, as if he had tasted only gall. Nor does it make any more confusion between the two ideas of sweet and bitter, that the same sort of body produces at one time one and at another time another idea by the taste, than it makes a confusion in two ideas of white and sweet, or white and round, that the same piece of sugar produces them both in the mind at the same time. And the ideas of orange-colour and azure that are produced in the mind by the same parcel of the infusion of *lignum nephriticum,* are no less distinct ideas than those of the same colours taken from two very different bodies.

Comparing.—The comparing them one with another, in respect of extent, degrees, time, place, or any other circumstances, is another operation of the mind about its ideas, and is that upon which depends all that large tribe of ideas, comprehended under relation; which of how vast an extent it is, I shall have occasion to consider hereafter.

Naming.—When children have by repeated sensations got ideas fixed in their memories, they begin by degrees to learn the use of signs. And when they have got the skill to apply the organs of speech to the framing of articulate sounds, they begin to make use of words to signify their ideas to others. These verbal signs they sometimes borrow from others, and sometimes make themselves, as one may observe among the new and unusual names children often give to things in their first use of language.

Abstracting.—The use of words then being to stand as outward marks of our internal ideas, and those ideas being taken from particular things, if every particular idea that we take in should have a distinct name, names must be endless. To prevent this, the mind makes the particular ideas, received from particular objects, to become general; which is done by considering them as they are in the mind such appearances separate from all other existences, and the circumstances of real existence, as time, place, or any other concomitant ideas. This is called "abstraction," whereby ideas taken from particular beings become general representatives of all of the same kind; and their names, general names, applicable to whatever exists conformable to such abstract ideas. Such precise, naked appearances in the mind, without considering how, whence, or with what others they came there, the understanding lays up (with names commonly annexed to them) as the standards to rank real existences into sorts, as they agree with these patterns, and to denominate them accordingly.

Method.—These, I think, are the first faculties and operations of the mind which it makes use of in understanding; and though they are exercised about all its ideas in general, yet the instances I have hitherto given have been chiefly in simple ideas; and I have subjoined the explication of these faculties of the mind to that of simple ideas, before I come to what I have to say concerning complex ones, for these following reasons:—

First, because, several of these faculties being exercised at first principally about simple ideas, we might, by following nature in its ordinary method, trace and discover them in their rise, progress, and gradual improvements.

Secondly, because, observing the faculties of the mind, how they operate about simple ideas, which are usually in most men's minds much more clear, precise, and distinct than complex ones, we may the better examine and learn how the mind abstracts, denominates, compares, and exercises its other operations about those which are complex, wherein we are much more liable to mistake.

Thirdly, because these very operations of the mind about ideas received from sensation are themselves, when reflected on, another set of ideas, derived from that other source of our knowledge which I call "reflection"; and therefore fit to be considered in this place after the simple ideas of sensation. Of compounding, comparing, abstracting, &c., I have but just spoken, having occasion to treat of them more at large in other places.

XII. OF COMPLEX IDEAS

Made by the mind out of simple ones.—We have hitherto considered those ideas, in the reception whereof the mind is only passive, which are those simple ones received from sensation and reflection before mentioned, whereof the mind cannot make one to itself, nor have any idea which does not wholly consist of them. But as the mind is wholly passive in the reception of all its simple ideas, so it exerts several acts of its own, whereby out of its simple ideas, as the materials and foundations of the rest, the others are framed. The acts of the mind wherein it exerts its power over its simple ideas are chiefly these three: (1.) Combining several simple ideas into one compound one; and thus all complex ideas are made. (2.) The second is bringing two ideas, whether simple or complex, together, and setting them by one another, so as to take a view of them at once, without uniting them into one; by which it gets all its ideas of relations. (3.) The third is separating them from all other ideas that accompany them in their real existence; this is called "abstraction": and thus all its general ideas are made. This shows man's power and its way of operation to be much-what the same in the material and intellectual world. For, the materials in both being such as he has no power over, either to make or destroy, all that man can do is either to unite them together, or to set them by one another, or wholly separate them.

Made voluntarily.—In this faculty of repeating and joining together its ideas, the mind has great power in varying and multiplying the objects of its thoughts infinitely beyond what sensation or reflection furnished it with; but all this still confined to those simple ideas which it received from those two sources, and which are the ultimate materials of all its compositions. For, simple ideas are all from things themselves; and of these the mind can have no more nor other than what are suggested to it. It can have no other ideas of sensible qualities than what come from without by the senses, nor any ideas of other kind of operations of a thinking substance than what it finds in itself; but when it has once got these simple ideas, it is not confined barely to observation, and what offers itself from without; it can, by its own power, put together those ideas it has, and make new complex ones which it never received so united.

Are either modes, substances, or relations.—Complex ideas, however compounded and decompounded, though their number be infinite, and the variety endless wherewith they fill and entertain the thoughts of men, yet I think they may be all reduced under these three heads: 1. Modes. 2. Substances. 3. Relations.

XIII. OF SIMPLE MODES; AND FIRST, OF THE SIMPLE MODES OF SPACE

Simple modes.—Though in the foregoing part I have often mentioned simple ideas, which are truly the materials of all our knowledge; yet, having treated of them there rather in the way that they come into the mind than as distinguished from others more compounded, it will not be perhaps amiss to take a view of some of them again under this consideration, and examine those different modifications of the same idea, which the mind either finds in things existing, or is able to make within itself, without the help of any extrinsical object, or any foreign suggestion.

Those modifications of any one simple idea (which I call "simple modes") are as perfectly different and distinct ideas in the mind as those of the greatest distance or contrariety; for the idea of two is as distinct from that of one as blueness from heat, or either of them from any number; and yet it is made up only of that simple idea of an unit repeated; and repetitions of this kind joined together make those distinct simple modes of a dozen, a gross, a million.

Idea of space.—I shall begin with the simple idea of space. I have showed above that we get the idea of space both by our sight and touch: which I think is so evident that it would be as needless to go to prove that men perceive by their sight a distance between bodies of different colours, or between the parts of the same body, as that they see colours themselves; nor is it less obvious that they can do so in the dark by feeling and touch.

Space and extension.—This space considered barely in length between any two beings, without considering anything else between them, is called "distance"; if considered in length, breadth, and thickness, I think it may be called "capacity"; the term "extension" is usually applied to it, in what manner soever considered.

XIV. OF DURATION, AND ITS SIMPLE MODES

Duration is fleeting extension.—There is another sort of distance or length, the idea whereof we get not from the permanent parts of space, but from the fleeting and perpetually perishing parts of succession: this we call "duration," the simple modes whereof are any different lengths of it whereof we have distinct ideas, as hours, days, years, &c., time, and eternity.

Its idea from reflection on the train of our ideas.—The answer of a great man to one who asked what time was, *Si non rogas intelligo* (which amounts to this: "The more I set myself to think of it the less I under-stand it,"), might perhaps persuade one that time, which reveals all other things, is itself not to be discovered. Duration, time, and eternity are not without reason thought to have something very abstruse in their nature. But however remote these may seem from our comprehension, yet if we trace them right to their originals, I doubt not but one of those sources of all our knowledge, viz., sensation and reflection, will be able to furnish us with these ideas as clear and distinct as many other which are thought much less obscure; and we shall find that the idea of eternity itself is derived from the same common original with the rest of our ideas.

To understand time and eternity aright, we ought with attention to consider what idea it is we have of duration, and how we came by it. It is evident to anyone who will but observe what passes in his own mind, that there is a train of ideas which constantly succeed one another in his understanding as long as he is awake. Reflection on these appearances of several ideas one after another in our minds, is that which furnishes us with the idea of succession; and the distance between any parts of that succession, or between the appearance of any two ideas in our minds, is that we call duration. For whilst we are thinking, or whilst we receive successively several ideas in our minds, we know that we do exist; and so we call the existence or the continuation of the existence of ourselves, or anything else commensurate to the succession of any ideas in our minds, the duration of ourselves, or any such other thing co-existing with our thinking.

The idea of succession not from motion.—Thus, by reflecting on the appearance of various ideas one after another in our understandings, we get the notion of succession; which if anyone should think we did rather get from our observation of motion by our senses, he will perhaps be of my mind, when he considers that even motion produces in his mind an idea of succession no otherwise than as it produces there a continued train of distinguishable ideas. For, a man, looking upon a body really moving, perceives yet no motion at all, unless that motion produces a constant train of successive ideas; v.g., a man becalmed at sea, out of sight of land, in a fair day may look on the sun, or sea, or ship, a whole hour together, and perceive no motion at all in either; though it be certain that two, and perhaps all of them, have moved during that time a great way; but as soon as he perceives either of them to have changed distance with some other body, as soon as this motion produces any new idea in him, then he per-ceives that there has been motion. But wherever a man is with all things at rest about him, without perceiving any motion at all, if during this hour of quiet he has been thinking, he will perceive the various ideas of his own thoughts in his own mind appearing one after another, and thereby observe and find succession where he could observe no motion.

This train the measure of other successions.—So that to me it seems, that the constant and regular succession of ideas in a waking man is, as it were, the measure and standard of all other successions; whereof if any one either exceeds the place of our ideas,—as where two sounds or pains, &c., take up in their succession the duration of but one idea, or else where any motion or succession is so slow that it keeps not pace with the ideas in our minds, or the quickness in which they take their turns; as when any one or more ideas in their ordinary course come into our mind between those which are offered to the sight by the different perceptible distances of a body in motion, or between sounds or smells following one another,—there also the sense of a constant, continued succession is lost, and we perceive it not but with certain gaps of rest between.

Time is duration set out by measures.—Having thus got the idea of duration, the next thing natural for the mind to do is, to get some measure of this common duration, whereby it might judge of its different lengths, and consider the distinct order wherein several things exist: without which a great part of our knowledge would be confused, and a great part of history be rendered very useless. This consideration of duration, as set out by certain periods, and marked by certain measures or epochs, is that, I think, which most properly we call "time."

A good measure of time must divide its whole duration into equal periods.—In the measuring of extension there is nothing more required but the application of the standard or measure we make use of to the thing of whose extension we would be informed. But in the measuring of duration this cannot be done, because no two different parts of succession can be put together to measure one another: and nothing being a measure of duration but duration, as nothing is of extension but extension, we cannot keep by us any standing unvarying measure of duration, which consists in a constant fleeting succession, as we can of certain lengths of extension, as inches, feet, yards, &c., marked out in permanent parcels of matter. Nothing then could serve well for a convenient measure of time but what has divided the whole length of its duration into apparently equal portions by constantly repeated periods. What portions of duration are not distinguished or considered as distinguished and measured by such periods come not so properly under the notion of time, as appears by such phrases as these, viz., "before all time," and "when time shall be no more."

Eternity.—By the same means, therefore, and from the same original, that we come to have the idea of time, we have also that idea which we call "eternity," viz., having got the idea of succession and duration, by reflecting on the train of our own ideas, caused in us either by the natural appearances of those ideas coming constantly of themselves into our waking thoughts, or else caused by external objects successively affecting our senses; and having from the revolutions of the sun got the ideas of certain lengths of duration, we can in our thoughts add such lengths of duration to one another as often as we please, and apply them, so added, to durations past or to come: and this we can continue to do on, without bounds or limits, and proceed *in infinitum,* and apply thus the length of the annual motion of the sun to duration, supposed before the sun's or any other motion had its being; which is no more difficult or absurd than to apply the notion I have of the moving of a shadow one hour to-day upon the sun-dial to the duration of something last night; v.g., the burning of a candle, which is now absolutely separate from all actual motion; and it is as impossible for the duration of that flame for an hour last night to co-exist with any motion that now is, or for ever shall be, as for any part of duration that was before the beginning of the world to co-exist with the motion of the sun now. But yet this hinders not but that, having the idea of the length of the motion of the shadow on a dial between the marks of two hours, I can as distinctly measure in my thoughts the duration of that candle-light last night as I can the duration of anything that does now exist; and it is no more than to think, that had the sun shone then on the dial, and moved after the same rate it doth now, the shadow on the dial would have passed from one hour-line to another whilst that flame of the candle lasted.

For as, in the history of the creation delivered by Moses, I can imagine that light existed three days before the sun was or had any motion, barely by thinking that the duration of light before the sun was created was so long as (if the sun had moved then as it doth now) would have been equal to three of his diurnal revolutions; so by the same way I can have an idea of the chaos, or angels being created, before there was either light or any continued motion, a minute, an hour, a day, a year, or one thousand years. For if I can but consider duration equal to one minute, before either the being or motion of any body, I can add one minute more till I come to sixty; and by the same way of adding minutes, hours, or years (i.e., such or such parts of the sun's revolution, or any other period whereof I have the idea), proceed *in infinitum,* and supposing a duration exceeding as many such periods as I can reckon, let me add whilst I will: which I think is the notion we have of eternity, of whose infinity we have no other notion than we have of the infinity of number, to which we can add for ever without end.

XV. OF DURATION AND EXPANSION CONSIDERED TOGETHER

Both capable of greater and less.—Though we have in the precedent chapters dwelt pretty long on the considerations of space and duration, yet they being ideas of general concernment, that have something very abstruse and peculiar in their nature, the comparing them one with another may perhaps be of use for their illustration; and we may have the more clear and distinct conception of them by taking a view of them together. Distance or space, in its simple abstract conception, to avoid confusion, I call "expansion," to distinguish it from extension, which by some is used to express this distance only as it is in the solid parts of matter, and so includes, or at least intimates, the idea of body; whereas, the idea of pure distance includes no such thing. I prefer also the word "expansion" to "space," because space is often applied to distance of fleeting successive parts, which never exist together, as well as to those which are permanent. In both these (viz., expansion and duration) the mind has this common idea of continued lengths, capable of greater or less quantities; for a man has as clear an idea of the difference of the length of an hour and a day as of an inch and a foot.

Expansion not bounded by matter.—The mind having got the idea of the length of any part of expansion, let it be a span, or a pace, or what length you will, can, as has been said, repeat that idea; and so adding it to the former, enlarge its idea of length, and make it equal to two spans, or two paces, and so, as often as it will, till it equals the distance of any parts of the earth one from another, and increase thus till it amounts to the distance of the sun or remotest star. By such a progression as this, setting out from the place where it is, or any other place, it can proceed and pass beyond all those lengths, and find nothing to stop its going on, either in or without body. It is true we can easily in our thoughts come to the end of solid extension; the extremity and bounds of all body, we have no difficulty to arrive at: but when the mind is there, it finds nothing to hinder its progress into this endless expansion: of that it can neither find nor conceive any end. Nor let anyone say, that beyond the bounds of body there is nothing at all, unless he will confine God within the limits of matter.

Nor duration by motion.—Just so is it in duration. The mind, having got the idea of any length of duration, can double, multiply, and enlarge it, not only beyond its own, but beyond the existence of all corporeal beings and all the measures of time, taken from the great bodies of the world and their motions. But yet everyone easily admits, that though we make duration boundless, as certainly it is, we cannot yet extend it beyond all being. God, everyone easily allows, fills eternity; and it is hard to find a reason why anyone should doubt that he likewise fills immensity. His infinite being is certainly as boundless one way as another; and methinks it ascribes a little too much to matter to say, "Where there is no body, there is nothing."

Time to duration, is as place to expansion.—Time in general is to duration as place to expansion. They are so much of those boundless oceans of eternity and immensity, as is set out and distinguished from the rest as it were by land-marks; and so are made use of to denote the position of finite real beings, in respect one to another, in those uniform infinite oceans of duration and space. These, rightly considered, are nothing but ideas of determinate distances, from certain known points fixed in distinguishable sensible things, and supposed to keep the same distance one from another. From such points fixed in sensible beings we reckon, and from them we measure our portions of those infinite quantities; which, so considered, are that which we call "time" and "place." For duration and space being in themselves uniform and boundless, the order and position of things without such known settled points would be lost in them; and all things would lie jumbled in an incurable confusion.

They belong to all beings.—WHERE and WHEN are questions belonging to all finite existences, and are by us always reckoned from some known parts of this sensible world, and from some certain epochs marked out to us by the motions observable in it. Without some such fixed parts or periods, the order of things would be lost to our finite understandings in the boundless, invariable oceans of duration and expansion; which comprehend in them all finite beings, and in their full extent belong only to the Deity. And therefore we are not to wonder that we comprehend them not, and do so often find our thoughts at a loss, when we would consider them either abstractedly in themselves, or as any way attributed to the first incomprehensible Being. But when applied to any particular finite beings, the extension of any body is so much of that infinite space as the bulk of that body takes up. And place is the position of any body, when considered at a certain distance from some other. As the idea of the particular duration of anything is an idea of that portion of infinite duration which passes during the existence of that thing, so the time when the thing existed is the idea of that space of duration which passed between some known and fixed period of duration, and the being of that thing. One shows the distance of the extremities of the bulk or existence of the same thing, as that it is a foot square, or lasted two years; the other shows the distance of it in place or existence from other fixed points of space or duration.

All the parts of extension are extension; and all the parts of duration are duration.—There is one thing more wherein space and duration have a great conformity; and that is, though they are justly reckoned amongst our simple ideas, yet none of the distinct ideas we have of either is without all manner of composition; it is the very nature of both of them to consist of parts: but their parts, being all of the same kind, and without the mixture of any other idea, hinder them not from having a place amongst simple ideas. Could the mind, as in number, come to so small a part of extension or duration as excluded divisibility, that would be, as it were, the indivisible unit or idea; by repetition of which, it would make its more enlarged ideas of extension and duration. But since the mind is not able to frame an idea of any space without parts, instead thereof it makes use of the common measures, which by familiar use in each country have imprinted themselves on the memory: (as inches, and feet; or cubits, and parasangs; and so seconds, minutes, hours, days, and years in duration) the mind makes use, I say, of such ideas as these, as simple ones; and these are the component parts of larger ideas, which the mind, upon occasion, makes by the addition of such known lengths which it is acquainted with.

On the other side, the ordinary smallest measure we have of either, is looked on as an unit in number, when the mind by division would reduce them into less fractions. Though on both sides, both in addition and division, either of space or duration, when the idea under consideration becomes very big or very small, its precise bulk becomes very obscure and confused; and it is the number of its repeated additions or divisions, that alone remains clear and distinct; as will easily appear to anyone who will let his thoughts loose in the vast expansion of space, or divisibility of matter. Every part of duration is duration too; and every part of extension is extension; both of them capable of addition or division *in infinitum*. But the least portions of either of them, whereof we have clear and distinct ideas, may perhaps be fittest to be considered by us as the simple ideas of that kind, out of which our complex modes of space, extension, and duration are made up, and into which they can again be distinctly resolved. Such a small part in duration may be called a "moment," and is the time of one idea in our minds, in the train of their ordinary succession there. The other, wanting a proper name, I know not whether I may be allowed to call "a sensible point," meaning thereby the least particle of matter or space we can discern, which is ordinarily about a minute, and to the sharpest eyes seldom less than thirty seconds, of a circle whereof the eye is the centre.

XVI. OF NUMBER

Number, the simplest and most universal idea.—Amongst all the ideas we have, as there is none suggested to the mind by more ways, so there is none more simple, than that of unity, or one. It has no shadow of variety of composition in it; every object our senses are employed about, every idea in our understandings, every thought of our minds, brings this idea along with it: and therefore it is the most intimate to our thoughts, as well as it is, in its agreement to all other things, the most universal idea we have. For number applies itself to men, angels, actions, thoughts,—everything that either doth exist or can be imagined.

Its modes made by addition.—By repeating this idea in our minds, and adding the repetitions together, we come by the complex ideas of the modes of it. Thus by adding one to one we have the complex idea of a couple: by putting twelve units together we have the complex idea of a dozen; and a score, or a million, or any other number.

Each mode distinct.—The simple modes of number are of all other the most distinct; every the least variation which is an unit, making each combination as clearly different from that which approacheth nearest to it, as the most remote: two being as distinct from one as two hundred; and the idea of two as distinct from the idea of three, as the magnitude of the whole earth is from that of a mite. This is not so in other simple modes, in which it is not so easy, nor perhaps possible, for us to distinguish betwixt two approaching ideas, which yet are really different. For who will undertake to find a difference between the white of this paper and that of the next degree to it? or can form distinct ideas of every the least excess in extension?

Therefore demonstrations in numbers the most precise.—The clearness and distinctness of each mode of number from all others, even those that approach nearest, makes me apt to think that demonstrations in numbers, if they are not more evident and exact than in extension, yet they are more general in their use, and more determinate in their application. But it is not so in extension, where whatsoever is more than just a foot, or an inch, is not distinguishable from the standard of a foot, or an inch; and in lines which appear of an equal length, one may be longer than the other by innumerable parts; nor can anyone assign an angle which shall be the next biggest to a right one.

Number measures all measurables.—This farther is observable in number, that it is that which the mind makes use of in measuring all things that by us are measurable, which principally are expansion and duration; and our idea of infinity even when applied to those seems to be nothing but the infinity of number. For what else are our ideas of eternity and immensity, but the repeated additions of certain ideas of imagined parts of duration and expansion, with the infinity of number, in which we can come to no end of addition? For such an inexhaustible stock, number, of all our other ideas, most clearly furnishes us with, as is obvious to everyone. For let a man collect into one sum as great a number as he pleases, this multitude, how great soever, lessens not one jot the power of adding to it, or brings him any nearer the end of the inexhaustible stock of number, where still there remains as much to be added as if none were taken out. And this endless addition or addibility (if anyone like the word better) of numbers, so apparent to the mind, is that,

I think, which gives us the clearest and most distinct idea of infinity; of which more in the following chapter.

XVII. OF INFINITY

How we come by the idea of infinity.—Everyone that has any idea of any stated lengths of space, as a foot, finds that he can repeat that idea; and, joining it to the former, make the idea of two feet, and, by the addition of a third, three feet, and so on, without ever coming to an end of his additions, whether of the same idea of a foot, or, if he pleases, of doubling it, or any other idea he has of any length, as a mile, or diameter of the earth, or of the *orbis magnus;* for, whichsoever of these he takes, and how often soever he doubles or any otherwise multiplies it, he finds that, after he has continued this doubling in his thoughts and enlarged his idea as much as he pleases, he has no more reason to stop, nor is one jot nearer the end of such addition than he was at first setting out: the power of enlarging his idea of space by farther additions remaining still the same, he hence takes the idea of infinite space.

Our idea of space boundless.—This, I think, is the way whereby the mind gets the idea of infinite space. It is a quite different consideration to examine whether the mind has the idea of such a boundless space actually existing, since our ideas are not always proofs of the existence of things; but yet, since this comes here in our way, I suppose I may say that we are apt to think that space in itself is actually boundless, to which imagination the idea of space or expansion of itself naturally leads us. For, it being considered by us either as the extension of body, or as existing by itself, without any solid matter taking it up (for of such a void space we have not only the idea, but I have proved, as I think, from the motion of body, its necessary existence), it is impossible the mind should be ever able to find or suppose any end of it, or be stopped anywhere in its progress in this space, how far soever it extends its thoughts.

And so of duration.—As, by the power we find in ourselves of repeating as often as we will any idea of space, we get the idea of immensity; so, by being able to repeat the idea of any length of duration we have in our minds, with all the endless addition of number, we come by the idea of eternity. For we find in ourselves, we can no more come to an end of such repeated ideas than we can come to the end of number; which everyone perceives he cannot. But here again it is another question, quite different from our having an idea of eternity, to know whether there were any real being whose duration has been eternal. And as to this, I say, he that considers something now existing must necessarily come to something eternal.

Difference between infinity of space and space infinite.—Though our idea of infinity arise from the contemplation of quantity, and the endless increase the mind is able to make in quantity, by the repeated additions of what portions thereof it pleases; yet, I guess, we cause great confusion in our thoughts when we join infinity to any supposed idea of quantity the mind can be thought to have, and so discourse or reason about an infinite quantity (viz.), an infinite space or an infinite duration. For our idea of infinity being, as I think, an endless growing idea, but the idea of any quantity the mind has being at that time terminated in that idea (for be it as great as it will, it can be no greater than it is), to join infinity to it, is to adjust a standing measure to a growing bulk; and therefore I think it is not an insignificant subtilty if I say that we are carefully to distinguish between the idea of *the infinity of space* and the idea of *a space infinite:* the first is nothing but a supposed endless progression of the mind over what repeated ideas of space it pleases; but to have actually in the mind the idea of a space infinite, is to suppose the mind already passed over, and actually to have a view of all those repeated ideas of space which an endless repetition can never totally represent to it; which carries in it a plain contradiction.

No positive idea of infinite.—Though it be hard, I think, to find anyone so absurd as to say he has the positive idea of an actual infinite number, the infinity whereof lies only in a power still of adding any combination of units to any former number, and that as long and as much as one will; the like also being in the infinity of space and duration, which power leaves always to the mind room for endless additions; yet there be those who imagine they have positive ideas of infinite duration and space. It would, I think, be enough to destroy any such positive idea of infinite to ask him that has it, whether he could add to it or no? which would easily show the mistake of such a positive idea. We can, I think, have no positive idea of any space or duration which is not made up of, and commensurate to, repeated numbers of feet or yards, or days and years; which are the common measures whereof we have the idea in our minds, and whereby we judge of the greatness of these sort of quantities. And therefore, since an idea of infinite space or duration must needs be made up of infinite parts, it can have no other infinity than that of number, capable still of farther addition; but not an actual positive idea of a number infinite. For, I think, it is evident that the addition of finite things together (as are all lengths whereof we have the positive ideas) can never otherwise produce the idea of infinite than as number does; which, consisting of additions of finite units one to another, suggests the idea of infinite only by a power we find we have of still increasing the sum, and adding more of the same kind, without coming one jot nearer the end of such progression.

XVIII. OF OTHER SIMPLE MODES

Modes of motion.—Though I have in the foregoing chapters shown how, from simple ideas taken in by sensation the mind comes to extend itself even to infinity; which, however it may of all others seem most remote from any sensible perception, yet at last hath nothing in it but what is made out of simple ideas received into the mind by the senses, and afterwards there put together by the faculty the mind has to repeat its own ideas: though, I say, these might be instances enough of simple modes of the simple ideas of sensation, and suffice to show how the mind comes by them; yet I shall, for method's sake, though briefly, give an account of some few more, and then proceed to more complex ideas.

Modes of tastes.—All compounded tastes and smells are also modes made up of these simple ideas of those senses. But they, being such as generally we have no names for, are less taken notice of, and cannot be set down in writing; and therefore must be left without enumeration to the thoughts and experience of my reader.

XIX. OF THE MODES OF THINKING

Sensation, remembrance, contemplation, &c.—When the mind turns its view inwards upon itself, and contemplates its own actions, thinking is the first that occurs. In it the mind observes a great variety of modifications, and from thence receives distinct ideas. Thus the perception which actually accompanies and is annexed to any impression on the body made by an external object, being distinct from all other modifications of thinking, furnishes the mind with a distinct idea which we call "sensation"; which is, as it were, the actual entrance of any idea into the understanding by the senses. The same idea, when it again recurs without the operation of the like object on the external sensory, is "remembrance": if it be sought after by the mind, and with pain and endeavour found, and brought again in view, it is "recollection": if it be held there long under attentive consideration, it is "contemplation": when ideas float in our mind without any reflection or regard of the understanding, it is that which the French call *réverie;* our language has scarce a name for it: when the ideas that offer themselves are taken notice of, and, as it were, registered in the memory, it is "attention": when the mind with great earnestness, and of choice, fixes its view on any idea, considers it on all sides, and will not be called off by the ordinary solicitation of other ideas, it is that we call "intention," or "study": "sleep" without dreaming is rest from all these: and "dreaming" itself is the having of ideas in the mind not suggested by any external objects or known occasion, nor under any choice or conduct of the understanding at all; and whether that which we call "ecstasy" be not dreaming with the eyes open, I leave to be examined.

XX. ON MODES OF PLEASURE AND PAIN

Pleasure and pain simple ideas.—Amongst the simple ideas which we receive both from sensation and reflection, pain and pleasure are two very considerable ones. For as in the body there is sensation barely in itself, or accompanied with pain or pleasure; so the thought or perception of the mind is simply so, or else accompanied also with pleasure or pain, delight or trouble, call it how you please. These, like other simple ideas, cannot be described, nor their names defined: the way of knowing them is, as of the simple ideas of the senses, only by experience. For to define them by the presence of good or evil, is no otherwise to make them known to us than by making us reflect on what we feel in ourselves, upon the several and various operations of good and evil upon our minds, as they are differently applied to or considered by us.

Good and evil, what.—Things then are good or evil only in reference to pleasure or pain. That we call "good," which is apt to cause or increase pleasure, or diminish pain, in us; or else to procure or preserve us the possession of any other good, or absence of any evil. And, on the contrary, we name that "evil," which is apt to produce or increase any pain, or diminish any pleasure, in us; or else to procure us any evil, or deprive us of any good. By "pleasure" and "pain," I must be understood to mean of body or mind, as they are commonly distinguished; though, in truth, they be only different constitutions of the mind, sometimes occasioned by disorder in the body, sometimes by thoughts in the mind.

Our passions moved by good and evil.—Pleasure and pain, and that which causes them, good and evil, are the hinges on which our passions turn: and if we reflect on ourselves, and observe how these, under various considerations, operate in us,—what modifications or tempers of mind, what internal sensations (if I may so call them) they produce in us,—we may thence form to ourselves the ideas of our passions.

XXI. OF POWER

This idea how got.—The mind being every day informed, by the senses, of the alteration of those simple ideas it observes in things without, and taking notice how one comes to an end and ceases to be, and another begins to exist which was not before; reflecting also, on what passes within itself, and observing a constant change of its ideas, sometimes by the impression of outward objects on the senses, and sometimes by the determination of its own choice; and concluding, from what it has so constantly observed to have been, that the like changes will for the future be made in the same things by like agents, and by the like ways; considers in one thing the possibility of having any of its simple ideas changed, and in another the possibility of making that change; and so comes by that idea which we call "power."

Power active and passive.—Power thus considered is twofold; viz., as able to make, or able to receive, any change: the one may be called "active," and the other "passive," power. Whether matter be not wholly destitute of active power, as its author, God, is truly above all passive power; and whether the intermediate state of created spirits be not that alone which is capable of both active and passive power, may be worth consideration. I shall not now enter into that inquiry; my present business being not to search into the original of power, but how we come by the idea of it. But since active powers make so great a part of our complex ideas of natural substances (as we shall see hereafter), and I mention them as such, according to common apprehension; yet they being not, perhaps, so truly active powers as our hasty thoughts are apt to represent them, I judge it not amiss, by this intimation, to direct our minds to the consideration of God and spirits, for the clearest idea of active power.

Whence the ideas of liberty and necessity.—Everyone, I think, finds in himself a power to begin or forbear, continue or put an end to, several actions in himself. From the consideration of the extent of this power of the mind over the actions of the man, which everyone finds in himself, arise the ideas of liberty and necessity.

Liberty, what.—All the actions that we have any idea of, reducing themselves, as has been said, to these two, viz., thinking and motion, so far as a man has a power to think or not to think, to move or not to move, according to the preference or direction of his own mind, so far is a man free. Wherever any performance and forbearance are not equally in a man's power, wherever doing or not doing will not equally follow upon the preference of his mind directing it, there he is not free, though perhaps the action may be voluntary. So that the idea of liberty is the idea of a power in any agent to do or forbear any particular action, according to the determination or thought of the mind, whereby either of them is preferred to the other; where either of them is not in the power of the agent, to be produced by him according to his volition, there he is not at liberty, that agent is under necessity. So that liberty cannot be where there is no thought, no volition, no will; but there may be thought, there may be will, there may be volition, where there is no liberty.

XXII. OF MIXED MODES

Mixed modes, what.—Having treated of simple modes in the foregoing chapters, and given several instances of some of the most considerable of them, to show what they are, and how we come by them: we are now, in the next place, to consider those we call "mixed modes": such are the complex ideas we mark by the names "obligation," "drunkenness," "a lie," &c., which, consisting of several combinations of simple ideas of different kinds, I have called "mixed modes," to distinguish them from the more simple modes, which consist only of simple ideas of the same kind. These mixed modes, being also such combinations of simple ideas as are not looked upon to be characteristical marks of any real beings that have a steady existence, but scattered and independent ideas put together by the mind, are thereby distinguished from the complex ideas of substances.

How we get the ideas of mixed modes.—There are therefore three ways whereby we get the complex ideas of mixed modes. (1.) By experience and observation of things themselves; thus by seeing two men wrestle or fence, we get the idea of wrestling or fencing. (2.) By invention, or voluntary putting together of several simple ideas in our own minds: so he that first invented printing, or etching, had an idea of it in his mind before it ever existed. (3.) Which is the most usual way, by explaining the names of actions we never saw, or notions we cannot see; and by enumerating, and thereby, as it were, setting before our imaginations all those ideas which go to the making them up, and are the constituent parts of them. For, having by sensation and reflection stored our minds with simple ideas, and by use got the names that stand for them, we can by those names represent to another any complex idea we would have him conceive; so that it has in it no simple ideas but what he knows, and has with us the same name for. For all our complex ideas are ultimately resolvable into simple ideas, of which they are compounded, and originally made up, though perhaps their immediate ingredients, as I may so say, are also complex ideas.

Mixed modes made also of other ideas.—I think I shall not need to remark here, that though power and action make the greatest part of mixed modes, marked by names and familiar in the minds and mouths of men, yet other simple ideas, and their several combinations, are not excluded; much less, I think, will it be necessary for me to enumerate all the mixed modes which have been settled, with names to them. That would be to make a dictionary of the greatest part of the words made use of in divinity, ethics, law, and politics, and several other sciences. All

that is requisite to my present design is, to show what sort of ideas
those are which I called "mixed modes": how the mind comes by them;
and that they are compositions made up of simple ideas got from sensation and reflection; which, I suppose, I have done.

XXIII. OF OUR COMPLEX IDEAS OF SUBSTANCES

Ideas of substance, how made.—The mind being, as I have declared,
furnished with a great number of the simple ideas conveyed in by the
senses, as they are found in exterior things, or by reflection on its own
operations, takes notice, also, that a certain number of these simple ideas
go constantly together; which being presumed to belong to one thing,
and words being suited to common apprehensions, and made use of for
quick despatch, are called, so united in one subject, by one name; which,
by inadvertency, we are apt afterward to talk of and consider as one
simple idea, which indeed is a complication of many ideas together: because, as I have said, not imagining how these simple ideas can subsist
by themselves, we accustom ourselves to suppose some *substratum* wherein
they do subsist, and from which they do result; which therefore we call
"substance."

Our idea of substance in general.—So that if anyone will examine
himself concerning his notion of pure substance in general, he will find
he has no other idea of it at all, but only a supposition of he knows not
what support of such qualities which are capable of producing simple
ideas in us; which qualities are commonly called "accidents." If anyone
should be asked, "What is the subject wherein colour or weight inheres?"
he would have nothing to say but, "The solid extended parts." And if
he were demanded, "What is it that solidity and extension inhere in?"
he would not be in a much better case than the Indian who, saying that
the world was supported by a great elephant, was asked, what the elephant rested on? to which his answer was, "A great tortoise": but being
again pressed to know what gave support to the broad-backed tortoise,
replied,—something, he knew not what. And thus here, as in all other
cases where we use words without having clear and distinct ideas, we
talk like children; who, being questioned what such a thing is which
they know not readily give this satisfactory answer,—that it is something;
which in truth signifies no more, when so used, either by children or men,
but that they know not what; and that the thing they pretend to know
and talk of, is what they have no distinct idea of at all, and so are perfectly ignorant of it, and in the dark. The idea, then, we have, to which
we give the general name "substance," being nothing but the supposed,
but unknown, support of those qualities we find existing, which we

imagine cannot subsist *sine re substante,* "without something to support them," we call that support *substantia;* which, according to the true import of the word, is, in plain English, "standing under," or "upholding."

No clear idea of substance in general.—Hence, when we talk or think of any particular sort of corporeal substances, as horse, stone, &c., though the idea we have of either of them be but the complication or collection of those several simple ideas of sensible qualities which we used to find united in the thing called "horse" or "stone"; yet because we cannot conceive how they should subsist alone, nor one in another, we suppose them existing in, and supported by, some common subject; which support we denote by the name "substance," though it be certain we have no clear or distinct idea of that thing we suppose a support.

Three sorts of ideas make our complex ones of substances.—The ideas that make our complex ones of corporeal substances are of these three sorts. First: The ideas of the primary qualities of things which are discovered by our senses, and are in them even when we perceive them not: such are the bulk, figure, number, situation, and motion of the parts of bodies, which are really in them, whether we take notice of them or no. Secondly: The sensible secondary qualities which, depending on these, are nothing but the powers those substances have to produce several ideas in us by our senses; which ideas are not in the things themselves otherwise than as anything is in its cause. Thirdly: The aptness we consider in any substance to give or receive such alterations of primary qualities as that the substance so altered should produce in us different ideas from what it did before; these are called "active and passive powers": all which powers, as far as we have any notice or notion of them, terminate only in sensible simple ideas. For, whatever alteration a loadstone has the power to make in the minute particles of iron, we should have no notion of any power it had at all to operate on iron, did not its sensible motion discover it; and I doubt not but there are a thousand changes that bodies we daily handle have a power to cause in one another, which we never suspect, because they never appear in sensible effects.

Powers make a great part of our complex ideas of substances.— Powers therefore justly make a great part of our complex ideas of substances. He that will examine his complex idea of gold, will find several of its ideas that make it up to be only powers: as the power of being melted, but of not spending itself in the fire, of being dissolved in *aqua regia,* are ideas as necessary to make up our complex idea of gold, as its colour and weight: which, if duly considered, are also nothing but different powers. For, to speak truly, yellowness is not actually in gold; but is a power in gold to produce that idea in us by our eyes, when placed in a due light: and the heat which we cannot leave out of our idea of the sun, is no more really in the sun than the white colour it introduces into wax. These are both equally powers in the sun, operating, by the motion and figure of its insensible parts, so on a man as to make him have the idea of heat; and so on wax as to make it capable to produce in a man the idea of white.

XXIV. OF COLLECTIVE IDEAS OF SUBSTANCES

One idea.—Besides these complex ideas of several single substances, as of man, horse, gold, violet, apple, &c., the mind hath also "complex collective ideas" of substances; which I so call, because such ideas are made up of many particular substances considered together, as united into one idea, and which so joined are looked on as one; v.g., the idea of such a collection of men as make an army, though consisting of a great number of distinct substances, is as much one idea as the idea of a man; and the great collective idea of all bodies whatsoever, signified by the name "world," is as much one idea as the idea of any the least particle of matter in it; it sufficing to the unity of any idea, that it be considered as one representation or picture, though made up of ever so many particulars.

Made by the power of composing in the mind.—These collective ideas of substances the mind makes by its power of composition, and uniting, severally, either simple or complex ideas into one, as it does by the same faculty make the complex ideas of particular substances, consisting of an aggregate of divers simple ideas united in one substance: and as the mind, by putting together the repeated ideas of unity, makes the collective mode or complex idea of any number, as a score, or a gross, &c., so by putting together several particular substances, it makes collective ideas of substances, as a troop, an army, a swarm, a city, a fleet: each of which everyone finds that he represents to his own mind by one idea, in one view; and so under that notion considers those several things as perfectly one, as one ship, or one atom. Nor is it harder to conceive how an army of ten thousand men should make one idea, than how a man should make one idea; it being as easy to the mind to unite into one the idea of a great number of men, and consider it as one, as it is to unite into one particular all the distinct ideas that make up the composition of a man, and consider them all together as one.

XXV. OF RELATION

Relation, what.—Besides the ideas, whether simple or complex, that the mind has of things, as they are in themselves, there are others it gets from their comparison one with another. The understanding, in the consideration of anything, is not confined to that precise object: it can carry any idea, as it were, beyond itself, or, at least, look beyond it, to see how it stands in conformity to any other. When the mind so considers one thing, that it does, as it were, bring it to and set it by another, and carry its view from one to the other: this is, as the words import, "relation" and "respect"; and the denominations given to positive things, intimating that respect, and serving as marks to lead the thoughts beyond the subject itself denominated to something distinct from it, are what we call "relatives"; and the things so brought together, "related."

Relation only betwixt two things.—Whatsoever doth or can exist, or be considered as one thing, is positive; and so not only simple ideas and substances, but modes also, are positive beings; though the parts of which they consist are very often relative one to another; but the whole together considered as one thing, and producing in us the complex idea of one thing, which idea is in our minds as one picture, though an aggregate of divers parts and under one name, it is a positive or absolute thing or idea. Thus a triangle, though the parts thereof, compared one to another, be relative, yet the idea of the whole is a positive absolute idea. The same may be said of a family, a tune, &c., for there can be no relation but betwixt two things, considered as two things. There must always be in relation two ideas, or things, either in themselves really separate, or considered as distinct, and then a ground or occasion for their comparison.

All things capable of relation.—Concerning relation in general, these things may be considered.

First: That there is no one thing, whether simple idea, substance, mode, or relation, or name of either of them, which is not capable of almost an infinite number of considerations in reference to other things; and therefore this makes no small part of men's thoughts and words.

The ideas of relations clearer often than of the subjects related.—Secondly: This farther may be considered concerning relation, that though it be not contained in the real existence of things, but something extraneous and superinduced; yet the ideas which relative words stand for are often clearer and more distinct than of those substances to which they do belong. The notion we have of a father or brother is a great deal clearer and more distinct than that we have of a man: or, if you will, paternity is a thing whereof it is easier to have a clear idea than of humanity: and I can much easier conceive what a friend is than what God. Because the knowledge of one action, or one simple idea, is oftentimes sufficient to give the notion of a relation: but to the knowing of any substantial being, an accurate collection of sundry ideas is necessary. A man, if he compares two things together, can hardly be supposed not to know what it is wherein he compares them: so that when he compares any things together, he cannot but have a very clear idea of that relation.

Relations all terminate in simple ideas.—Thirdly: Though there be a great number of considerations wherein things may be compared one with another, and so a multitude of relations; yet they all terminate in, and are concerned about, those simple ideas either of sensation or reflection, which I think to be the whole materials of all our knowledge.

Terms leading the mind beyond the subject denominated are relative.—Fourthly: That relation being the considering of one thing with another, which is extrinsical to it, it is evident that all words that necessarily lead the mind to any other ideas than are supposed really to exist in that thing to which the word is applied, are relative words.

XXVI. OF CAUSE AND EFFECT AND OTHER RELATIONS

Whence their ideas got.—In the notice that our senses take of the constant vicissitude of things, we cannot but observe that several particular both qualities and substances begin to exist; and that they receive this their existence from the due application and operation of some other being. From this observation we get our ideas of cause and effect. That which produces any simple or complex idea, we denote by the general name "cause"; and that which is produced, "effect." Thus finding that in that substance which we call "wax" fluidity, which is a simple idea that was not in it before, is constantly produced by the application of a certain degree of heat, we call the simple idea of heat, in relation to fluidity in wax, *the cause* of it, and fluidity *the effect*. So also finding that the substance, wood, which is a certain collection of simple ideas so called, by the application of fire is turned into another substance called "ashes," i.e., another complex idea, consisting of a collection of simple ideas, quite different from that complex idea which we call "wood," we consider fire, in relation to ashes, as cause, and the ashes, as effect. So that whatever is considered by us to conduce or operate to the producing any particular simple idea, or collection of simple ideas, whether substance or mode, which did not before exist, hath thereby in our minds the relation of a cause, and so is denominated by us.

XXVII. OF IDENTITY AND DIVERSITY

Identity of substances. Identity of modes.—We have the ideas but of three sorts of substances: 1. God. 2. Finite intelligences. 3. Bodies. First: God is without beginning, eternal, unalterable, and everywhere; and therefore concerning his identity, there can be no doubt. Secondly: Finite spirits having had each its determinate time and place of beginning to exist, the relation to that time and place will always determine to each of them its identity as long as it exists. Thirdly: The same will hold of every particle of matter, to which no addition or subtraction of matter being made, it is the same. For though these three sorts of substances, as we term them, do not exclude one another out of the same place: yet we cannot conceive but that they must necessarily each of them exclude any of the same kind out of the same place: or else the notions and names of "identity and diversity" would be in vain, and there could be no such distinction of substances, or anything else, one from another.

Principium individuationis.—From what has been said, it is easy to discover, what is so much inquired after, the *principium individuationis;* and that, it is plain, is existence itself, which determines a being of any sort to a particular time and place incommunicable to two beings of the same kind. This, though it seems easier to conceive in simple substances or modes, yet, when reflected on, is not more difficult in compounded ones, if care be taken to what it is applied; v.g., let us suppose an atom, i.e., a continued body under one immutable superficies, existing in a determined time and place; it is evident, that, considered in any instant of its existence, it is, in that instant, the same with itself. For, being at that instant what it is and nothing else, it is the same, and so must continue as long as its existence is continued; for so long it will be the same and no other. In like manner, if two or more atoms be joined together into the same mass, every one of those atoms will be the same, by the foregoing rule: and whilst they exist united together, the mass, consisting of the same atoms, must be the same mass, or the same body, let the parts be ever so differently jumbled: but if one of these atoms be taken away, or one new one added, it is no longer the same mass, or the same body.

In the state of living creatures, their identity depends not on a mass of the same particles, but on something else. For in them the variation of great parcels of matter alters not the identity; an oak, growing from a plant to a great tree, and then lopped, is still the same oak: and a colt, grown up to a horse, sometimes fat, sometimes lean, is all the while the same horse: though, in both these cases, there may be a manifest change of the parts; so that truly they are not either of them the same masses of matter, though there be truly one of them the same oak, and the other the same horse. The reason whereof is, that, in these two cases of a mass of matter and a living body, identity is not applied to the same thing.

Consciousness makes the same person.—But though the same immaterial substance or soul does not alone, wherever it be, and in whatsoever state, make the same man; yet it is plain, consciousness, as far as ever it can be extended, should it be to ages past, unites existences and actions, very remote in time, into the same person, as well as it does the existence and actions of the immediately preceding moment: so that whatever has the consciousness of present and past actions is the same person to whom they both belong.

Self depends on consciousness.—Self is that conscious thinking thing (whatever substance made up of, whether spiritual or material, simple or compounded, it matters not) which is sensible or conscious of pleasure and pain, capable of happiness or misery, and so is concerned for itself, as far as that consciousness extends. Thus everyone finds, that whilst comprehended under that consciousness, the little finger is as much a part of itself as what is most so. Upon separation of this little finger, should this consciousness go along with the little finger, and leave the rest of the body, it is evident the little finger would be the person, the same person; and self then would have nothing to do with the rest of the body. As in this case it is the consciousness that goes along with the substance, when one part is separate from another, which makes the same person, and constitutes this inseparable self, so it is in reference to substances remote in time. That with which the consciousness of this present thinking thing can join itself makes the same person, and is one self with it, and with nothing else; and so attributes to itself and owns all the actions of that thing as its own, as far as that consciousness reaches, and no farther; as everyone who reflects will perceive.

Consciousness alone makes self.—Nothing but consciousness can unite remote existences into the same person; the identity of substance will not do it. For, whatever substance there is, however framed, without consciousness there is no person: and a carcass may be a person, as well as any sort of substance be so without consciousness.

Could we suppose two distinct incommunicable consciousnesses acting the same body, the one constantly by day, the other by night; and, on the other side, the same consciousness acting by intervals two distinct bodies: I ask, in the first case, whether the day and the night man would not be two as distinct persons as Socrates and Plato? and whether, in the second case, there would not be one person in two distinct bodies, as much as one man is the same in two distinct clothings? Nor is it at all material to say, that this same and this distinct consciousness, in the cases above mentioned, is owing to the same and distinct immaterial substances, bringing it with them to those bodies; which, whether true or no, alters not the case: since it is evident the personal identity would equally be determined by the consciousness, whether that consciousness were annexed to some individual immaterial substance or no. For, granting that the thinking substance in man must be necessarily supposed immaterial, it is evident that immaterial thinking thing may sometimes part with its past consciousness, and be restored to it again, as appears in the forgetfulness men often have of their past actions, and the mind many times recovers the memory of a past consciousness which it had lost for twenty years together. Make these intervals of memory and forgetfulness to take their turns regularly by day and night, and you have two persons with the same immaterial spirit, as much as in the former instance two persons with the same body. So that self is not determined by identity or diversity of substance, which it cannot be sure of, but only by identity of consciousness.

The difficulty from ill use of names.—To conclude: Whatever substance begins to exist, it must, during its existence, necessarily be the same: whatever compositions of substances begin to exist, during the union of those substances, the concrete must be the same; whatsoever mode begins to exist, during its existence it is the same: and so if the composition be of distinct substances and different modes, the same rule holds. Whereby it will appear, that the difficulty or obscurity that has been about this matter rather rises from the names ill used, than from any obscurity in things themselves. For whatever makes the specific idea to which the name is applied, if that idea be steadily kept to, the distinction of any thing into the same and diverse will easily be conceived, and there can arise no doubt about it.

XXVIII. OF OTHER RELATIONS

Proportional.—Besides the before-mentioned occasions of time, place, and casualty of comparing, or referring things one to another, there are, as I have said, infinite others, some whereof I shall mention.

First: The first I shall name, is some one simple idea, which, being capable of parts or degrees, affords an occasion of comparing the subjects wherein it is to one another, in respect of that simple idea, v.g., "whiter, sweeter, bigger, equal, more," &c. These relations, depending on the equality and excess of the same simple idea in several subjects, may be called, if one will, "proportional"; and that these are only conversant about those simple ideas received from sensation or reflection, is so evident that nothing need be said to evince it.

Natural.—Secondly: Another occasion of comparing things together, or considering one thing so as to include in that consideration some other thing, is the circumstances of their origin or beginning; which, being not afterwards to be altered, make the relations depending thereon as lasting as the subjects to which they belong; v.g., father and son, brothers, cousins-german, &c., which have their relations by one community of blood, wherein they partake in several degrees; countrymen, i.e., those who were born in the same country or track of ground; and these I call "natural relations": wherein we may observe, that mankind have fitted their notions and words to the use of common life, and not to the truth and extent of things. For it is certain that in reality the relation is the same betwixt the begetter and the begotten in the several races of other animals as well as men: but yet it is seldom said, "This bull is the grandfather of such a calf"; or that two pigeons are cousins-german.

Instituted.—Thirdly: Sometimes the foundation of considering things with reference to one another, is some act whereby anyone comes by a moral right, power, or obligation to do something. Thus a general is one that hath power to command an army; and an army under a general is a collection of armed men obliged to obey one man. A citizen or a burgher is one who has a right to certain privileges in this or that place. All this sort depending upon men's wills or agreement in society, I call "instituted," or "voluntary," and may be distinguished from the natural, in that they are, most if not all of them, some way or other alterable and separable from the persons to whom they have sometimes belonged, though neither of the substances so related be destroyed. Now, though these are all reciprocal, as well as the rest, and contain in them a reference of two things one to the other; yet, because one of the two things often wants a relative name importing that reference, men usually take no notice of it, and the relation is commonly overlooked, v.g., a patron and client are easily allowed to be relations: but a constable or dictator are not so readily, at first hearing, considered as such; because there is no peculiar name for those who are under the command of a dictator or constable, expressing a relation to either of them; though it be certain that either of them hath a certain power over some others; and so is so far related to them, as well as a patron is to his client, or general to his army.

Moral.—Fourthly: There is another sort of relation, which is the conformity or disagreement men's voluntary actions have to a rule to which they are referred, and by which they are judged of; which, I think, may be called "moral relation," as being that which denominates our moral actions, and deserves well to be examined, there being no part of knowledge wherein we should be more careful to get determined ideas, and avoid, as much as may be, obscurity and confusion. Human actions, when, with their various ends, objects, manners, and circumstances, they are framed into distinct complex ideas, are, as has been shown, so many mixed modes, a great part whereof have names affixed to them. Thus, supposing gratitude to be a readiness to acknowledge and return kindness received; polygamy to be the having more wives than one at once: when we frame these notions thus in our minds, we have there so many determined ideas of mixed modes. But this is not all that concerns our actions; it is not enough to have determined ideas of them, and to know what names belong to such and such combinations of ideas. We have a farther and greater concernment; and that is, to know whether such actions so made up are morally good or bad.

These three laws the rules of moral good and evil.—These three, then, first, the law of God, secondly, the law of politic societies, thirdly, the law of fashion, or private censure—are those to which men variously compare their actions: and it is by their conformity to one of these laws that they take their measures, when they would judge of their moral rectitude, and denominate their actions good or bad.

Morality is the relation of actions to these rules.—Whether the rule to which, as to a touchstone, we bring our voluntary actions to examine them by, and try their goodness, and accordingly to name them; which is, as it were, the mark of the value we set upon them: whether, I say, we take that rule from the fashion of the country, or the will of a law-maker, the mind is easily able to observe the relation any action hath to it, and to judge whether the action agrees or disagrees with the rule; and so hath a notion of moral goodness or evil, which is either conformity or not conformity of any action to that rule: and therefore is often called "moral rectitude." This rule being nothing but a collection of several simple ideas, the conformity thereto is but so ordering the action that the simple ideas belonging to it may correspond to those which the law requires. And thus we see how moral beings and notions are founded on, and terminated in, these simple ideas we have received from sensation or reflection.

XXIX. OF CLEAR AND OBSCURE, DISTINCT AND CONFUSED IDEAS

"Clear" and "obscure" explained by sight.—The perception of the mind being most aptly explained by words relating to the sight, we shall best understand what is meant by "clear" and "obscure" in our ideas, by reflecting on what we call "clear" and "obscure" in the objects of sight. Light being that which discovers to us visible objects, we give the name of "obscure" to that which is not placed in a light sufficient to discover minutely to us the figure and colours which are observable in it, and which in a better light would be discernible. In like manner our simple ideas are clear, when they are such as the objects themselves, from whence they were taken, did or might, in a well-ordered sensation or perception, present them. Whilst the memory retains them thus, and can produce them to the mind whenever it has occasion to consider them, they are clear ideas. So far as they either want anything of that original exactness, or have lost any of their first freshness, and are, as it were, faded or tarnished by time, so far are they obscure. Complex ideas, as they are made up of simple ones, so they are clear when the ideas that go to their composition

are clear; and the number and order of those simple ideas, that are the ingredients of any complex one, is determinate and certain.

Distinct and confused, what.—As a clear idea is that whereof the mind has such a full and evident perception as it does receive from an outward object operating duly on a well-disposed organ, so a distinct idea is that wherein the mind perceives a difference from all other, and a confused idea is such an one as is not sufficiently distinguishable from another from which it ought to be different.

Confusion concerns always two ideas.—Confusion, making it a difficulty to separate two things that should be separated, concerns always two ideas; and those most which most approach one another. Whenever therefore we suspect any idea to be confused, we must examine what other it is in danger to be confounded with, or which it cannot easily be separated from; and that will always be found an idea belonging to another name, and so should be a different thing, from which yet it is not sufficiently distinct; being either the same with it, or making a part of it, or, at least, as properly called by that name as the other it is ranked under; and so keeps not that difference from that other idea, which the different names import.

Causes of confusion.—This, I think, is the confusion proper to ideas, which still carries with it a secret reference to names. At least, if there be any other confusion of ideas this is that which most of all disorders men's thoughts and discourses: ideas, as ranked under names, being those that for the most part men reason of within themselves, and always those which they commune about with others. And therefore where there are supposed two different ideas, marked by two different names, which are not as distinguishable as the sounds that stand for them, there never fails to be confusion; and where any ideas are distinct, as the ideas of those two sounds they are marked by, there can be between them no confusion. The way to prevent it is to collect and unite into one complex idea, as precisely as is possible, all those ingredients whereby it is differenced from others; and to them so united in a determinate number and order, apply steadily the same name. But this neither accommodating men's ease or vanity, or serving any design but that of naked truth, which is not always the thing aimed at, such exactness is rather to be wished than hoped for. And since the loose application of names to undetermined, variable, and almost no ideas serves both to cover our own ignorance, as well as to perplex and confound others, which goes for learning and superiority in knowledge, it is no wonder that most men should use it themselves whilst they complain of it in others. Though, I think, no small part of the confusion to be found in the notions of men might, by care and ingenuity, be avoided; yet I am far from concluding it everywhere wilful. Some ideas are so complex, and made up of so many parts, that the memory does not easily retain the very same precise combination of simple ideas under one name; much less are we able constantly to divine for what precise complex idea such a name stands in another man's use of it. From the first of these follows confusion in a man's own reasonings and opinions within himself; from the latter frequent confusion in discoursing and arguing with others. But having more at large treated of words, their defects and abuses, in the following book, I shall here say no more of it.

XXX. OF REAL AND FANTASTICAL IDEAS

Real ideas are conformable to their archetypes.—Besides what we have already mentioned concerning ideas, other considerations belong to them, in reference to things from whence they are taken, or which they may be supposed to represent; and thus, I think, they may come under a threefold distinction; and are,

First: Either real or fantastical.

Secondly: Adequate or inadequate.

Thirdly: True or false.

First: By "real ideas," I mean such as have a foundation in nature; such as have a conformity with the real being and existence of things, or with their archetypes. "Fantastical or chimerical," I call such as have no foundation in nature, nor have any conformity with that reality of being to which they are tacitly referred as to their archetypes. If we examine the several sorts of ideas before mentioned, we shall find, that,

Simple ideas all real.—First: Our simple ideas are all real, all agree to the reality of things. Not that they are all of them the images or representations of what does exist; the contrary whereof, in all but the primary qualities of bodies, hath been already showed. But though whiteness and coldness are no more in snow than pain is; yet those ideas of whiteness and coldness, pain, &c., being in us the effects of powers in things without us, ordained by our Maker to produce in us such sensations, they are real ideas in us, whereby we distinguish the qualities that are really in things themselves.

Mixed modes made of consistent ideas are real.—Secondly: Mixed modes and relations having no other reality but what they have in the minds of men, there is nothing more required to those kinds of ideas to make them real but that they be so framed that there be a possibility of existing conformable to them. These ideas, being themselves archetypes, cannot differ from their archetypes, and so cannot be chimerical, unless anyone will jumble together in them inconsistent ideas. Indeed, as any of them have the names of a known language assigned to them, by which he that has them in his mind would signify them to others, so bare possibility of existing is not enough; they must have a conformity to the ordinary signification of the name that is given them, that they may not be thought fantastical: as if a man would give the name of "justice" to that idea which common use calls "liberality." But this fantasticalness relates more to propriety of speech, than reality of ideas. For a man to be undisturbed in danger, sedately to consider what is fittest to be done, and to execute it steadily, is a mixed mode or a complex idea of an action which may exist. But to be undisturbed in danger, without using one's reason or industry, is what is also possible to be; and so is as real an idea as the other. Though the first of these, having the name "courage" given to it, may, in respect of that name, be a right or a wrong idea: but the other, whilst it has not a common received name of any known language assigned to it, is not capable of any deformity, being made with no reference to anything but itself.

Ideas of substance are real when they agree with the existence of things.—Thirdly: Our complex ideas of substances, being made all of them in reference to things existing without us, and intended to be representations of substances as they really are, are no farther real than as they are such combinations of simple ideas as are really united, and co-exist in things without us. On the contrary, those are fantastical which are made up of such collections of simple ideas as were really never united, never were found together in any substance.

XXXI. OF ADEQUATE AND INADEQUATE IDEAS

Adequate ideas are such as perfectly represent their archetypes.—Of our real ideas, some are adequate, and some are inadequate. Those I call "adequate" which perfectly represent those archetypes which the mind supposes them taken from; which it intends them to stand for, and to which it refers them. Inadequate ideas are such which are but a partial or incomplete representation of those archetypes to which they are referred. Upon which account it is plain,

Simple ideas all adequate.—First: That all our simple ideas are adequate. Because being nothing but the effects of certain powers in things, fitted and ordained by God to produce such sensations in us, they cannot but be correspondent and adequate to those powers: and we are sure they agree to the reality of things.

Modes are all adequate.—Secondly: Our complex ideas of modes, being voluntary collections of simple ideas which the mind puts together, without reference to any real archetypes or standing patterns existing any-where, are and cannot but be adequate ideas. Because they, not being in-tended for copies of things really existing, but for archetypes made by the mind to rank and denominate things by, cannot want any thing; they having each of them that combination of ideas, and thereby that perfection, which the mind intended they should: so that the mind acquiesces in them, and can find nothing wanting.

Ideas of substances, as referred to real essences, not adequate.— Thirdly: What ideas we have of substances, I have above showed. Now, those ideas have in the mind a double reference. (1.) Sometimes they are referred to a supposed real essence of each species of things. (2.) Sometimes they are only designed to be pictures and representations in the mind of things that do exist by ideas of those qualities that are discoverable in them. In both which ways, these copies of those originals and archetypes are imperfect and inadequate.

First: It is usual for men to make the names of substances stand for things, as supposed to have certain real essences, whereby they are of this or that species: and names standing for nothing but the ideas that are in men's minds, they must consequently refer their ideas to such real essences as to their archetypes. That men (especially such as have been bred up in the learning taught in this part of the world), do suppose certain specific essences of substances, which each individual, in its several kinds, is made conformable to and partakes of, is so far from needing proof, that it will be thought strange if anyone should do otherwise. And thus they ordinarily apply the specific names they rank particular substances under, to things, as distinguished by such specific real essences. Who is there almost who would not take it amiss if it should be doubted whether he called himself "man" with any other meaning than as having the real essence of a man? And yet if you demand what those real essences are, it is plain men are ignorant, and know them not. From whence it follows, that the ideas they have in their minds, being referred to real essences, as to archetypes which are unknown, must be so far from being adequate, that they cannot be supposed to be any representation of them at all.

Ideas of substances, as collections of their qualities, are all inadequate. —Secondly: Those who, neglecting that useless supposition of unknown real essences whereby they are distinguished, endeavour to copy the substances that exist in the world by putting together the ideas of those sensible qualities which are found co-existing in them, though they come much nearer a likeness of them, than those who imagine they-know-notwhat real specific essences; yet they arrive not at perfectly adequate ideas of those substances they would thus copy into their minds; nor do those copies exactly and fully contain all that is to be found in their archetypes. Because those qualities and powers of substances, whereof we make their complex ideas, are so many and various that no man's complex idea contains them all. That our complex ideas of substances do not contain in them all the simple ideas that are united in the things themselves, is evident, in that men do rarely put into their complex idea of any substance all the simple ideas they do know to exist in it. Because endeavouring to make the signification of their specific names as clear and as little cumbersome as they can, they make their specific ideas of the sorts of substances, for the most part, of a few of those simple ideas which are to be found in them: but these having no original precedency or right to be put in and make the specific idea, more than others that are left out, it is plain that, both these ways, our ideas of substances are deficient and inadequate. These simple ideas, whereof we make our complex ones of substances, are all of them (bating only the figure and bulk of some sorts) powers; which being relations to other substances, we can never be sure that we know all the powers that are in any one body, till we have tried what changes it is fitted to give to, or receive from, other substances in their several ways of application: which being impossible to be tried upon any one body, much less upon all, it is impossible we should have adequate ideas of any substance made up of a collection of all its properties.

Ideas of substances, as collections of their qualities, are all inadequate. —So that all our complex ideas of substances are imperfect and inadequate. Which would be so also in mathematical figures, if we were to have our complex ideas of them only by collecting their properties in reference to other figures. How uncertain and imperfect would our ideas be of an ellipsis, if we had no other idea of it but some few of its properties! Whereas, having in our plain idea the whole essence of that figure, we from thence discover those properties, and demonstratively see how they flow and are inseparable from it.

Ideas of modes and relations are archetypes, and cannot but be adequate.—Thirdly: Complex ideas of modes and relations are originals and archetypes; are not copies, nor made after the pattern of any real existence, to which the mind intends them to be conformable, and exactly to answer. These being such collections of simple ideas that the mind itself puts together, and such collections that each of them contains in it precisely all that the mind intends it should, they are archetypes and essences of modes that may exist; and so are designed only for and belong only to such modes as, when they do exist, have an exact conformity with those complex ideas. The ideas thereof of modes and relations cannot but be adequate.

XXXII. OF TRUE AND FALSE IDEAS

Truth and falsehood properly belong to propositions.—Though truth and falsehood belong, in propriety of speech, only to propositions, yet ideas are oftentimes termed "true or false," though I think that when ideas themselves are termed "true or false," there is still some secret or tacit proposition which is the foundation of that denomination: as we shall see, if we examine the particular occasions wherein they come to be called "true or false." In all which we shall find some kind of affirmation or negation, which is the reason of that denomination. For our ideas being nothing but bare appearances or perceptions in our minds, cannot properly and simply in themselves be said to be true or false, no more than a single name of anything can be said to be true or false.

Metaphysical truth contains a tacit proposition.—Indeed, both ideas and words may be said to be true in a metaphysical sense of the word "truth," as all other things that any way exist are said to be true; i.e., really to be such as they exist. Though in things called "true," even in that sense, there is, perhaps, a secret reference to our ideas, looked upon as the standards of that truth, which amounts to a mental proposition, though it be usually not taken notice of.

No idea, as an appearance in the mind, true or false.—But it is not in that metaphysical sense of truth which we inquire here, when we examine whether our ideas are capable of being true or false; but in the more ordinary acceptation of those words, and so, I say, that the ideas in our minds being only so many perceptions or appearances there, none of them are false; the idea of a centaur having no more falsehood in it, when it appears in our minds, than the name "centaur" has falsehood in it, when it is pronounced by our mouths, or written on paper. For, truth or falsehood lying always in some affirmation or negation, mental or verbal, our ideas are not capable, any of them, of being false, till the mind passes some judgment on them; that is, affirms or denies something of them.

Ideas referred to anything may be true or false.—Whenever the mind refers any of its ideas to anything extraneous to them, they are then capable to be called true or false. Because the mind in such a reference makes a tacit supposition of their conformity to that thing; which supposition, as it happens to be true or false, so the ideas themselves come to be denominated.

Simple ideas may be false in reference to others of the same name, but are least liable to be so.—First, then, I say, that when the truth of our ideas is judged of by the conformity they have to the ideas which other men have and commonly signify by the same name, they may be any of them false. But yet simple ideas are least of all liable to be mistaken: because a man by his senses, and every day's observation, may easily satisfy himself what the simple ideas are which their several names that are in common use stand for, they being but few in number, and such as, if he doubts or mistakes in, he may easily rectify by the objects they are to be found in. Therefore it is seldom that anyone mistakes in his names of simple ideas, or applies the name "red" to the idea of "green," or the name "sweet" to the idea "bitter": much less are men apt to confound the names of ideas belonging to different senses, and call a colour by the name of a taste, etc., whereby it is evident, that the simple ideas they call by any name are commonly the same that others have and mean when they use the same names.

Ideas of mixed modes most liable to be false in this sense.—Complex ideas are much more liable to be false in this respect; and the complex ideas of mixed modes much more than those of substances: because in substances some remarkable sensible qualities, serving ordinarily to distinguish one sort from another, easily preserve those who take any care in the use of their words from applying them to sorts of substances to which they do not at all belong. But in mixed modes we are much more uncertain, it being not so easy to determine of several actions whether they are to be called "justice" or "cruelty," "liberality" or "prodigality." And so, in referring our ideas to those of other men called by the same names, ours may be false; and the idea in our minds, which we express by the word "justice," may, perhaps, be that which ought to have another name.

First: Simple ideas in this sense not false, and why.—First: Our simple ideas being barely such perceptions as God has fitted us to receive, and given power to external objects to produce in us by established laws and ways, suitable to his wisdom and goodness, though incomprehensible to us; their truth consists in nothing else but in such appearances as are produced in us, and must be suitable to those powers he has placed in external objects, or else they could not be produced in us: and thus answering those powers, they are, what they should be, true ideas. Nor do they become liable to any imputation of falsehood, if the mind judges these ideas to be in the things themselves.

Secondly: Modes not false.—Secondly: Neither can our complex ideas of modes, in reference to the essence of anything really existing, be false. Because whatever complex idea I have of any mode, it hath no reference to any pattern existing, and made by nature: it is not supposed to contain in it any other ideas than what it hath, nor to represent anything but such a complication of ideas as it does.

Thirdly: Ideas of substances when false.—Thirdly: Our complex ideas of substances, being all referred to patterns in things themselves, may be false. That they are all false when looked upon as the representations of the unknown essences of things, is so evident that there needs nothing to be said of it. I shall therefore pass over that chimerical supposition, and consider them as collections of simple ideas in the mind, taken from combinations of simple ideas existing together constantly in things, of which patterns they are the supposed copies: and in this reference of them to the existence of things, they are false ideas: (1.) When they put together simple ideas, which in the real existence of things have no union; as when to the shape and size that exist together in a horse, is joined in the same complex idea the power of barking like a dog; which three ideas, however put together into one in the mind, were never united in nature; and this therefore may be called a false idea of a horse. (2.) Ideas of substances are in this respect also false, when, from any collection of simple ideas that do always exist together, there is separated by a direct negation, any other simple idea which is constantly joined with them.

Ideas in themselves neither true nor false.—Any idea, then, which we have in our minds, whether conformable or not to the existence of things, or to any ideas in the minds of other men, cannot properly for this alone be called false. For these representations, if they have nothing in them but what is really existing in things without, cannot be thought false, being exact representations of something: nor yet if they have anything in them differing from the reality of things, can they properly be said to be false representations or ideas of things they do not represent.

More properly to be called "right" or "wrong."—Upon the whole matter, I think that our ideas, as they are considered by the mind, either in reference to the proper signification of their names, or in reference to the reality of things, may very fitly be called "right" or "wrong" ideas, according as they agree or disagree to those patterns to which they are referred. But if anyone had rather call them "true" or "false," it is fit he use a liberty which everyone has to call things by those names he thinks best; though, in propriety of speech, "truth" or "falsehood" will, I think, scarce agree to them, but as they, some way or other, virtually contain in them some mental proposition. The ideas that are in a man's mind, simply considered, cannot be wrong, unless complex ones, wherein inconsistent parts are jumbled together. All other ideas are in themselves right; and the knowledge about them, right and true knowledge: but when we come to refer them to anything, as to their patterns and archetypes, then they are capable of being wrong, as far as they disagree with such archetypes.

XXXIII. OF THE ASSOCIATION OF IDEAS

Something unreasonable in most men.—There is scarce anyone that does not observe something that seems odd to him, and is in itself really extravagant, in the opinions, reasonings, and actions of other men. The least flaw of this kind, if at all different from his own, everyone is quick-sighted enough to espy in another, and will by the authority of reason forwardly condemn, though he be guilty of much greater unreasonableness in his own tenets and conduct, which he never perceives, and will very hardly, if at all, be convinced of.

A degree of madness.—I shall be pardoned for calling it by so harsh a name as "madness," when it is considered, that opposition to reason deserves that name, and is really madness; and there is scarce a man so free from it but that if he should always, on all occasions, argue or do as in some cases he constantly does, would not be thought fitter for Bedlam than civil conversation. I do not here mean when he is under the power of an unruly passion, but in the steady calm course of his life. That which will yet more apologize for this harsh name, and ungrateful imputation on the greatest part of mankind, is, that inquiring a little by the by into the nature of madness, I found it to spring from the very same root, and to depend on the very same cause, we are here speaking of. This consideration of the thing itself, at a time when I thought not the least on the subject which I am now treating of, suggested it to me. And if this be a weakness to which all men are so liable, if this be a taint which so universally infects mankind, the greater care should be taken to lay it open under its due name, thereby to excite the greater care in its prevention and cure.

From a wrong connexion of ideas.—Some of our ideas have a natural correspondence and connexion one with another; it is the office and excellency of our reason to trace these, and hold them together in that union and correspondence which is founded in their peculiar beings. Besides this, there is another connexion of ideas wholly owing to chance or custom: ideas that in themselves are not at all of kin, come to be so united in some men's minds that it is very hard to separate them; they always keep in company, and the one no sooner at any time comes into the understanding, but its associate appears with it; and if they are more than two which are thus united, the whole gang, always inseparable, show themselves together.

A great cause of errors.—This wrong connexion in our minds of ideas, in themselves loose and independent one of another, has such an influence, and is of so great force, to set us awry in our actions, as well moral as natural, passions, reasonings, and notions themselves, that perhaps there is not any one thing that deserves more to be looked after.

Book Three

1. OF WORDS OR LANGUAGE IN GENERAL

Man fitted to form articulate sounds.—God, having designed man for a sociable creature, made him not only with an inclination and under a necessity to have fellowship with those of his own kind, but furnished him also with language, which was to be the great instrument and common tie of society. Man therefore had by nature his organs so fashioned as to be fit to frame articulate sounds, which we call "words." But this was not enough to produce language; for parrots and several other birds will be taught to make articulate sounds distinct enough, which yet by no means are capable of language.

To make them signs of ideas.—Besides articulate sounds, therefore, it was farther necessary that he should be able to use these sounds as signs of internal conceptions, and to make them stand as marks for the ideas within his own mind; whereby they might be made known to others, and the thoughts of men's minds be conveyed from one to another.

To make general signs.—But neither was this sufficient to make words so useful as they ought to be. It is not enough for the perfection of language that sounds can be made signs of ideas, unless those signs can be so made use of as to comprehend several particular things: for the multiplication of words would have perplexed their use, had every particular thing need of a distinct name to be signified by. To remedy this inconvenience, language had yet a farther improvement in the use of general terms, whereby one word was made to mark a multitude of particular existences: which advantageous use of sounds was obtained only by the difference of the ideas they were made signs of: those names becoming general which are made to stand for general ideas, and those remaining particular where the ideas they are used for are particular.

Words ultimately derived from such as signify sensible ideas.—It may also lead us a little towards the original of all our notions and knowledge, if we remark how great a dependence our words have on common sensible ideas; and how those which are made use of to stand for actions and notions quite removed from sense, have their rise from thence, and from obvious sensible ideas are transferred to more abstruse significations, and made to stand for ideas that come not under the cognizance of our senses.

Distribution.—But, to understand better the use and force of language as subservient to instruction and knowledge, it will be convenient to consider,

First: To what it is that names, in the use of language, are immediately applied.

Secondly: Since all (except proper) names are general, and so stand not particularly for this or that single thing, but for sorts and ranks of things, it will be necessary to consider, in the next place, what the sorts and kinds, or, if you rather like the Latin names, what the *species* and *genera* of things are, wherein they consist, and how they come to be made. These being (as they ought) well looked into, we shall the better come to find the right use of words, the natural advantages and defects of language, and the remedies that ought to be used to avoid the inconveniences of obscurity or uncertainty in the signification of words; without which it is impossible to discourse with any clearness or order concerning knowledge: which being conversant about propositions, and those most commonly universal ones, has greater connexion with words than perhaps is suspected.

II. OF THE SIGNIFICATION OF WORDS

Words are sensible signs necessary for communication.—Man, though he have great variety of thoughts, and such from which others as well as himself might receive profit and delight, yet they are all within his own breast, invisible, and hidden from others, nor can of themselves be made to appear. The comfort and advantage of society not being to be had without communication of thoughts, it was necessary that man should find out some external sensible signs, whereby those invisible ideas which his thoughts are made up of might be made known to others. For this purpose nothing was so fit, either for plenty or quickness, as those articulate sounds which, with so much ease and variety, he found himself able to make.

Words are the sensible signs of his ideas who uses them.—The use men have of these marks being either to record their own thoughts for the assistance of their own memory, or, as it were, to bring out their ideas, and lay them before the view of others: words in their primary or immediate signification stand for nothing but the ideas in the mind of him that uses them, how imperfectly soever or carelessly those ideas are collected from the things which they are supposed to represent. When a man speaks to another, it is that he may be understood; and the end of speech is, that those sounds, as marks, may make known his ideas to the hearer. That, then, which words are the marks of are the ideas of the speaker: nor can anyone apply them, as marks, immediately to any thing else but the ideas that he himself hath. For, this would be to make them signs of his own conceptions, and yet apply them to other ideas; which would be to make them signs and not signs of his ideas at the same time; and so, in effect to have no signification at all. Words being voluntary signs, they cannot be voluntary signs imposed by him on things he knows not. That would be to make them signs of nothing, sounds without signification. A man cannot make his words the signs either of qualities in things, or of conceptions in the mind of another, whereof he has none in his own. Till he has some ideas of his own, he cannot suppose them to correspond with the conceptions of another man, nor can he use any signs for them: for thus they would be the signs of he knows not what, which is in truth to be the signs of nothing. But when he represents to himself other men's ideas by some of his own, if he consent to give them the same names that other men do, it is still to his own ideas; to ideas that he has, and not to ideas that he has not.

Words often secretly referred.—But though words, as they are used by men, can properly and immediately signify nothing but the ideas that are in the mind of the speaker, yet they in their thoughts give them a secret reference to two other things.

First: To the ideas in other men's minds.—First: They suppose their words to be marks of the ideas in the minds also of other men, with whom they communicate: for else they should talk in vain, and could not be understood, if the sounds they applied to one idea were such as by the hearer were applied to another, which is to speak two languages.

Secondly: To the reality of things.—Secondly: Because men would not be thought to talk barely of their own imaginations, but of things as really they are; therefore they often suppose their words to stand also for the reality of things.

Their signification perfectly arbitrary.—Words, by long and familiar use, as has been said, come to excite in men certain ideas so constantly and readily, that they are apt to suppose a natural connexion between them. But that they signify only men's peculiar ideas, and that by a perfectly arbitrary imposition, is evident in that they often fail to excite in others (even that use the same language) the same ideas we take them to be the signs of: and every man has so inviolable a liberty to make words stand for what ideas he pleases, that no one hath the power to make others have the same ideas in their minds that he has, when they use the same words that he does.

III. OF GENERAL TERMS

The greatest part of words general.—All things that exist being particulars, it may perhaps be thought reasonable that words, which ought to be conformed to things, should be so too, I mean in their signification: but yet we find the quite contrary. The far greatest part of words, that make all languages, are general terms: which has not been the effect of neglect or chance, but of reason and necessity.

For every particular thing to have a name is impossible.—First: It is impossible that every particular thing should have a distinct peculiar name. For the signification and use of words depending on that connexion which the mind makes between its ideas and the sounds it uses as signs of them, it is necessary, in the application of names to things, that the mind should have distinct ideas of the things, and retain also the particular name that belongs to every one, with its peculiar appropriation to that idea. But it is beyond the power of human capacity to frame and retain distinct ideas of all the particular things we meet with: every bird and beast men saw, every tree and plant that affected the senses, could not find a place in the most capacious understanding.

And useless.—Secondly: If it were possible, it would yet be useless, because it would not serve to the chief end of language. Men would in vain heap up names of particular things, that would not serve them to communicate their thoughts. Men learn names, and use them in talk with others, only that they may be understood: which is then only done when, by use or consent, the sound I make by the organs of speech excites, in another man's mind who hears it, the idea I apply it to in mine when I speak it. This cannot be done by names applied to particular things, whereof I alone having the ideas in my mind, the names of them could not be significant or intelligible to another who was not acquainted with all those very particular things which had fallen under my notice.

How general words are made.—The next thing to be considered is, how general words come to be made. For, since all things that exist are only particulars, how come we by general terms, or where find we those general natures they are supposed to stand for? Words become general by being made the signs of general ideas: and ideas become general by separating from them the circumstances of time, and place, and any other ideas that may determine them to this or that particular existence. By this way of abstraction they are made capable of representing more individuals than one; each of which, having in it a conformity to that abstract idea, is (as we call it) of that sort.

General and universal are creatures of the understanding.—To return to general words: it is plain, by what has been said, that general and universal belong not to the real existence of things; but are the inventions and creatures of the understanding, made by it for its own use, and concern only signs, whether words or ideas. Words are general, as has been said, when used for signs of general ideas, and so are applicable indifferently to many particular things; and ideas are general when they are set up as the representatives of many particular things: but universality belongs not to things themselves, which are all of them particular in their existence, even those words and ideas which in their signification are general. When therefore we quit particulars, the generals that rest are only creatures of our own making, their general nature being nothing but the capacity they are put into by the understanding of signifying or representing many particulars. For the signification they have is nothing but a relation that by the mind of man is added to them.

IV. OF THE NAMES OF SIMPLE IDEAS

Names of simple ideas, modes, and substances, have each something peculiar.—Though all words, as I have shown, signify nothing immediately but the ideas in the mind of the speaker, yet, upon a nearer survey, we shall find that the names of simple ideas, mixed modes and natural substances, have each of them something peculiar, and different from the other.

What a definition is.—I think it is agreed, that a definition is nothing else but "the showing the meaning of one word by several other not synonymous terms." The meaning of words being only the ideas they are made to stand for by him that uses them, the meaning of any term is then showed, or the word is defined, when by other words the idea it is made the sign of and annexed to in the mind of the speaker is, as it were, represented or set before the view of another; and thus its signification ascertained. This is the only use and end of definitions; and therefore the only measure of what is or is not a good definition.

Simple ideas, why undefinable.—This being premised, I say, that "the names of simple ideas," and those only, "are capable of being defined." The reason whereof is this, that the several terms of a definition signifying several ideas, they can all together by no means represent an idea which has no composition at all: and therefore a definition (which is properly nothing but the showing the meaning of one word by several others not signifying each the same thing) can in the names of simple ideas have no place.

The names of complex ideas, when to be made intelligible by words. —Simple ideas, as has been showed, can only be got by experience from those objects which are proper to produce in us those perceptions. When by this means we have our minds stored with them, and know the names for them, then we are in a condition to define, and by definition to understand, the names of complex ideas that are made up of them. But when any term stands for a simple idea that a man has never yet had in his mind, it is impossible, by any words, to make known its meaning to him. When any term stands for an idea a man is acquainted with, but is ignorant that that term is the sign of it, there another name, of the same idea which he has been accustomed to, may make him understand its meaning. But in no case whatsoever is any name of any simple idea capable of a definition.

V. OF THE NAMES OF MIXED MODES AND RELATIONS

They stand for abstract ideas, as other general names.—The names of mixed modes being general, they stand, as has been showed, for sorts or species of things, each of which has its peculiar essence. The essences of these species also, as has been showed, are nothing but the abtract ideas in the mind, to which the name is annexed. Thus far the names and essences of mixed modes have nothing but what is common to them with other ideas: but if we take a little nearer survey of them, we shall find that they have something peculiar, which, perhaps, may deserve our attention.

First: The ideas they stand for are made by the understanding.—The first particularity I shall observe in them is, that the abstract ideas, or, if you please, the essences of the several species of mixed modes, are made by the understanding: wherein they differ from those of simple ideas; in which sort the mind has no power to make any one, but only receives such as are presented to it by the real existence of things operating upon it.

Secondly: Made arbitrarily, and without patterns.—In the next place, these essences of the species of mixed modes are not only made by the mind, but made very arbitrarily, made without patterns, or reference to any real existence; wherein they differ from those of substances, which carry with them the supposition of some real being from which they are taken, and to which they are conformable. But in its complex ideas of mixed modes, the mind takes a liberty not to follow the existence of things exactly. It unites and retains certain collections as so many distinct specific ideas; whilst others, that as often occur in nature, and are as plainly suggested by outward things, pass neglected without particular names or specifications. Nor does the mind, in these of mixed modes, as in the complex ideas of substances, examine them by the real existence of things, or verify them by patterns containing such peculiar compositions in nature.

But still subservient to the end of language.—But though these complex ideas, or essences of mixed modes, depend on the mind, and are made by it with great liberty; yet they are not made at random, and jumbled together without any reason at all. Though these complex ideas be not always copied from nature, yet they are always suited to the end for which abstract ideas are made: and though they be combinations made of ideas, that are loose enough, and have as little union in themselves, as several other, to which the mind never gives a connexion that combines them into one idea: yet, they are always made for the convenience of communication, which is the chief end of language. The use of language is by short sounds, to signify with ease and despatch general conceptions; wherein not only abundance of particulars may be contained, but also a great variety of independent ideas collected into one complex one. In the making therefore of the species of mixed modes, men have had regard only to such combinations as they had occasion to mention one to another. Those they have combined into distinct complex ideas, and given names to; whilst others that in nature have as near a union, are left loose and unregarded.

VI. OF THE NAMES OF SUBSTANCES

The common names of substances stand for sorts.—The common names of substances, as well as other general terms, stand for sorts: which is nothing else but the being made signs of such complex ideas, wherein several particular substances do or might agree, by virtue of which they are capable of being comprehended in one common conception, and be signified by one name. I say, "do or might agree": for though there be but one sun existing in the world, yet the idea of it being abstracted, so that more substances might each agree in it; it is as much a sort as if there were as many suns as there are stars. They want not their reasons who think there are, and that each fixed star would answer the idea the name "sun" stands for, to one who were placed in a due distance; which, by the way, may show us how much the sorts, or if you please, *genera* and *species,* of things depend on such collections of ideas as men have made, and not on the real nature of things: since it is not impossible but that, in propriety of speech, that might be a sun to one which is a star to another.

The essence of each sort is the abstract idea.—The measure and boundary of each sort or species whereby it is constituted that particular sort and distinguished from others, is that we call its "essence," which is nothing but that abstract idea to which that name is annexed: so that every thing contained in that idea is essential to that sort. This, though it be all the essence of natural substances that we know, or by which we distinguish them into sorts; yet I call it by a peculiar name, the "nominal essence," to distinguish it from that real constitution of substances upon which depends this nominal essence, and all the properties of that sort; which therefore, as has been said, may be called the "real essence."

Nothing essential to individuals.—That "essence," in the ordinary use of the word, relates to sorts, and that it is considered in particular beings no farther than they are ranked into sorts, appears from hence: that take but away the abstract ideas by which we sort individuals, and rank them under common names, and then the thought of anything essential to any of them instantly vanishes: we have no notion of the one without the other; which plainly shows their relation. It is necessary for me to be as I am: God and nature has made me so: but there is nothing I have is essential to me.

The nominal essence bounds the species.—The next thing to be considered is, by which of those essences it is that substances are determined into sorts or species; and that, it is evident, is by the nominal essence. For it is that alone that the name, which is the mark of the sort, signifies. It is impossible therefore that any thing should determine the sorts of things which we rank under general names, but that idea which that name is designed as a mark for; which is that, as has been shown, which we call the "nominal essence." Why do we say, "This is a horse, and that a mule; this is an animal, that an herb"? How comes any particular thing to be of this or that sort, but because it has that nominal essence, or, which is all one, agrees to that abstract idea that name is annexed to? And I desire anyone but to reflect on his own thoughts when he hears or speaks any of those or other names of substances, to know what sort of essences they stand for.

And that the species of things to us are nothing but the ranking them under distinct names, according to the complex ideas in us, and not according to precise, distinct, real essences in them, is plain from hence, that we find many of the individuals that are ranked into one sort, called by one common name, and so received as being of one species, have yet qualities depending on their real constitutions, as far different one from another as from others from which they are accounted to differ specifically. This, as it is easy to be observed by all who have to do with natural bodies, so chymists especially are often, by sad experience, convinced of it, when they, sometimes in vain, seek for the same qualities in one parcel of sulphur, antimony, or vitriol, which they have found in others. For though they are bodies of the same species, having the same nominal essence, under the same name; yet do they often, upon severe ways of examination, betray qualities so different one from another as to frustrate the expectation and labour of very wary chymists. But if things were distinguished into species according to their real essences, it would be as impossible to find different properties in any two individual substances of the same species, as it is to find different properties in two circles or two equilateral triangles. That is properly the essence to us which determines every particular to this or that *classis;* or, which is the same thing, to this or that general name: and what can that be else but that abstract idea to which that name is annexed? and so has, in truth, a reference, not so much to the being of particular things as to their general denominations.

Difficulties against a certain number of real essences.—To distinguish substantial beings into species, according to the usual supposition, that there are certain precise essences or forms of things whereby all the individuals existing are by nature distinguished into species, these things are necessary:

First: To be assured that nature, in the production of things, always designs them to partake of certain regulated, established essences, which are to be the models of all things to be produced. This, in that crude sense it is usually proposed, would need some better explication before it can fully be assented to.

Secondly: It would be necessary to know whether nature always attains that essence it designs in the production of things. The irregular and monstrous births that in divers sorts of animals have been observed, will always give us reason to doubt of one or both of these.

Thirdly: It ought to be determined whether those we call "monsters" be really a distinct species according to the scholastic notion of the word "species"; since it is certain that every thing that exists has its particular constitution: and yet we find, that some of these monstrous productions have few or none of those qualities which are supposed to result from and accompany the essence of that species from whence they derive their originals, and to which by their descent they seem to belong.

Our nominal essences of substances, not perfect collections of properties.—Fourthly: The real essences of those things which we distinguish into species, and as so distinguished we name, ought to be known; i.e., we ought to have ideas of them. But since we are ignorant in these four points, the supposed real essences of things stand us not instead for the distinguishing substances into species.

Fifthly: The only imaginable help in this case would be, that having framed perfect complex ideas of the properties of things, flowing from their different real essences, we should thereby distinguish them into species. But neither can this be done: for, being ignorant of the real essence itself, it is impossible to know all those properties that flow from it, and are so annexed to it that, any one of them being away, we may certainly conclude that that essence is not there, and so the thing is not of that species. We can never know what are the precise number of properties depending on the real essence of gold; any one of which failing, the real essence of gold, and consequently gold, would not be there, unless we knew the real essence of gold itself, and by that determined that species. By the word "gold" here, I must be understood to design a particular piece of matter, v.g., the last guinea that was coined. For if it should stand here in its ordinary signification for that complex idea which I or anyone else calls "gold," i.e., for the nominal essence of gold, it would be jargon: so hard is it to show the various meaning and imperfection of words, when we have nothing else but words to do it by.

By all which it is clear, that our distinguishing substances into species by names, is not at all founded on their real essences; nor can we pretend to arrange and determine them exactly into species according to internal essential differences.

But such a collection as our name stands for.—But since, as has been remarked, we have need of general words, though we know not the real essences of things; all we can do is to collect such a number of simple ideas as by examination we find to be united together in things existing, and thereof to make one complex idea. Which, though it be not the real essence of any substance that exists, is yet the specific essence to which our name belongs, and is convertible with it; by which we may at least try the truth of these nominal essences. For example: some there be that say, that the essence of body is extension; if it be so, we can never mistake in putting the essence of any thing for the thing itself. Let us, then, in discourse put extension for body; and when we would say that body moves, let us say that extension moves, and see how it will look. He that should say, that one extension by impulse moves another extension, would, by the bare expression, sufficiently show the absurdity of such a notion. The "essence" of any thing in respect of us, is the whole complex idea comprehended and marked by that name; and in substances, besides the several distinct simple ideas that make them up, the confused one of substance, or of an unknown support and cause of their union, is always a part: and therefore the essence of body is not bare extension, but an extended solid thing; and so to say, "An extended solid thing moves or impels another," is all one, and as intelligible, as to say, "Body moves or impels." Likewise to say that "a rational animal is capable of conversation," is all one as to say, "a man." But no one will say, that rationality is capable of conversation, because it makes not the whole essence to which we give the name "man."

The more general our ideas are, the more incomplete and partial they are.—If the number of simple ideas that make the nominal essence of the lowest species or first sorting of individuals, depends on the mind of man variously collecting them, it is much more evident that they do so in the more comprehensive *classes,* which by the masters of logic are called *genera.* These are complex ideas designedly imperfect: and it is visible at first sight that several of those qualities that are to be found in the things themselves, are purposely left out of generical ideas. For as the mind, to make general ideas comprehending several particulars, leaves out those of time, and place, and such other that make them incommunicable to more than one individual; so, to make other yet more general ideas that may comprehend different sorts, it leaves out those qualities that distinguish them, and puts into its new collection only such ideas as are common to several sorts.

The same convenience that made men express several parcels of yellow matter coming from Guinea and Peru under one name, sets them also upon making of one name that may comprehend both gold, and silver, and some other bodies of different sorts. This is done by leaving out those qualities which are peculiar to each sort; and retaining a complex idea made up of those that are common to them all. To which the name "metal" being annexed, there is a genus constituted; the essence whereof being that abstract idea, containing only malleableness and fusibility, with certain degrees of weight and fixedness, wherein some bodies of several kinds agree, leaves out the colour, and other qualities peculiar to gold and silver, and the other sorts comprehended under the name "metal." Whereby it is plain that men follow not exactly the patterns set them by nature, when they make their general ideas of substances; since there is no body to be found which has barely malleableness and fusibility in it, without other qualities as inseparable as those. But men, in making their general ideas, seeking more the convenience of language and quick despatch by short and comprehensive signs, than the true and precise nature of things as they exist, have, in the framing their abstract ideas, chiefly pursued that end, which was, to be furnished with store of general and variously comprehensive names. So that in this whole business of *genera* and *species,* the genus, or more comprehensive, is but a partial conception of what it is in the species, and the species but a partial idea of what is to be found in each individual. If, therefore, anyone will think that a man, and a horse, and an animal, and a plant, &c., are distinguished by real essences made by nature, he must think nature to be very liberal of these real essences, making one for body, another for an animal, and another for a horse, and all these essences liberally bestowed upon Bucephalus. But if we would rightly consider what is done in all these *genera* and *species,* or sorts, we should find that there is no new thing made, but only more or less comprehensive signs whereby we may be enabled to express, in a few syllables, great numbers of particular things, as they agree in more or less general conceptions which we have framed to that purpose. In all which we may observe, that the more general term is always the name of a less complex idea; and that each genus is but a partial conception of the species comprehended under it. So that, if these abstract general ideas be thought to be complete, it can only be in respect of a certain established relation between them and certain names which are made use of to signify them; and not in respect of any thing existing, as made by nature.

This all accommodated to the end of speech.—This is adjusted to the true end of speech, which is, to be the easiest and shortest way of communicating our notions. For thus he that would make and discourse of things as they agreed in the complex idea of extension and solidity, needed but use the word "body," to denote all such. He that to these would join others, signified by the words "life," "sense," and "spontaneous motion," needed but use the word "animal," to signify all which partook of those ideas: and he that had made a complex idea of a body, with life, sense, and motion, with the faculty of reasoning, and a certain shape joined to it, needed but use the short monosyllable "man," to express all particulars that correspond to that complex idea. This is the proper business of *genus* and *species;* and this men do, without any consideration of real essences or substantial forms, which come not within the reach of our knowledge when we think of those things; nor within the signification of our words when we discourse with others.

VII. OF ABSTRACT AND CONCRETE TERMS

Abstract terms not predicable one of another, and why.—The ordinary words of language, and our common use of them, would have given us light into the nature of our ideas, if they had been but considered with attention. The mind, as has been shown, has a power to abstract its ideas, and so they become essences, general essences, whereby the sorts of things are distinguished. Now each abstract idea being distinct, so that of any two the one can never be the other, the mind will, by its intuitive knowledge, perceive their difference; and therefore in propositions no two whole ideas can ever be affirmed one of another. All our affirmations, then, are only inconcrete, which is the affirming not one abstract idea to be another, but one abstract idea to be joined to another; which abstract ideas, in substances, may be of any sort; in all the rest, are little else but of relations; and in substances the most frequent are of powers.

They show the difference of our ideas.—This distinction of names shows us also the difference of our ideas: for if we observe them, we shall find that our simple ideas have all abstract as well as concrete names: the one whereof is (to speak the language of grammarians) a substantive, the other an adjective; as, "whiteness, white, sweetness, sweet." The like also holds in our ideas of modes and relations, as, "justice, just, equality, equal"; only with this difference, that some of the concrete names of relations, amongst men chiefly, are substantives, as *paternitas, pater;* whereof it were easy to render a reason. But as to our ideas of substances, we have very few or no abstract names at all.

VIII. OF THE IMPERFECTION OF WORDS

Words are used for recording and communicating our thoughts.—From what has been said in the foregoing chapters, it is easy to perceive what imperfection there is in language, and how the very nature of words makes it almost unavoidable for many of them to be doubtful and uncertain in their significations. To examine the perfection or imperfection of words, it is necessary first to consider their use and end: for as they are more or less fitted to attain that, so they are more or less perfect. We have, in the former part of this discourse, often, upon occasion, mentioned a double use of words.

First: One for the recording of our own thoughts.

Secondly: The other for the communicating of our thoughts to others.

Any words will serve for recording.—As to the first of these, for the recording our own thoughts for the help of our own memories, whereby, as it were, we talk to ourselves, any words will serve the turn. For, since sounds are voluntary and indifferent signs of any ideas, a man may use what words he pleases to signify his own ideas to himself: and there will be no imperfection in them, if he constantly use the same sign for the same idea: for then he cannot fail of having his meaning understood, wherein consists the right use and perfection of language.

Communication by words civil or philosophical.—Secondly: As to communication of words, that too has a double use.

I. Civil.

II. Philosophical.

First: By their civil use, I mean such a communication of thoughts and ideas by words as may serve for the upholding common conversation and commerce about the ordinary affairs and conveniences of civil life, in the societies of men one amongst another.

Secondly: By the philosophical use of words, I mean such an use of them as may serve to convey the precise notions of things, and to express, in general propositions, certain and undoubted truths which the mind may rest upon and be satisfied with, in its search after true knowledge. These two uses are very distinct; and a great deal less exactness will serve in the one than in the other, as we shall see in what follows.

The imperfection of words is the doubtfulness of their signification.—The chief end of language in communication being to be understood, words serve not well for that end, neither in civil nor philosophical discourse, when any word does not excite in the hearer the same idea which it stands for in the mind of the speaker. Now since sounds have no natural connexion with our ideas, but have all their signification from the arbitrary imposition of men, the doubtfulness and uncertainty of their signification, which is the imperfection we here are speaking of, has its cause more in the ideas they stand for, than in any incapacity there is in one sound more than in another to signify any idea: for in that regard, they are all equally perfect.

That then which makes doubtfulness and uncertainty in the signification of some more than other words, is the difference of ideas they stand for.

With this imperfection, they may serve for civil, but not well for philosophical, use.—It is true, as to civil and common conversation, the general names of substances, regulated in their ordinary signification by some obvious qualities (as by the shape and figure in things of known seminal propagation, and in other substances for the most part by colour, joined with some other sensible qualities) do well enough to design the things men would be understood to speak of: and so they usually conceive well enough the substances meant by the word "gold" or "apple," to distinguish the one from the other. But in philosophical inquiries and debates, where general truths are to be established, and consequences drawn from positions laid down, there the precise signification of the names of substances will be found not only not to be well established, but also very hard to be so. For example: He that shall make malleableness, or a certain degree of fixedness, a part of his complex idea of gold, may make propositions concerning gold, and draw consequences from them, that will truly and clearly follow from gold taken in such a signification: but yet such as another man can never be forced to admit, nor be convinced of their truth, who makes not malleableness, or the same degree of fixedness, part of that complex idea that the name "gold," in his use of it, stands for.

The names of simple ideas the least doubtful.—From what has been said it is easy to observe, what has been before remarked, viz., that the names of simple ideas are, of all others, the least liable to mistakes, and that for these reasons: first, because the ideas they stand for, being each but one single perception, are much easier got and more clearly retained than the more complex ones; and therefore are not liable to the uncertainty which usually attends those compounded ones of substances and mixed modes, in which the precise number of simple ideas that make them up are not easily agreed, and so readily kept in the mind. And, secondly, because they are never referred to any other essence but barely that perception they immediately signify: which reference is that which renders the significations of the names of substances naturally so perplexed, and gives occasion to so many disputes. Men that do not perversely use their words, or on purpose set themselves to cavil, seldom mistake, in any language which they are acquainted with, the use and signification of the names of simple ideas: white and sweet, yellow and bitter, carry a very obvious meaning with them, which everyone precisely comprehends, or easily perceives he is ignorant of, and seeks to be informed. But what precise collection of simple ideas modesty or frugality stand for in another's use, is not so certainly known. And, however we are apt to think we well enough know what is meant by "gold" or "iron," yet the precise complex idea others make them the signs of is not so certain: and I believe it is very seldom that in speaker and hearer they stand for exactly the same collection. Which must needs produce mistakes and disputes, when they are made use of in discourses wherein men have to do with universal propositions, and would settle in their minds universal truths, and consider the consequences that follow from them.

This should teach us moderation in imposing our own sense of old authors.—Sure I am, that the signification of words, in all languages, depending very much on the thoughts, notions, and ideas of him that uses them, must unavoidably be of great uncertainty to men of the same language and country. This is so evident in the Greek authors, that he that shall peruse their writings will find, in almost every one of them, a distinct language, though the same words. But when to this natural difficulty in every country there shall be added different countries and remote ages, wherein the speakers and writers had very different notions, tempers, customs, ornaments and figures of speech, &c., every one of which influenced the signification of their words then, though to us now they are lost and unknown, it would become us to be charitable one to another in our interpretations or misunderstanding of those ancient writings; which, though of great concernment to be understood, are liable to the unavoidable difficulties of speech, which (if we except the names of simple ideas, and some very obvious things) is not capable, without a constant defining the terms, of conveying the sense and intention of the speaker without any manner of doubt and uncertainty to the hearer. And in discourses of religion, law, and morality, as they are matters of the highest concernment, so there will be the greatest difficulty.

IX. OF THE ABUSE OF WORDS

Abuse of words.—Besides the imperfection that is naturally in language, and the obscurity and confusion that is so hard to be avoided in the use of words, there are several wilful faults and neglects which men are guilty of in this way of communication, whereby they render these signs less clear and distinct in their signification than naturally they need to be.

First: Words without any, or without clear, ideas.—First: In this kind, the first and most palpable abuse is, the using of words without clear and distinct ideas; or, which is worse, signs without any thing signified. Of these there are two sorts:—

I. One may observe, in all languages, certain words that, if they be examined, will be found, in their first original and their appropriated use, not to stand for any clear and distinct ideas. These, for the most part, the several sects of philosophy and religion have introduced. For their authors or promoters, either affecting something singular, and out of the way of common apprehensions, or to support some strange opinions, or cover some weakness of their hypothesis, seldom fail to coin new words, and such as, when they come to be examined, may justly be called "insignificant terms." For, having either had no determinate collection of ideas annexed to them when they were first invented, or at least such as, if well examined, will be found inconsistent, it is no wonder if afterwards, in the vulgar use of the same party, they remain empty sounds with little or no signification, amongst those who think it enough to have them often in their mouths, as the distinguishing characters of their church or school, without much troubling their heads to examine what are the precise ideas they stand for.

II. Others there be who extend this abuse yet farther, who take so little care to lay by words which, in their primary notation, have scarce any clear and distinct ideas which they are annexed to, that, by an unpardonable negligence, they familiarly use words which the propriety of language has affixed to very important ideas, without any distinct meaning at all.

Secondly: Unsteady application of them.—Secondly: Another great abuse of words is inconsistency in the use of them. It is hard to find a discourse written of any subject, especially of controversy, wherein one shall not observe, if he read with attention, the same words (and those commonly the most material in the discourse, and upon which the argument turns) used sometimes for one collection of simple ideas, and sometimes for another, which is a perfect abuse of language. Words being intended for signs of my ideas, to make them known to others, not by any natural signification, but by a voluntary imposition, it is plain cheat and abuse when I make them stand sometimes for one thing and sometimes for another: the wilful doing whereof can be imputed to nothing but great folly or greater dishonesty.

Thirdly: Affected obscurity by wrong application.—Another abuse of language is an affected obscurity, by either applying old words to new and unusual significations, or introducing new and ambiguous terms without defining either: or else putting them so together as may confound their ordinary meaning. Though the peripatetic philosophy has been most eminent in this way, yet other sects have not been wholly clear of it. There is scarce any of them that are not cumbered with some difficulties (such is the imperfection of human knowledge), which they have been fain to cover with obscurity of terms and to confound the signification of words, which, like a mist before people's eyes, might hinder their weak parts from being discovered.

Fourthly: Taking them for things.—Fourthly: Another great abuse of words is the taking them for things. This, though it, in some degree, concerns all names in general, yet more particularly affects those of substances. To this abuse those men are most subject who confine their thoughts to any one system, and give themselves up into a firm belief of the perfection of any received hypothesis: whereby they come to be persuaded, that the terms of that sect are so suited to the nature of things that they perfectly correspond with their real existence.

Fifthly: Setting them for what they cannot signify.—Fifthly: Another abuse of words is the setting them in the place of things which they do [not] or can by no means signify. We may observe, that, in the general names of substances, whereof the nominal essences are only known to us when we put them into propositions, and affirm or deny any thing about them, we do most commonly tacitly suppose or intend they should stand for the real essence of a certain sort of substances.

Sixthly: A supposition that words have a certain and evident significa-tion.—Sixthly: There remains yet another more general, though perhaps less observed, abuse of words; and that is, that men having by a long and familiar use annexed to them certain ideas, they are apt to imagine so near and necessary a connexion between the names and the significa-tion they use them in, that they forwardly suppose one cannot but under-stand what their meaning is, and therefore one ought to acquiesce in the words delivered; as if it were past doubt that, in the use of those common received sounds, the speaker and hearer had necessarily the same precise ideas. Whence, presuming that when they have in discourse used any term, they have thereby, as it were, set before others the very thing they talk of; and so likewise taking the words of others as naturally standing for just what they themselves have been accustomed to apply them to; they never trouble themselves to explain their own or understand clearly others' meaning. From whence commonly proceeds noise and wrangling, without improvement or information; whilst men take words to be the constant, regular marks of agreed notions, which, in truth, are no more but the voluntary and unsteady signs of their own ideas. And yet men think it strange if, in discourse or (where it is often absolutely necessary) in dispute, one sometimes asks the meaning of their terms; though the arguings one may every day observe in conversation make it evident that there are few names of complex ideas which any two men use for the same just precise collection.

Seventhly: Figurative speech also an abuse of language.—Since wit and fancy finds easier entertainment in the world than dry truth and real knowledge, figurative speeches and allusion in language will hardly be admitted as an imperfection or abuse of it. I confess, in discourses where we seek rather pleasure and delight, than information and improve-ment, such ornaments as are borrowed from them can scarce pass for faults. But yet, if we would speak of things as they are, we must allow that all the art of rhetoric, besides order and clearness, all the artificial and figurative application of words eloquence hath invented, are for nothing else but to insinuate wrong ideas, move the passions, and thereby mislead the judgment; and so indeed are perfect cheats: and therefore, however laudable or allowable oratory may render them in harangues and popular addresses, they are certainly, in all discourses that pretend to inform or instruct, wholly to be avoided; and, where truth and knowl-edge are concerned, cannot but be thought a great fault either of the language or person that makes use of them.

X. OF THE REMEDIES OF THE FOREGOING IMPERFECTIONS AND ABUSES

To REMEDY the defects of speech before mentioned to some degree, and to prevent the inconveniences that follow from them, I imagine the observation of these following rules may be of use, till somebody better able shall judge it worth his while to think more maturely on this matter, and oblige the world with his thoughts on it.

First remedy: To use no word without an idea.—First: A man should take care to use no word without a signification, no name without an idea for which he makes it stand. This rule will not seem altogether needless to anyone who shall take the pains to recollect how often he has met with such words as "instinct," "sympathy," and "antipathy," &c., in the discourse of others, so made use of as he might easily conclude, that those that used them had no ideas in their minds to which they applied them; but spoke them only as sounds, which usually served instead of reasons on the like occasions. Not but that these words and the like have very proper significations in which they may be used; but there being no natural connexion between any words and any ideas, these and any other may be learned by rote, and pronounced or writ by men, who have no ideas in their minds to which they have annexed them, and for which they make them stand; which is necessary they should, if men would speak intelligibly even to themselves alone.

Secondly: To have distinct ideas annexed to them in modes.—Secondly: It is not enough a man uses his words as signs of some ideas: those ideas he annexes them to, if they be simple, must be clear and distinct; if complex, must be determinate; i.e., the precise collection of simple ideas settled in the mind, with that sound annexed to it as the sign of that precise determined collection, and no other. This is very necessary in names of modes, and especially moral words; which, having no settled objects in nature from whence their ideas are taken as from their original, are apt to be very confused. "Justice" is a word in every man's mouth, but most commonly with a very undetermined, loose signification: which will always be so unless a man has in his mind a distinct comprehension of the component parts that complex idea consists of: and if it be decompounded, must be able to resolve it still on till he at last comes to the simple ideas that make it up: and unless this be done, a man makes an ill use of the word, let it be "justice," for example, or any other. I do not say, a man needs stand to recollect, and make this analysis at large, every time the word "justice" comes in his way: but this, at least, is necessary, that he have so examined the signification of that name, and settled the idea of all its parts in his mind, that he can do it when he pleases. If one who makes this complex idea of justice to be such a treatment of the person or goods of another as is according to law, hath not a clear and distinct idea what law is, which makes a part of his complex idea of justice, it is plain his idea of justice itself will be confused and imperfect. This exactness will, perhaps, be judged very troublesome; and therefore most men will think they may be excused from settling the complex ideas of mixed modes so precisely in their minds. But yet I must say, till this be done it must not be wondered that they have a great deal of obscurity and confusion in their own minds, and a great deal of wrangling in their discourses with others.

And conformable in substances.—In the names of substances, for a right use of them something more is required than barely determined ideas. In these the names must also be conformable to things as they exist: but of this, I shall have occasion to speak more at large by and by. This exactness is absolutely necessary in inquiries after philosophical knowledge, and in controversies about truth. And though it would be well, too, if it extended itself to common conversation and the ordinary affairs of life; yet, I think, that is scarce to be expected. Vulgar notions suit vulgar discourses: and both, though confused enough, yet serve pretty well the market and the wake. Merchants and lovers, cooks and tailors, have words wherewithal to despatch their ordinary affairs; and so, I think, might philosophers and disputants too, if they had a mind to understand, and to be clearly understood.

Thirdly: Propriety.—Thirdly: It is not enough that men have ideas, determined ideas, for which they make these signs stand; but they must also take care to apply their words, as near as may be, to such ideas as common use has annexed them to. For, words, especially of languages already framed, being no man's private possession, but the common measure of commerce and communication, it is not for anyone, at pleasure, to change the stamp they are current in, nor alter the ideas they are affixed to; or at least when there is a necessity to do so, he is bound to give notice of it. Men's intentions in speaking are, or at least should be, to be understood; which cannot be without frequent explanations, demands, and other the like incommodious interruptions, where men do not follow common use. Propriety of speech is that which gives our thoughts entrance into other men's minds with the greatest ease and advantage; and therefore deserves some part of our care and study, especially in the names of moral words.

Fourthly: To make known their meaning.—Fourthly: But because common use has not so visibly annexed any signification to words, as to make men know always certainly what they precisely stand for; and because men in the improvement of their knowledge come to have ideas different from the vulgar and ordinary received ones, for which they must either make new words (which men seldom venture to do, for fear of being thought guilty of affectation or novelty), or else must use old ones in a new signification; therefore after the observation of the foregoing rules, it is sometimes necessary for the ascertaining the signification of words, to declare their meaning; where either common use has left it uncertain and loose (as it has in most names of very complex ideas), or where the term, being very material in the discourse, and that upon which it chiefly turns, is liable to any doubtfulness or mistake.

Book Four

I. OF KNOWLEDGE IN GENERAL

Our knowledge conversant about our ideas.—Since the mind, in all its thoughts and reasonings, hath no other immediate object but its own ideas, which it alone does or can contemplate, it is evident that our knowledge is only conversant about them.

Knowledge is the perception of the agreement or disagreement of two ideas.—Knowledge then seems to me to be nothing but the perception of the connexion and agreement, or disagreement and repugnancy, of any of our ideas. In this alone it consists. Where this perception is, there is knowledge; and where it is not, there, though we may fancy, guess, or believe, yet we always come short of knowledge.

This agreement fourfold.—But, to understand a little more distinctly, wherein this agreement or disagreement consists, I think we may reduce it all to these four sorts: (1.) Identity, or diversity. (2.) Relation. (3.) Co-existence, or necessary connexion. (4.) Real existence.

First: Of identity or diversity.—First: As to the first sort of agreement or disagreement, viz., identity or diversity. It is the first act of the mind, when it has any sentiments or ideas at all, to perceive its ideas, and, so far as it perceives them, to know each what it is, and thereby also to perceive their difference, and that one is not another. This is so absolutely necessary, that without it there could be no knowledge, no reasoning, no imagination, no distinct thoughts at all. By this the mind clearly and infallibly perceives each idea to agree with itself, and to be what it is; and all distinct ideas to disagree, i.e., the one not to be the other: and this it does without pains, labour, or deduction, but at first view, by its natural power of perception and distinction.

Secondly: Relative.—Secondly: The next sort of agreement or disagreement the mind perceives in any of its ideas may, I think, be called "relative," and is nothing but the perception of the relation between any two ideas, of what kind soever, whether substances, modes, or any other. For, since all distinct ideas must eternally be known not to be the same, and so be universally and constantly denied one of another: there could be no room for any positive knowledge at all, if we could not perceive any relation between our ideas, and find out the agreement or disagreement they have one with another, in several ways the mind takes of comparing them.

Thirdly: Of co-existence.—Thirdly: The third sort of agreement or disagreement to be found in our ideas, which the perception of the mind is employed about, is co-existence, or non-co-existence in the same subject; and this belongs particularly to substances.

Fourthly: Of real existence.—Fourthly: The fourth and last sort is that of actual real existence agreeing to any idea. Within these four sorts of agreement or disagreement is, I suppose, contained all the knowledge we have or are capable of; for, all the inquiries that we can make concerning any of our ideas, all that we know or can affirm concerning any of them, is, that it is or is not the same with some other; that it does or or does not always co-exist with some other idea in the same subject; that it has this or that relation to some other idea; or that it has a real existence without the mind.

Knowledge actual or habitual.—There are several ways wherein the mind is possessed of truth, each of which is called "knowledge."

First: There is "actual knowledge," which is the present view the mind has of the agreement or disagreement of any of its ideas, or of the relation they have one to another.

Secondly: A man is said to know any proposition which having been once laid before his thoughts, he evidently perceived the agreement or disagreement of the ideas whereof it consists; and so lodged it in his memory, that whenever that proposition comes again to be reflected on, he, without doubt or hesitation, embraces the right side, assents to and is certain of the truth of it. This, I think, one may call "habitual knowledge"; and thus a man may be said to know all those truths which are lodged in his memory by a foregoing clear and full perception, whereof the mind is assured past doubt as often as it has occasion to reflect on them.

Habitual knowledge twofold.—Of habitual knowledge there are also, vulgarly speaking, two degrees:—

First: The one is of such truths laid up in the memory as, whenever they occur to the mind, it actually perceives the relation is between those ideas. And this is in all those truths whereof we have an intuitive knowledge, where the ideas themselves, by an immediate view, discover their agreement or disagreement one with another.

Secondly: The other is of such truths, whereof the mind having been convinced, it retains the memory of the conviction without the proofs.

II. OF THE DEGREES OF OUR KNOWLEDGE

Intuitive.—All our knowledge consisting, as I have said, in the view the mind has of its own ideas, which is the utmost light and greatest certainty we, with our faculties and in our way of knowledge, are capable of, it may not be amiss to consider a little the degrees of its evidence. The different clearness of our knowledge seems to me to lie in the different way of perception the mind has of the agreement or disagreement of any of its ideas. For if we will reflect on our own ways of thinking, we shall find that sometimes the mind perceives the agreement or disagreement of two ideas immediately by themselves, without the intervention of any other: and this, I think, we may call "intuitive knowledge." For in this the mind is at no pains of proving or examining, but perceives the truth, as the eye doth light, only by being directed towards it.

Demonstrative.—The next degree of knowledge is, where the mind perceives the agreement or disagreement of any ideas, but not immediately. Though wherever the mind perceives the agreement or disagreement of any of its ideas, there be certain knowledge; yet it does not always happen that the mind sees that agreement or disagreement which there is between them, even where it is discoverable; and in that case remains in ignorance, and at most gets no farther than a probable conjecture. The reason why the mind cannot always perceive presently the agreement or disagreement of two ideas, is, because those ideas concerning whose agreement or disagreement the inquiry is made, cannot by the mind be so put together as to show it. In this case then, when the mind cannot so bring its ideas together as, by their immediate comparison and, as it were, juxtaposition or application one to another, to perceive their agreement or disagreement, it is fain, by the intervention of other ideas (one or more, as it happens), to discover the agreement or disagreement which it searches; and this is that which we call "reasoning."

Sensitive knowledge of particular existence.—These two, viz., intuition and demonstration, are the degrees of our knowledge; whatever comes short of one of these, with what assurance soever embraced, is but faith or opinion, but not knowledge, at least in all general truths. There is, indeed, another perception of the mind employed about the particular existence of finite beings without us; which, going beyond bare probability, and yet not reaching perfectly to either of the foregoing degrees of certainty, passes under the name of "knowledge." There can be nothing more certain, than that the idea we receive from an external object is in our minds; this is intuitive knowledge. But whether there be any thing more than barely that idea in our minds, whether we can thence certainly infer the existence of any thing without us which corresponds to that idea, is that whereof some men think there may be a question made; because men may have such ideas in their minds when no such thing exists, no such object affects their senses. But yet here, I think, we are provided with an evidence that puts us past doubting; for I ask anyone, whether he be not invincibly conscious to himself of a different perception when he looks on the sun by day, and thinks on it by night; when he actually tastes wormwood, or smells a rose, or only thinks on that savour or odour? We as plainly find the difference there is between any idea revived in our minds by our own memory, and actually coming into our minds by our senses, as we do between any two distinct ideas.

III. OF THE EXTENT OF HUMAN KNOWLEDGE

KNOWLEDGE, as has been said, lying in the perception of the agreement or disagreement of any of our ideas, it follows from hence, that,

First: No farther than we have ideas.—First: We can have knowledge no farther than we have ideas.

Secondly: No farther than we can perceive their agreement or disagreement.—Secondly: That we can have no knowledge farther than we can have perception of that agreement or disagreement: which perception being, (1.) either by intuition, or the immediate comparing any two ideas; or, (2.) by reason, examining the agreement or disagreement of two ideas by the intervention of some others; or, (3.) by sensation, perceiving the existence of particular things; hence it also follows,

Thirdly: Intuitive knowledge extends itself not to all the relations of all our ideas.—Thirdly: That we cannot have an intuitive knowledge that shall extend itself to all our ideas, and all that we would know about them; because we cannot examine and perceive all the relations they have one to another by juxtaposition, or an immediate comparison one with another.

Fourthly: Nor demonstrative knowledge.—Fourthly: It follows also, from what is above observed, that our rational knowledge cannot reach to the whole extent of our ideas: because between two different ideas we would examine, we cannot always find such mediums as we can connect one to another with an intuitive knowledge, in all the parts of the deduction; and wherever that fails, we come short of knowledge and demonstration.

Fifthly: Sensitive knowledge narrower than either.—Fifthly: Sensitive knowledge, reaching no farther than the existence of things actually present to our senses, is yet much narrower than either of the former.

Sixthly: Our knowledge therefore narrower than our ideas.—From all which it is evident, that the extent of our knowledge comes not only short of the reality of things, but even of the extent of our own ideas.

How far our knowledge reaches.—The affirmations or negations we make concerning the ideas we have, may, as I have before intimated in general, be reduced to these four sorts, viz., identity, co-existence, relation, and real existence. I shall examine how far our knowledge extends in each of these:—

First: Our knowledge of identity and diversity, as far as our ideas.—First: As to identity and diversity, in this way of the agreement or disagreement of ideas, our intuitive knowledge is as far extended as our ideas themselves; and there can be no idea in the mind which does not presently, by an intuitive knowledge, perceive to be what it is, and to be different from any other.

Secondly: Of co-existence, a very little way.—Secondly: As to the second sort, which is the agreement or disagreement of our ideas in co-existence, in this our knowledge is very short, though in this consists the greatest and most material part of our knowledge concerning substances.

Thirdly: Of other relations, it is not easy to say how far.—As to the third sort of our knowledge, viz., the agreement or disagreement of any of our ideas in any other relation: this, as it is the largest field of our knowledge, so it is hard to determine how far it may extend: because the advances that are made in this part of knowledge depending on our sagacity in finding intermediate ideas that may show the relations and habitudes of ideas, whose co-existence is not considered, it is a hard matter to tell when we are at an end of such discoveries, and when reason has all the helps it is capable of for the finding of proofs, or examining the agreement or disagreement of remote ideas.

Fourthly: Of real existence. We have an INTUITIVE *knowledge of our own,* DEMONSTRATIVE *of God's,* SENSITIVE *of some few other things.*—As to the fourth sort of our knowledge, viz., of the real actual existence of things, we have an intuitive knowledge of our own existence; a demonstrative knowledge of the existence of a God; of the existence of anything else, we have no other but a sensitive knowledge, which extends not beyond the objects present to our senses.

Our ignorance great.—Our knowledge being so narrow, as I have showed, it will, perhaps, give us some light into the present state of our minds, if we look a little into the dark side, and take a view of our ignorance: which, being infinitely larger than our knowledge, may serve much to the quieting of disputes and improvement of useful knowledge, if, discovering how far we have clear and distinct ideas, we confine our thoughts within the contemplation of those things that are within the reach of our understandings, and launch not out into that abyss of darkness out of a presumption that nothing is beyond our comprehension. But to be satisfied of the folly of such a conceit, we need not go far. He that knows any thing, knows this in the first place, that he need not seek long for instances of his ignorance. The meanest and most obvious things that come in our way have dark sides, that the quickest sight cannot penetrate into. The clearest and most enlarged understandings of thinking men find themselves puzzled and at a loss in every particle of matter. We shall the less wonder to find it so when we consider the causes of our ignorance, which, from what has been said, I suppose, will be found to be chiefly these three:

FIRST: Want of ideas.

SECONDLY: Want of a discoverable connexion between the ideas we have.

THIRDLY: Want of tracing and examining our ideas.

First: One cause of it, want of ideas, either such as we have no conception of.—First: There are some things, and those not a few, that we are ignorant of for want of ideas.

First: All the simple ideas we have are confined to those we receive from corporeal objects by sensation, and from the operations of our own minds as the objects of reflection. But how much these few and narrow inlets are disproportionate to the vast whole extent of all beings, will not be hard to persuade those who are not so foolish as to think their span the measure of all things.

Or want of such ideas as particularly we have not, because of their remoteness.—Secondly: Another great cause of ignorance is the want of ideas we are capable of. As the want of ideas which our faculties are not able to give us shuts us wholly from those views of things which it is reasonable to think other beings, perfecter than we, have, of which we know nothing; so the want of ideas I now speak of keeps us in ignorance of things we conceive capable of being known to us. Bulk, figure, and motion, we have ideas of. But though we are not without ideas of these primary qualities of bodies in general, yet not knowing what is the particular bulk, figure, and motion of the greatest part of the bodies of the universe, we are ignorant of the several powers, efficacies, and ways of operation, whereby the effects which we daily see are produced. These are hid from us in some things by being too remote; and, in others, by being too minute.

Secondly: Want of a discoverable connexion between ideas we have. —Secondly: What a small part of the substantial beings that are in the universe the want of ideas leaves open to our knowledge, we have seen. In the next place, another cause of ignorance of no less moment is a want of a discoverable connexion between those ideas which we have. For wherever we want that, we are utterly uncapable of universal and certain knowledge; and are, as in the former case, left only to observation and experiment; which how narrow and confined it is, how far from general knowledge, we need not be told.

Thirdly: Want of tracing our ideas.—Thirdly: Where we have adequate ideas, and where there is a certain and discoverable connexion between them, yet we are often ignorant for want of tracing those ideas which we have or may have; and for want of finding out those intermediate ideas which may show us what habitude of agreement or disagreement they have one with another. And thus many are ignorant of mathematical truths, not out of any imperfection of their faculties, or uncertainty in the things themselves; but for want of application in acquiring, examining, and by due ways comparing those ideas. That which has most contributed to hinder the due tracing of our ideas, and finding out their relations and agreements or disagreements one with another has been, I suppose, the ill use of words. It is impossible that men should ever truly seek, or certainly discover, the agreement or disagreement of ideas themselves, whilst their thoughts flutter about, or stick only in sounds of doubtful and uncertain significations.

IV. OF THE REALITY OF HUMAN KNOWLEDGE

IT IS EVIDENT the mind knows not things immediately, but only by the intervention of the ideas it has of them. Our knowledge therefore is real only so far as there is a conformity between our ideas and the reality of things. But what shall be here the criterion? How shall the mind, when it perceives nothing but its own ideas, know that they agree with things themselves? This, though it seems not to want difficulty, yet I think there be two sorts of ideas that we may be assured agree with things.

As, first, all simple ideas do.—First: The first are simple ideas, which since the mind, as has been showed, can by no means make to itself, must necessarily be the product of things operating on the mind in a natural way, and producing therein those perceptions which by the wisdom and will of our Maker they are ordained and adapted to. From whence it follows, that simple ideas are not fictions of our fancies, but the natural and regular productions of things without us really operating upon us; and so carry with them all the conformity which is intended, or which our state requires; for they represent to us things under those appearances which they are fitted to produce in us, whereby we are enabled to distinguish the sorts of particular substances, to discern the states they are in, and so to take them for our necessities, and apply them to our uses.

Secondly: All complex ideas except of substances.—Secondly: All our complex ideas except those of substances being archetypes of the mind's own making, not intended to be the copies of any thing, nor referred to the existence of any thing, as to their originals, cannot want any conformity necessary to real knowledge. For that which is not designed to represent any thing but itself, can never be capable of a wrong representation, nor mislead us from the true apprehension of any thing by its dislikeness to it; and such, excepting those of substances, are all our complex ideas: which, as I have showed in another place, are combinations of ideas which the mind by its free choice puts together without considering any connexion they have in nature. And hence it is, that in all these sorts the ideas themselves are considered as the archetypes, and things no otherwise regarded but as they are conformable to them. So that we cannot but be infallibly certain, that all the knowledge we attain concerning these ideas is real, and reaches things themselves; because in all our thoughts, reasonings, and discourses of this kind, we intend things no farther than as they are conformable to our ideas. So that in these we cannot miss of a certain and undoubted reality.

V. OF TRUTH IN GENERAL

What truth is.—"What is truth?" was an inquiry many ages since; and it being that which all mankind either do or pretend to search after, it cannot but be worth our while carefully to examine wherein it consists; and so acquaint ourselves with the nature of it, as to observe how the mind distinguishes it from falsehood.

A right joining or separating of signs; i.e., ideas or words.—Truth then seems to me, in the proper import of the word, to signify nothing but the joining or separating of signs, as the things signified by them do agree or disagree one with another. The joining or separating of signs here meant, is what by another name we call "proposition." So that truth properly belongs only to propositions: whereof there are two sorts, viz., mental and verbal; as there are two sorts of signs commonly made use of, viz., ideas and words.

Which make mental or verbal propositions.—To form a clear notion of truth, it is very necessary to consider truth of thought, and truth of words, distinctly one from another: but yet it is very difficult to treat them asunder; because it is unavoidable, in treating of mental propositions, to make use of words; and then the instances given of mental propositions cease immediately to be barely mental, and become verbal. For, a mental proposition being nothing but a bare consideration of the ideas as they are in our minds stripped of names, they lose the nature of purely mental propositions as soon as they are put into words.

Mental propositions are very hard to be treated of.—And that which makes it yet harder to treat of mental and verbal propositions separately, is, that most men, if not all, in their thinking and reasonings within themselves, make use of words instead of ideas, at least when the subject of their meditation contains in it complex ideas. Which is a great evidence of the imperfection and uncertainty of our ideas of that kind, and may, if attentively made use of, serve for a mark to show us what are those things we have clear and perfect established ideas of, and what not.

When mental propositions contain real truth, and when verbal.—Everyone's experience will satisfy him that the mind, either by perceiving or supposing the agreement or disagreement of any of its ideas, does tacitly within itself put them into a kind of proposition affirmative or negative, which I have endeavoured to express by the terms "putting together" and "separating." But this action of the mind, which is so familiar to every thinking and reasoning man, is easier to be conceived by reflecting on what passes in us when we affirm or deny, than to be explained by words. When ideas are so put together or separated in the mind, as they or the things they stand for do agree or not, that is, as I may call it "mental truth." But truth of words is something more, and that is the affirming or denying of words one of another, as the ideas they stand for agree or disagree: and this again is twofold; either purely verbal and trifling, which I shall speak of, or real and instructive, which is the object of that real knowledge which we have spoken of already.

Moral and metaphysical truth.—Besides truth taken in the strict sense before mentioned, there are other sorts of truths; as, (1.) Moral truth, which is speaking things according to the persuasion of our own minds, though the proposition we speak agree not to the reality of things. (2.) Metaphysical truth, which is nothing but the real existence of things conformable to the ideas to which we have annexed their names. This, though it seems to consist in the very beings of things, yet when considered a little nearly will appear to include a tacit proposition, whereby the mind joins that particular thing to the idea it had before settled with a name to it.

VI. OF UNIVERSAL PROPOSITIONS, THEIR TRUTH AND CERTAINTY

Treating of words necessary to knowledge.—Though the examining and judging of ideas by themselves, their names being quite laid aside, be the best and surest way to clear and distinct knowledge; yet, through the prevailing custom of using sounds for ideas, I think it is very seldom practised. Everyone may observe how common it is for names to be made use of instead of the ideas themselves, even when men think and reason within their own breasts; especially if the ideas be very complex, and made up of a great collection of simple ones. This makes the consideration of words and propositions so necessary a part of the treatise of knowledge, that it is very hard to speak intelligibly of the one without explaining the other.

General truths hardly to be understood but in verbal propositions.— All the knowledge we have being only of particular or general truths, it is evident that whatever may be done in the former of these, the latter, which is that which with reason is most sought after, can never be well made known, and is very seldom apprehended, but as conceived and expressed in words. It is not therefore out of our way, in the examination of our knowledge, to inquire into the truth and certainty of universal propositions.

Certainty twofold, of truth and of knowledge.—But that we may not be misled in this case by that which is the danger everywhere, I mean by the doubtfulness of terms, it is fit to observe that certainty is twofold; certainty of truth, and certainty of knowledge. Certainty of truth is, when words are so put together in propositions as exactly to express the agreement or disagreement of the ideas they stand for, as really it is. Certainty of knowledge is, to perceive the agreement or disagreement of ideas, as expressed in any proposition. This we usually call "knowing," or "being certain of the truth of any proposition."

No proposition can be known to be true, where the essence of each species mentioned is not known.—Now, because we cannot be certain of the truth of any general proposition unless we know the precise bounds and extent of the species its terms stand for, it is necessary we should know the essence of each species, which is that which constitutes and bounds it. This, in all simple ideas and modes, is not hard to do. For in these the real and nominal essence being the same, or, which is all one, the abstract idea, which the general term stands for, being the sole essence and boundary that is or can be supposed of the species, there can be no doubt how far the species extends, or what things are comprehended under each term: which it is evident are all that have an exact conformity with the idea it stands for, and no other. But in substances, wherein a real essence distinct from the nominal is supposed to constitute, determine, and bound the species, the extent of the general word is very uncertain: because, not knowing this real essence, we cannot know what is or is not of that species, and consequently what may or may not with certainty be affirmed of it.

Because co-existence of ideas in few cases is to be known.—The complex ideas that our names of the species of substances properly stand for, are collections of such qualities as have been observed to co-exist in an unknown substratum which we call "substance"; but what other qualities necessarily co-exist with such combinations, we cannot certainly know, unless we can discover their natural dependence; which in their primary qualities we can go but a very little way in; and in all their secondary qualities we can discover no connexion at all, for the reasons mentioned, viz., (1.) Because we know not the real constitutions of substances, on which each secondary quality particularly depends. (2.) Did we know that it would serve us only for experimental (not universal) knowledge; and reach with certainty no farther than that bare instance; because our understandings can discover no conceivable connexion between any secondary quality, and any modification whatsoever of any of the primary ones. And therefore there are very few general propositions to be made concerning substances which can carry with them undoubted certainty.

As far as any such co-existence can be known, so far universal propositions may be certain. But this will go but a little way, because—The more, indeed, of these co-existing qualities we unite into one complex idea, under one name, the more precise and determinate we make the signification of that word; but yet never make it thereby more capable of universal certainty in respect of other qualities not contained in our complex idea; since we perceive not their connexion or dependence one on another, being ignorant both of that real constitution in which they are all founded, and also how they flow from it. For the chief part of our knowledge concerning substances is not, as in other things, barely of the relation of two ideas that may exist separately; but, is of the necessary connexion and co-existence of several distinct ideas in the same subject, or of their repugnances so to co-exist. Could we begin at the other end, and discover what it was wherein that colour consisted, what made a body lighter or heavier, what texture of parts made it malleable, fusible, and fixed, and fit to be dissolved in this sort of liquor, and not in another; if (I say) we had such an idea as this of bodies, and could perceive wherein all sensible qualities originally consist, and how they are produced, we might frame such abstract ideas of them as would furnish us with matter of more general knowledge, and enable us to make universal propositions that should carry general truth and certainty with them. But whilst our complex ideas of the sorts of substances are so remote from that internal real constitution on which their sensible qualities depend, and are made up of nothing but an imperfect collection of those apparent qualities our senses can discover, there can be very few general propositions concerning substances, of whose real truth we can be certainly assured; since there are but few simple ideas of whose connexion and necessary co-existence we can have certain and undoubted knowledge.

Wherein lies the general certainty of propositions.—To conclude:

general propositions, of what kind soever, are then only capable of certainty, when the terms used in them stand for such ideas whose agreement or disagreement as there expressed, is capable to be discovered by us. And we are then certain of their truth or falsehood, when we perceive the ideas the terms stand for to agree or not agree, according as they are affirmed or denied one of another. Whence we may take notice, that general certainty is never to be found but in our ideas. Whenever we go to seek it elsewhere in experiment or observations without us, our knowledge goes not beyond particulars. It is the contemplation of our own abstract ideas that alone is able to afford us general knowledge.

VII. OF MAXIMS

They are self-evident.—There are a sort of propositions which, under the name of "maxims and axioms," have passed for principles of science: and, because they are self-evident, have been supposed innate, although nobody ever went about to show the reason and foundation of their clearness or cogency.

Wherein that self-evidence consists.—Knowledge, as has been shown, consists in the perception of the agreement or disagreement of ideas: now where that agreement or disagreement is perceived immediately by itself, without the intervention or help of any other, there our knowledge is self-evident. This will appear to be so to anyone who will but consider any of those propositions which, without any proof, he assents to at first sight; for in all of them he will find that the reason of his assent is from that agreement or disagreement which the mind, by an immediate comparing them, finds in those ideas, answering the affirmation or negation in the proposition.

These axioms do not much influence our other knowledge.—In the next place let us consider what influence these received maxims have upon the other parts of our knowledge. The rules established in the schools, that all reasonings are *ex præcognitis et præconcessis,* seem to lay the foundation of all other knowledge in these maxims, and to suppose them to be *præcognita;* whereby I think are meant these two things: first, that these axioms are those truths that are first known to the mind; and, secondly, that upon them the other parts of our knowledge depend.

Because they are not the truths we first knew.—First: That they are not the truths first known to the mind is evident to experience, as we have shown in another place.

Who perceives not, that a child certainly knows that a stranger is not its mother, that its sucking-bottle is not the rod, long before he knows that it is impossible for the same thing to be, and not to be? And how many truths are there about numbers which it is obvious to observe that the mind is perfectly acquainted with, and fully convinced of, before it ever thought on these general maxims to which mathematicians in their arguings do sometimes refer them! Whereof the reason is very plain: for, that which makes the mind assent to such propositions being nothing else but the perception it has of the agreement or disagreement of its ideas, according as it finds them affirmed or denied one of another in words it understands, and every idea being known to be what it is, and every two distinct ideas being known not to be the same, it must necessarily follow, that such self-evident truths must be first known which consist of ideas that are first in the mind; and the ideas first in the mind, it is evident, are those of particular things, from whence, by slow degrees, the understanding proceeds to some few general ones; which, being taken from the ordinary and familiar objects of sense, are settled in the mind with general names to them. Thus particular ideas are first received and distinguished, and so knowledge got about them; and next to them the less general or specific, which are next to particular: for, abstract ideas are not so obvious or easy to children or the yet unexercised mind, as particular ones. If they seem so to grown men, it is only because by constant and familiar use they are made so: for when we nicely reflect upon them, we shall find that general ideas are fictions and contrivances of the mind, that carry difficulty with them, and do not so easily offer themselves as we are apt to imagine.

Because on them the other parts of our knowledge do not depend.— Secondly: From what has been said, it plainly follows that these magnified maxims are not the principles and foundations of all our other knowledge. For, if there be a great many other truths which have as much self-evidence as they, and a great many that we know before them, it is impossible they should be the principles from which we deduce all other truths.

What use these general maxims have.—What shall we then say? Are these general maxims of no use? By no means; though perhaps their use is not that which it is commonly taken to be. But since doubting in the least of what hath been by some men ascribed to these maxims may be apt to be cried out against, as overturning the foundations of all the sciences, it may be worth while to consider them with respect to other parts of our knowledge, and examine more particularly to what purposes they serve.

To come therefore to the use that is made of maxims.

(1.) They are of use, as has been observed, in the ordinary methods of teaching sciences as far as they are advanced: but of little or none in advancing them farther.

(2.) They are of use in disputes, for the silencing of obstinate wranglers, and bringing those contests to some conclusion.

Maxims, if care be not taken in the use of words, may prove contradictions.—One thing farther, I think, it may not be amiss to observe concerning these general maxims; that they are so far from improving or establishing our minds in true knowledge, that if our notions be wrong, loose, or unsteady, and we resign up our thoughts to the sound of words, rather than fix them on settled determined ideas of things; I say, these general maxims will serve to confirm us in mistakes; and in such a way of use of words which is most common, will serve to prove contradictions.

VIII. OF TRIFLING PROPOSITIONS

Some propositions bring no increase to our knowledge.—Whether the maxims treated of in the foregoing chapter be of that use to real knowledge as is generally supposed, I leave to be considered. This, I think, may confidently be affirmed, that there are universal propositions which, though they be certainly true, yet they add no light to our understandings, bring no increase to our knowledge. Such are,

As, first, identical propositions.—First: All purely identical propositions. These obviously and at first blush appear to contain no instruction in them: for when we affirm the said term of itself, whether it be barely verbal, or whether it contains any clear and real idea, it shows us nothing but what we must certainly know before, whether such a proposition be either made by or proposed to us.

Secondly: When a part of any complex idea is predicated of the whole. —Secondly: Another sort of trifling propositions is, when a part of the complex idea is predicated of the name of the whole; a part of the definition, of the word defined. Such propositions can only serve to show the disingenuity of one who will go from the definition of his own terms, by reminding him sometimes of it; but carry no knowledge with them but of the signification of words, however certain they be.

Thirdly: Using words variously is trifling with them.—Though yet concerning most words used in discourses, especially argumentative and controversial, there is this more to be complained of, which is the worst sort of trifling, and which sets us yet farther from the certainty of knowledge we hope to attain by them, or find in them, viz., that most writers are so far from instructing us in the nature and knowledge of things, that they use their words loosely and uncertainly, and do not, by using them constantly and steadily in the same significations, make plain and clear deductions of words one from another, and make their discourses coherent and clear (how little soever it were instructive); which were not difficult to do, did they not find it convenient to shelter their ignorance or obstinacy under the obscurity and perplexedness of their terms: to which, perhaps, inadvertency and ill custom do in many men much contribute.

IX. OF OUR KNOWLEDGE OF EXISTENCE

General certain propositions concern not existence.—Hitherto we have only considered the essences of things, which, being only abstract ideas, and thereby removed in our thoughts from particular existence, give us no knowledge of real existence at all. Where, by the way, we may take notice, that universal propositions, of whose truth or falsehood we can have certain knowledge, concern not existence; and farther, that all particular affirmations or negations that would not be certain if they were made general, are only concerning existence; they declaring only the accidental union or separation of ideas in things existing, which in their abstract natures have no known necessary union or repugnancy.

A threefold knowledge of existence.—But leaving the nature of propositions, and different ways of predication, to be considered more at large in another place, let us proceed now to inquire concerning our knowledge of the existence of things, and how we come by it. I say then, that we have the knowledge of our own existence by intuition; of the existence of God by demonstration; and of other things by sensation.

Our knowledge of our own existence is intuitive.—As for our own existence, we perceive it so plainly and so certainly that it neither needs nor is capable of any proof. For nothing can be more evident to us than our own existence.

X. OF OUR KNOWLEDGE OF THE EXISTENCE OF A GOD

We are capable of knowing certainly that there is a God.—Though God has given us no innate ideas of himself; though he has stamped no original characters on our minds, wherein we may read his being; yet, having furnished us with those faculties our minds are endowed with, he hath not left himself without witness; since we have sense, perception, and reason, and cannot want a clear proof of him as long as we carry ourselves about us. Nor can we justly complain of our ignorance in this great point, since he has so plentifully provided us with the means to discover and know him, so far as is necessary to the end of our being, and the great concernment of our happiness. But though this be the most obvious truth that reason discovers, and though its evidence be (if I mistake not) equal to mathematical certainty; yet it requires thought and attention, and the mind must apply itself to a regular deduction of it from some part of our intuitive knowledge, or else we shall be as uncertain and ignorant of this as of other propositions which are in themselves capable of clear demonstration. To show, therefore, that we are capable of knowing, i.e., being certain, that there is a God, and how we may come by this certainty, I think we need go no farther than ourselves, and that undoubted knowledge we have of our own existence.

Man knows that he himself is.—I think it is beyond question, that man has a clear perception of his own being; he knows certainly that he exists, and that he is something. He that can doubt whether he be any thing or no, I speak not to; no more than I would argue with pure nothing, or endeavour to convince nonentity that it were something.

He knows also that nothing cannot produce a being, therefore something eternal.—In the next place, man knows by an intuitive certainty that bare nothing can no more produce any real being, than it can be equal to two right angles. If a man knows not that nonentity, or the absence of all being, cannot be equal to two right angles, it is impossible he should know any demonstration in Euclid. If therefore we know there is some real being, and that nonentity cannot produce any real being, it is an evident demonstration, that from eternity there has been something; since what was not from eternity had a beginning; and what had a beginning must be produced by something else.

That Eternal Being must be most powerful.—Next, it is evident, that what had its being and beginning from another, must also have all that which is in and belongs to its being from another too. All the powers it has, must be owing to and received from the same source. This eternal source, then, of all being, must also be the source and original of all power; and so this Eternal Being must be also the most powerful.

And most knowing.—Again: a man finds in himself perception and knowledge. We have then got one step farther; and we are certain now that there is not only some being, but some knowing, intelligent being in the world.

And therefore God.—Thus from the consideration of ourselves, and what we infallibly find in our own constitutions, our reason leads us to the knowledge of this certain and evident truth, that there is an eternal, most powerful, and most knowing Being; which whether anyone will please to call "God," it matters not. The thing is evident; and from this idea, duly considered, will easily be deduced all those other attributes which we ought to ascribe to this Eternal Being.

From what has been said, it is plain to me we have a more certain knowledge of the existence of a God, than of any thing our senses have not immediately discovered to us. Nay, I presume I may say, that we more certainly know that there is a God, than that there is any thing else without us. When I say "we know," I mean there is such a knowledge within our reach which we cannot miss, if we will but apply our minds to that as we do to several other inquiries.

XI. OF OUR KNOWLEDGE OF THE EXISTENCE OF OTHER THINGS

It is to be had only by sensation.—The knowledge of our own being we have by intuition. The existence of a God reason clearly makes known to us, as has been shown.

The knowledge of the existence of any other thing, we can have only by sensation: for, there being no necessary connexion of real existence with any idea a man hath in his memory, nor of any other existence but that of God with the existence of any particular man, no particular man can know the existence of any other being, but only when by actual operating upon him it makes itself perceived by him. For, the having the idea of any thing in our mind no more proves the existence of that thing than the picture of a man evidences his being in the world, or the visions of a dream make thereby a true history.

This, though not so certain as demonstration, yet may be called "knowledge," and proves the existence of things without us.—The notice we have by our senses of the existing of things without us, though it be not altogether so certain as our intuitive knowledge, or the deductions of our reason employed about the clear abstract ideas of our own minds; yet it is an assurance that deserves the name of knowledge. If we persuade ourselves that our faculties act and inform us right concerning the existence of those objects that affect them, it cannot pass for an ill-grounded confidence: for I think nobody can, in earnest, be so sceptical as to be uncertain of the existence of those things which he sees and feels. At least, he that can doubt so far (whatever he may have with his own thoughts) will never have any controversy with me: since he can never be sure I say any thing contrary to his opinion. As to myself, I think God has given me assurance enough of the existence of things without me; since, by their different application, I can produce in myself both pleasure and pain, which is one great concernment of my present state. This is certain, the confidence that our faculties do not herein deceive us is the greatest assurance we are capable of concerning the existence of material beings. For we cannot act any thing but by our faculties, nor talk of knowledge itself but by the help of those faculties which are fitted to apprehend even what knowledge is. But, besides the assurance we have from our senses themselves, that they do not err in the information they give us of the existence of things without us, when they are affected by them, we are farther confirmed in this assurance by other concurrent reasons.

First: Because we cannot have them but by the inlet of the senses.—First: It is plain those perceptions are produced in us by exterior causes affecting our senses, because those that want the organs of any sense never can have the ideas belonging to that sense produced in their minds. This is too evident to be doubted: and therefore we cannot but be assured that they come in by the organs of that sense, and no other way.

Secondly: Because an idea from actual sensation and another from memory are very distinct perceptions.—Secondly: Because sometimes I find that I cannot avoid the having those ideas produced in my mind: for though when my eyes are shut, or windows fast, I can at pleasure recall to my mind the ideas of light or the sun, which former sensations had lodged in my memory; so I can at pleasure lay by that idea, and take into my view that of the smell of a rose, or taste of sugar. But if I turn my eyes at noon towards the sun, I cannot avoid the ideas which the light or sun then produces in me. So that there is a manifest difference between the ideas laid up in my memory (over which, if they were there only, I should have constantly the same power to dispose of them, and lay them by at pleasure), and those which force themselves upon me and I cannot avoid having. And therefore it must needs be some exterior cause, and the brisk acting of some objects without me, whose efficacy I cannot resist, that produces those ideas in my mind, whether I will or no.

Thirdly: Pleasure or pain, which accompanies actual sensation, accompanies not the returning of those ideas without the external objects.—Thirdly: Add to this, that many of those ideas are produced in us with pain, which afterwards we remember without the least offence.

Fourthly: Our senses assist one another's testimony of the existence of outward things.—Fourthly: Our senses, in many cases, bear witness to the truth of each other's report concerning the existence of sensible things without us. He that sees a fire may, if he doubt whether it be any thing more than a bare fancy, feel it too, and be convinced by putting his hand in it; which certainly could never be put into such exquisite pain by a bare idea or phantom, unless that the pain be a fancy too; which yet he cannot, when the burn is well, by raising the idea of it, bring upon himself again.

XII. OF THE IMPROVEMENT OF OUR KNOWLEDGE

Knowledge is not from maxims.—It having been the common received opinion amongst men of letters, that maxims were the foundation of all knowledge; and that the sciences were each of them built upon certain *præcognita,* from whence the understanding was to take its rise, and by which it was to conduct itself in its inquiries into the matters belonging to that science; the beaten road of the Schools has been to lay down in the beginning one or more general propositions as foundations whereon to build the knowledge that was to be had of that subject. These doctrines thus laid down for foundations of any science were called "principles," as the beginnings from which we must set out, and look no farther backwards in our inquiries, as we have already observed.

But from the comparing clear and distinct ideas.—But if any one will consider, he will find that the great advancement and certainty of real knowledge, which men arrived to in these sciences, was not owing to the influence of these principles, nor derived from any peculiar advantage they received from two or three general maxims laid down in the beginning; but from the clear, distinct, complete ideas their thoughts were employed about, and the relation of equality and excess so clear between some of them, that they had an intuitive knowledge, and by that a way to discover it in others, and this without the help of those maxims.

XIII. SOME FARTHER CONSIDERATIONS CONCERNING OUR KNOWLEDGE

Our knowledge partly necessary, partly voluntary.—Our knowledge, as in other things, so in this, has a great conformity with our sight, that it is neither wholly necessary, nor wholly voluntary. If our knowledge were altogether necessary, all men's knowledge would not only be alike, but every man would know all that is knowable; and if it were only voluntary, some men so little regard or value it, that they would have extreme little or none at all. Men that have senses cannot choose but receive some ideas by them; and if they have memory, they cannot but retain some of them; and if they have any distinguishing faculty, cannot but perceive the agreement or disagreement of some of them one with another; as he that has eyes, if he will open them by day, cannot but see some objects, and perceive a difference in them. But though a man with his eyes open in the light cannot but see, yet there be certain objects which he may choose whether he will turn his eyes to; there may be in his reach a book containing pictures and discourses, capable to delight and instruct him, which yet he may never have the will to open, never take the pains to look into.

The application voluntary; but we know as things are, not as we please.—There is also another thing in a man's power; and that is, though he turns his eyes sometimes towards an object, yet he may choose whether he will curiously survey it, and with an intent application endeavour to observe accurately all that is visible in it. But yet what he does see, he cannot see otherwise than he does. Just thus is it with our understanding; all that is voluntary in our knowledge is the employing or withholding any of our faculties from this or that sort of objects, and a more or less accurate survey of them; but, they being employed, our will hath no power to determine the knowledge of the mind one way or other; that is done only by the objects themselves, as far as they are clearly discovered. And therefore as far as men's senses are conversant about external objects, the mind cannot but receive those ideas which are presented by them, and be informed of the existence of things without; and so far as men's thoughts converse with their own determined ideas, they cannot but in some measure observe the agreement and disagreement that is to be found amongst some of them, which is so far knowledge: and if they have names for those ideas which they have thus considered, they must needs be assured of the truth of those propositions which express that agreement or disagreement they perceive in them, and be undoubtedly convinced of those truths. For what a man sees, he cannot but see; and what he perceives, he cannot but know that he perceives.

XIV. OF JUDGMENT

Our knowledge being short, we want something else.—The understanding faculties being given to man, not barely for speculation, but also for the conduct of his life, man would be at a great loss if he had nothing to direct him but what has the certainty of true knowledge. For, that being very short and scanty, as we have seen, he would be often utterly in the dark, and in most of the actions of his life perfectly at a stand, had he nothing to guide him in the absence of clear and certain knowledge.

Judgment supplies the want of knowledge.—The faculty which God has given man to supply the want of clear and certain knowledge, in cases where that cannot be had, is judgment: whereby the mind takes its ideas to agree or disagree; or, which is the same, any proposition to be true or false, without perceiving a demonstrative evidence in the proofs. The mind sometimes exercises this judgment out of necessity, where demonstrative proofs and certain knowledge are not to be had; and sometimes out of·laziness, unskilfulness, or haste, even where demonstrative and certain proofs are to be had.

Judgment is the presuming things to be so without perceiving it.— Thus the mind has two faculties conversant about truth and falsehood,—

First: Knowledge, whereby it certainly perceives, and is undoubtedly satisfied of the agreement or disagreement of any ideas.

Secondly: Judgment, which is the putting ideas together, or separating them from one another in the mind, when their certain agreement or disagreement is not perceived, but presumed to be so; which is, as the word imports, taken to be so before it certainly appears. And if it so unites or separates them as in reality things are, it is right judgment.

XV. OF PROBABILITY

Probability is the appearance of agreement upon fallible proofs.—As demonstration is the showing the agreement or disagreement of two ideas by the intervention of one or more proofs, which have a constant, immutable, and visible connexion one with another; so probability is nothing but the appearance of such an agreement or disagreement by the intervention of proofs, whose connexion is not constant and immutable, or at least is not perceived to be so; but is, or appears for the most part to be so, and is enough to induce the mind to judge the proposition to be true or false, rather than the contrary.

It is to supply the want of knowledge.—Our knowledge, as has been shown, being very narrow, and we not happy enough to find certain truth in every thing which we have occasion to consider, most of the propositions we think, reason, discourse, nay, act upon, are such as we cannot have undoubted knowledge of their truth; yet some of them border so near upon certainty, that we make no doubt at all about them, but assent to them as firmly, and act according to that assent as resolutely, as if they were infallibly demonstrated, and our knowledge of them was perfect and certain. But, these being degrees herein, from the very neighbourhood of certainty and demonstration, quite down to improbability and unlikeliness, even to the confines of impossibility; and also degrees of assent from full assurance and confidence, quite down to conjecture, doubt, and distrust; I shall come now (having, as I think, found out the bounds of human knowledge and certainty) in the next place, to consider the several degrees and grounds of probability, and assent or faith.

Being that which makes us presume things to be true before we know them to be so.—Probability is likeliness to be true; the very notation of the word signifying such a proposition for which there be arguments or proofs to make it pass, or be received, for true. The entertainment the mind gives this sort of propositions is called "belief," "assent," or "opinion," which is the admitting or receiving any proposition for true, upon arguments or proofs that are found to persuade us to receive it as true, without certain knowledge that it is so. And herein lies the difference between probability and certainty, faith and knowledge, that in all the parts of knowledge there is intuition; each immediate idea, each step has its visible and certain connexion: in belief not so. That which makes me believe, is something extraneous to the thing I believe; something not evidently joined on both sides to, and so not manifestly showing the agreement or disagreement of, those ideas that are under consideration.

The grounds of probability are two; conformity with our own experi-

ence, or the testimony of others' experience.—Probability, then, being to supply the defect of our knowledge, and to guide us where that fails, is always conversant about propositions whereof we have no certainty, but only some inducements to receive them for true. The grounds of it are, in short, these two following:—

First: The conformity of any thing with our own knowledge, observation and experience.

Secondly: The testimony of others, vouching their observation and experience. In the testimony of others, is to be considered, (1.) The number. (2.) The integrity. (3.) The skill of the witnesses. (4.) The design of the author, where it is a testimony out of a book cited. (5.) The consistency of the parts and circumstances of the relation. (6.) Contrary testimonies.

XVI. OF THE DEGREES OF ASSENT

Our assent ought to be regulated by the grounds of probability.—The grounds of probability we have laid down in the foregoing chapter, as they are the foundations on which our assent is built, so are they also the measure whereby its several degrees are or ought to be regulated: only we are to take notice, that whatever grounds of probability there may be, they yet operate no further on the mind, which searches after truth and endeavours to judge right, than they appear at least in the first judgment or search that the mind makes. I confess, in the opinions men have and firmly stick to in the world, their assent is not always from an actual view of the reasons that at first prevailed with them; it being in many cases almost impossible, and in most very hard, even for those who have very admirable memories, to retain all the proofs which upon a due examination made them embrace that side of the question. It suffices that they have once with care and fairness sifted the matter as far as they could; and that they have searched into all the particulars that they could imagine to give any light to the question, and with the best of their skill cast up the account upon the whole evidence: and thus, having once found on which side the probability appeared to them after as full and exact an inquiry as they can make, they lay up the conclusion in their memories as a truth they have discovered; and for the future they remain satisfied with the testimony of their memories, that this is the opinion that, by the proofs they have once seen of it, deserves such a degree of their assent as they afford it.

These cannot always be actually in view, and then we must content ourselves with the remembrance that we once saw ground for such a degree of assent.—This is all that the greatest part of men are capable of doing in regulating their opinions and judgments, unless a man will exact of them either to retain distinctly in their memories all the proofs concerning any probable truth, and that too in the same order and regular deduction of consequences in which they have formerly placed or seen them; which sometimes is enough to fill a large volume upon one single question: or else they must require a man, for every opinion that he embraces, every day to examine the proofs: both which are impossible. It is unavoidable therefore that the memory be relied on in the case, and that men be persuaded of several opinions whereof the proofs are not actually in their thoughts; nay, which perhaps they are not able actually to recall. Without this the greatest part of men must be either very sceptics, or change every moment, and yield themselves up to whoever, having lately studied the question, offers them arguments; which, for want of memory, they are not able presently to answer.

The ill consequence of this, if our former judgment were not rightly made.—I cannot but own that men's sticking to their past judgment, and adhering firmly to conclusions formerly made, is often the cause of great obstinacy in error and mistake. But the fault is not, that they rely on their memories for what they have before well judged, but because they judged before they had well examined.

Probability is either of matter-of-fact or speculation.—But, to return to the grounds of assent, and the several degrees of it: we are to take notice that the propositions we receive upon inducements of probability are of two sorts; either concerning some particular existence, or, as it is usually termed, "matter-of-fact," which, falling under observation, is capable of human testimony; or else concerning things which, being beyond the discovery of our senses, are not capable of any such testimony.

The concurrent experience of all other men with ours, produces assurance approaching to knowledge.—Concerning the first of these, viz., particular matter-of-fact:—

First: Where any particular thing, consonant to the constant observation of ourselves and others in the like case, comes attested by the concurrent reports of all that mention it, we receive it as easily and build as firmly upon it as if it were certain knowledge; and we reason and act thereupon with as little doubt as if it were perfect demonstration.

Unquestionable testimony and experience for the most part produce confidence.—Secondly: The next degree of probability is, when I find by my own experience, and the agreement of all others that mention it, a thing to be for the most part so; and that the particular instance of it is attested by many and undoubted witnesses; v.g., history giving us such an account of men in all ages, and my own experience, as far as I had an opportunity to observe, confirming it, that most men prefer their private advantage to the public; if all historians that write of Tiberius say, that Tiberius did so, it is extremely probable. And in this case, our assent has a sufficient foundation to raise itself to a degree which we may call "confidence."

Fair testimony, and the nature of the thing indifferent, produce also confident belief.—Thirdly: In things that happen indifferently, as "that a bird should fly this or that way," "that it should thunder on a man's right or left hand," &c., when any particular matter-of-fact is vouched by the concurrent testimony of unsuspected witnesses, there our assent is also unavoidable.

XVII. OF REASON

Wherein reasoning consists.—If general knowledge, as has been shown, consists in a perception of the agreement or disagreement of our own ideas, and the knowledge of the existence of all things without us be had only by our senses; what room then is there for the exercise of any other faculty but outward sense and inward perception? What need is there of reason? Very much; both for the enlargement of our knowledge and regulating our assent: for it hath to do both in knowledge and opinion, and is necessary and assisting to all our other intellectual faculties, and indeed contains two of them, viz., sagacity and illation. By the one it finds out, and by the other it so orders, the intermediate ideas as to discover what connexion there is in each link of the chain, whereby the extremes are held together; and thereby, as it were, to draw into view the truth sought for, which is that we call "illation" or "inference," and consists in nothing but the perception of the connexion there is between the ideas in each step of the deduction, whereby the mind comes to see either the certain agreement or disagreement of any two ideas, as in demonstration, in which it arrives at knowledge; or their probable connexion, on which it gives or withholds its assent, as in opinion. Sense and intuition reach but a very little way. The greatest part of our knowledge depends upon deductions and intermediate ideas: and in those cases where we are fain to substitute assent instead of knowledge, and take propositions for true without being certain they are so, we have need to find out, examine, and compare the grounds of their probability. In both these cases the faculty which finds out the means, and rightly applies them to discover certainty in the one and probability in the other, is that which we call "reason." For, as reason perceives the necessary and indubitable connexion of all the ideas or proofs one to another in each step of any demonstration that produces knowledge, so it likewise perceives the probable connexion of all the ideas or proofs one to another, in every step of a discourse to which it will think assent due. This is the lowest degree of that which can be truly called "reason." For, where the mind does not perceive this probable connexion, where it does not discern whether there be any such connexion or no, there men's opinions are not the product of judgment or the consequence of reason, but the effects of chance and hazard, of a mind floating at all adventures, without choice and without direction.

Its four parts.—So that we may in reason consider these four degrees: The first and highest is the discovering and finding out of proofs; the second, the regular and methodical disposition of them, and laying them in a clear and fit order, to make their connexion and force be plainly and easily perceived; the third is the perceiving their connexion; and the fourth, a making a right conclusion. These several degrees may be observed in any mathematical demonstration: it being one thing, to perceive the connexion of each part as the demonstration is made by another; another, to perceive the dependence of the conclusion on all the parts; a third, to make out a demonstration clearly and neatly one's self; and something different from all these, to have first found out those intermediate ideas or proofs by which it is made.

XVIII. OF FAITH AND REASON, AND THEIR DISTINCT PROVINCES

Necessary to know their boundaries.—It has been above shown, (1.) That we are of necessity ignorant, and want knowledge of all sorts where we want ideas. (2.) That we are ignorant, and want rational knowledge where we want proofs. (3.) That we want general knowledge and certainty as far as we want clear and determined specific ideas. (4.) That we want probability to direct our assent in matters where we have neither knowledge of our own nor testimony of other men to bottom our reason upon.

From these things thus premised, I think we may come to lay down the measures and boundaries between faith and reason; the want whereof may possibly have been the cause, if not of great disorders, yet at least of great disputes, and perhaps mistakes, in the world: for till it be resolved how far we are to be guided by reason, and how far by faith, we shall in vain dispute and endeavour to convince one another in matters of religion.

Faith and reason what, as contradistinguished.—I find every sect, as far as reason will help them, make use of it gladly; and, where it fails them, they cry out, "It is matter of faith, and above reason." And I do not see how they can argue with anyone, or ever convince a gainsayer, who makes use of the same plea, without setting down strict boundaries between faith and reason, which ought to be the first point established in all questions where faith has anything to do.

Reason therefore here, as contradistinguished to faith, I take to be the discovery of the certainty or probability of such propositions or truths which the mind arrives at by deduction made from such ideas which it has got by the use of its natural faculties, viz., by sensation or reflection.

Faith, on the other side, is the assent to any proposition, not thus made out by the deductions of reason, but upon the credit of the proposer, as coming from God in some extraordinary way of communication. This way of discovering truths to men we call "revelation."

If the boundaries be not set between faith and reason, no enthusiasm or extravagancy in religion can be contradicted.—If the provinces of faith and reason are not kept distinct by these boundaries, there will, in matter of religion, be no room for reason at all; and those extravagant opinions and ceremonies that are to be found in the several religions of the world will not deserve to be blamed; for to this crying up of faith in opposition to reason, we may, I think, in good measure, ascribe those absurdities that fill almost all the religions which possess and divide mankind. For men, having been principled with an opinion that they must not consult reason in the things of religion, however apparently contradictory to common sense and the very principles of all their knowledge, have let loose their fancies and natural superstition; and have been by them led into so strange opinions and extravagant practices in religion, that a considerate man cannot but stand amazed at their follies, and judge them so far from being acceptable to the great and wise God, that he cannot avoid thinking them ridiculous and offensive to a sober, good man. So that, in effect, religion, which should most distinguish us from beasts, and ought most peculiarly to elevate us as rational creatures above brutes, is that wherein men often appear most irrational, and more senseless than beasts themselves.

XIX. OF ENTHUSIASM

Love of truth necessary.—He that would seriously set upon the search of truth, ought in the first place, to prepare his mind with a love of it; for he that loves it not will not take much pains to get it, nor be much concerned when he misses it. There is nobody in the commonwealth of learning who does not profess himself a lover of truth; and there is not a rational creature that would not take it amiss to be thought otherwise of. And yet, for all this, one may truly say, there are very few lovers of truth for truth's sake, even amongst those who persuade themselves that they are so. How a man may know whether he be so in earnest, is worth inquiry: and I think there is this one unerring mark of it, viz., the not entertaining any proposition with greater assurance than the proofs it is built upon will warrant. Whoever goes beyond this measure of assent, it is plain, receives not truth in the love of it; loves not truth for truth's sake, but for some other by-end.

Force of enthusiasm.—Upon this occasion I shall take the liberty to consider a third ground of assent, which, with some men, has the same authority and is as confidently relied on, as either faith or reason: I mean enthusiasm: which, laying by reason, would set up revelation without it; whereby in effect it takes away both reason and revelation, and substitutes in the room of it the ungrounded fancies of a man's own brain, and assumes them for a foundation both of opinion and conduct.

Reason and revelation.—Reason is natural revelation, whereby the eternal Father of light, and Fountain of all knowledge, communicates to mankind that portion of truth which he has laid within the reach of their natural faculties. Revelation is natural reason enlarged by a new set of discoveries communicated by God immediately, which reason vouches the truth of by the testimony and proofs it gives that they come from God. So that he that takes away reason to make way for revelation, puts out the light of both; and does much-what the same as if he would persuade a man to put out his eyes, the better to receive the remote light of an invisible star by a telescope.

Enthusiasm mistaken for seeing and feeling.—Though the odd opinions and extravagant actions enthusiasm has run men into were enough to warn them against this wrong principle, so apt to misguide them both in their belief and conduct; yet the love of something extraordinary, the ease and glory it is to be inspired and be above the common and natural ways of knowledge, so flatters many men's laziness, ignorance, and vanity, that when once they are got into this way of immediate revelation, of illumination without search, and of certainty without proof and without examination, it is a hard matter to get them out of it. Reason is lost upon them; they are above it: they see the light infused into their understandings, and cannot be mistaken; it is clear and visible there like the light of bright sunshine; shows itself, and needs no other proof but its own evidence; they feel the hand of God moving them within, and the impulses of the Spirit, and cannot be mistaken in what they feel. Thus they support themselves, and are sure reason hath nothing to do with what they see and feel in themselves; what they have a sensible experience of, admits no doubt, needs no probation.

XX. OF WRONG ASSENT, OR ERROR

Causes of error.—Knowledge being to be had only of visible certain truth, error is not a fault of our knowledge, but a mistake of our judgment, giving assent to that which is not true.

But if assent be grounded on likelihood, if the proper object and motive of our assent be probability, and that probability consists in what is laid down in the foregoing chapters, it will be demanded, how men come to give their assents contrary to probability? For there is nothing more common than contrariety of opinions; nothing more obvious than that one man wholly disbelieves what another only doubts of, and a third steadfastly believes and firmly adheres to. The reasons whereof, though they may be very various yet, I suppose, may be all reduced to these four: (1.) Want of proofs. (2.) Want of ability to use them. (3.) Want of will to use them. (4.) Wrong measures of probability.

First: Want of proofs.—First: By "want of proofs," I do not mean only the want of those proofs which are nowhere extant, and so are nowhere to be had; but the want even of those proofs which are in being, or might be procured. And thus men want proofs who have not the convenience or opportunity to make experiments and observations themselves, tending to the proof of any proposition; nor likewise the convenience to inquire into and collect the testimonies of others: and in this state are the greatest part of mankind who are given up to labour, and enslaved to the necessity of their mean condition, whose lives are worn out only in the provisions for living.

Secondly: Want of skill to use them.—Secondly: Those who want skill to use those evidences they have of probabilities, who cannot carry a train of consequences in their heads, nor weigh exactly the preponderancy of contrary proofs and testimonies making every circumstance its due allowance, may be easily misled to assent to positions that are not probable. There are some men of one, some but of two syllogisms, and no more; and others that can but advance one step farther. These cannot always discern that side on which the strongest proofs lie, cannot constantly follow that which in itself is the more probable opinion.

Thirdly: Want of will to use them.—Thirdly: There are another sort of people that want proofs, not because they are out of their reach, but because they will not use them; who, though they have riches and leisure enough, and want neither parts nor other helps, are yet never the better for them. Their hot pursuit of pleasure, or constant drudgery in business, engages some men's thoughts elsewhere; laziness and oscitancy in general, or a particular aversion for books, study, and meditation, keep others from any serious thoughts at all; and some, out of fear that an impartial inquiry would not favour those opinions which best suit their prejudices, lives, and designs, content themselves, without examination, to take upon trust what they find convenient and in fashion.

Fourthly: Wrong measures of probability, whereof.—Fourthly: There remains yet the last sort, who, even where the real probabilities appear, and are plainly laid before them, do not admit of the conviction, nor yield unto manifest reasons, but do either suspend their assent, or give it to the less probable opinion. And to this danger are those exposed who have taken up wrong measures of probability, which are, (1.) Propositions that are not in themselves certain and evident, but doubtful and false, taken up for principles. (2.) Received hypotheses. (3.) Predominant passions or inclinations. (4.) Authority.

XXI. OF THE DIVISION OF THE SCIENCES

Three sorts.—All that can fall within the compass of human understanding being either, first, the nature of things as they are in themselves, their relations, and their manner of operation: or, secondly, that which man himself ought to do, as a rational and voluntary agent, for the attainment of any end, especially happiness: or, thirdly, the ways and means whereby the knowledge of both the one and the other of these is attained and communicated: I think science may be divided properly into these three sorts:—

First: Physica.—First: The knowledge of things as they are in their own proper beings, their constitutions, properties, and operations, whereby I mean not only matter and body, but spirits also, which have their proper natures, constitutions, and operations, as well as bodies. The end of this is bare speculative truth: and whatsoever can afford the mind of man any such falls under this branch, whether it be God himself, angels, spirits, bodies, or any of their affections, as number, and figure, &c.

Secondly: Practica.—Secondly: The skill of right applying our own powers and actions for the attainment of things good and useful. The most considerable under this head is ethics, which is the seeking out those rules and measures of human actions which lead to happiness, and the means to practise them. The end of this is not bare speculation and the knowledge of truth; but right, and a conduct suitable to it.

Thirdly: Thirdly: The third branch may be called the "doctrine of signs," the most usual whereof being words; the business whereof is to consider the nature of signs the mind makes use of for the understanding of things, or conveying its knowledge to others. For, since the things the mind contemplates are none of them, besides itself, present to the understanding, it is necessary that something else, as a sign or representation of the thing it considers, should be present to it: and these are ideas. And because the scene of ideas that make one man's thoughts cannot be laid open to the immediate view of another, nor laid up anywhere but in the memory, a not very sure repository; therefore, to communicate our thoughts to one another, as well as record them for our own use, signs of our ideas are also necessary. Those which men have found most convenient, and therefore generally make use of, are articulate sounds. The consideration, then, of ideas and words as the great instruments of knowledge, makes no despicable part of their contemplation who would take a view of human knowledge in the whole extent of it. And perhaps, if they were distinctly weighed and duly considered, they would afford us another sort of logic and critic than what we have been hitherto acquainted with.

This is the first division of the objects of knowledge.—This seems to me the first and most general, as well as natural, division of the objects of our understanding. For a man can employ his thoughts about nothing but either the contemplation of things themselves for the discovery of truth; or about the things in his own power, which are his own actions, for the attainment of his own ends; or the signs the mind makes use of, both in the one and the other, and the right ordering of them for its clearer information. All which three, viz., things as they are in themselves knowable, actions as they depend on us in order to happiness, and the right use of signs in order to knowledge, being *toto cælo* different, they seemed to me to be the three great provinces of the intellectual world, wholly separate and distinct one from another.

THE CRITIQUE
OF PURE REASON

by

IMMANUEL KANT

CONTENTS

Critique of Pure Reason

IMMANUEL KANT

1724–1804

IMMANUEL KANT was born at Königsberg, East Prussia, on April 22, 1724, and never traveled more than forty miles from his birthplace during the entire eighty years of his life.

The grandfather of Kant was an emigrant from Scotland who spelled his name "Cant," a name not uncommon in the north of Scotland. His son, the father of the philosopher, changed the spelling to Kant, since the "C" was often pronounced "S" by the East Prussians.

Kant's father was a fairly prosperous saddler of Königsberg. Both he and Immanuel's mother were devotees of the Pietistic movement which was then strong in their section of the country. At Königsberg the Pietists were kind and gentle and believed that life's tragedies should be met with simple faith in the rightness of things. They emphasized the spiritual rather than the material side of life. The strong influence of this attitude is seen in Kant's later thinking and writing.

When, however, in his tenth year Kant entered the Collegium Fredericianum, another side of Pietism was revealed to him. This consisted of formalism and intellectual restraint —fixed hours of prayer and a compulsory morality which resulted in hypocrisy and affectation.

During his early schooling Kant planned to enter the ministry. He studied theology diligently, but he soon found his chief interest to lie in the classics. He became the school's most proficient Latin scholar. This interest lingered with him throughout his life, and his mastery of the Latin writers is evident in much of his published work.

At sixteen Kant entered the University of Königsberg, where he turned from the classics to physics and mathematics.

By this time he had definitely decided that his future was not in the Church. Because of the death of his father in 1746, Kant was forced to earn his living as a private tutor. Although he disliked the drudgery of teaching, he felt that his association with youngsters of noble birth would polish off the rough edges of his personality and his style.

In 1755, through the influence of a friend named Richter, Kant was enabled to resume his university studies. In the fall of that year he was graduated as doctor and qualified as *Privat-dozent*—a man permitted to teach at the university for fees. For fifteen years Kant continued in this capacity at the university. Twice he failed to gain an appointment as professor at Königsberg. Other offers were made him, but he refused them all, determined to remain at home. His lectures were gaining in popularity, and his reputation was growing all the time. At first he confined his teaching largely to physics, but gradually he expanded his scholastic activities until they embraced nearly all the phases of philosophy.

Kant's principles of teaching were few but definite. He insisted that his students should obtain a firm foundation of their subject before they began to speculate. He would never give his hearers a ready-made philosophy, since for him no such philosophy existed. Rather he would so teach his students that they might be able to build their own systems of philosophy. Kant concentrated his attention upon the average minds among his pupils. In defense of this attitude he argued that the geniuses would take care of themselves, the dunces were beyond remedy, and those of the middle group alone needed help if they were to succeed.

In 1770 Kant was given the chair of logic and metaphysics at Königsberg, and eleven years later he gave to the world one of the greatest books in the history of human thought—the *Critique of Pure Reason*. This was followed in 1783 by the *Prolegomena,* an attempt to state the argument of the *Critique* in more readable form and to amplify some of the more obscure arguments. Then, in 1787, a second edition of the *Critique,* with some modifications, appeared. This is the edition which is condensed in this volume.

The publication of the *Critique of Pure Reason* made Kant famous. Within ten years after the appearance of the *Critique,* his philosophy was being expounded in all the leading universities of the country. Pupils came from all over Germany to study with him, and scholars made pilgrimages to

Königsberg to see him and to talk with him. Indeed, he was taken as an oracle on almost every phase of human knowledge, from medicine to metaphysics.

And he received honors on every side. The prime minister of Frederick the Great, Count Zedlitz, to whom Kant had dedicated his *Critique,* brought it to the attention of persons powerful in the state. While Zedlitz remained in office, Kant enjoyed every favor of the court.

But this was not to last. Upon the death of Frederick the Great, Frederick William II came to the throne. He was a dissipated man of weak character, entranced by spiritualism and mysticism. The liberating forces that had brought about the French Revolution terrified him. Zedlitz was dismissed, and Wöllner, a bigot, was placed at the head of the department of religion and education. Also, a board of censors was appointed. This group sought to prohibit Kant from writing, but did not succeed.

In 1794, when Kant was about ready to publish his *Religion within the Boundaries of Pure Reason,* he first sought advice from the theological faculty of Königsberg. They told him to go ahead with the publication, and he did so. But immediately a royal mandate was issued and he was prohibited from writing or speaking on theology. Kant accepted this prohibition as "the duty of a subject" during the lifetime of the ruler. Upon his death and the coming to power of his successor, a man of more liberal ideas, Kant published an account of the controversy and again turned his attention to religious matters.

This struggle with the ruling powers, however, seems to have taken all the ambition out of Kant. In 1794 he withdrew largely from society, and in 1795 he gave up all his classes save one on logic and metaphysics. Then, in 1797, after forty-two years of academic work, he retired from the university. The spirit of the man was broken.

From this point on, Kant declined in strength and his mind began to disintegrate. His memory failed him, strings of words and melodies from his childhood raced through his mind, his nights were disturbed by horrifying dreams and his days with a strange restlessness.

On February 12, 1804, Kant died affirming that, despite all that had happened to him and the many injustices which a bigoted and none too intelligent ruler had heaped upon him, "I have not lost my feeling for humanity."

Besides the *Critique of Pure Reason,* Kant completed two other works of major importance in the history of philosophy. These are the *Critique of Practical Reason* and the *Critique of Judgment.* These works form a trinity of Kant's thought. The first is an analysis of pure reason showing its limits and its possibilities. The second carries over this method to the field of ethics, while in the third Kant discusses the problems growing out of the beauty and purposiveness of Nature.

The world we live in, observes Kant, cannot be understood through our senses; but it can be understood through our intellect, or reason. We can "see" the world only with our "inner" eye. And what do we see when we thus focus our inner eye upon the mystery of the world? We see that we cannot be positive about anything, that we must dispose of all definite assertions about man and nature, life and death, body and soul, matter and mind, and spirit and God.

At this point, however, Kant hesitates. His kindly soul, as Heine points out, is unable to deprive his old servant Lampe of his belief in God. "For without his God, the poor fellow cannot be happy; and people really ought to be happy in this world." And so Kant acknowledges the necessity of God in this world. *Accept* a belief in God because you *need* such a belief. For, if you believe in God, you thereby assume a *moral obligation*—Kant calls it the *categorical imperative*—in accordance with God's will.

This belief in God and the consequent acceptance of a moral obligation, continues Kant, leads us to the belief that we have a free will to choose between what is morally right and morally wrong. And it leads us to the further belief that after what we call "death" there is a continuance of life in which the consequences of our right and wrong actions will be finally adjudged.

These "truths"—asserts Kant—can be revealed not only to the philosopher but even to the layman if he directs the inner eye of his mind upon the two great mysteries of the world—"the starry heavens above, and the moral law within."

And then, having made all these positive assertions, Kant finishes his argument upon a note of doubt. The pity of the poet within him gives way to the impartiality of the philosopher. "All this is what I think. But how do I know that what I think is right?"

THE CRITIQUE OF PURE REASON

INTRODUCTION

THAT all our knowledge begins with experience there can be no doubt. But, though all our knowledge begins with experience, it by no means follows, that all arises out of experience. For, on the contrary, it is quite possible that our empirical knowledge is a compound of that which we receive through impressions, and that which the faculty of cognition supplies from itself (sensuous impressions giving merely the *occasion*), an addition which we cannot distinguish from the original element given by sense, till long practice has made us attentive to, and skilful in separating it. It is, therefore, a question which requires close investigation, and is not to be answered at first sight—whether there exists a knowledge altogether independent of experience, and even of all sensuous impressions? Knowledge of this kind is called *a priori,* in contradistinction to empirical knowledge, which has its sources *a posteriori,* that is, in experience.

By the term 'knowledge *a priori'* we shall in the sequel understand, not such as is independent of this or that kind of experience, but such as is absolutely so of *all* experience. Opposed to this is empirical knowledge, or that which is possible only *a posteriori,* that is, through experience. Knowledge *a priori* is either pure or impure. Pure knowledge *a priori* is that with which no empirical element is mixed up.

2

The question now is as to a *criterion,* by which we may securely distinguish a pure from an empirical cognition. Now, in the first place, if we have a proposition which contains the idea of necessity in its very conception, it is a judgment *a priori;* if, moreover, it is not derived from any other proposition, unless from one equally involving the idea of necessity, it is absolutely *a priori.* Secondly, an empirical judgment never exhibits strict and absolute, but only assumed and comparative universality; therefore, the most we can say is—so far as we have hitherto observed, there is no exception to this or that rule. If, on the other hand, a judgment carries with it strict and absolute universality, that is, admits of no possible exception, it is not derived from experience, but is valid absolutely *a priori*.

Not only in judgments, however, but even in conceptions, is an *a priori* origin manifest. For example, if we take away by degrees from our conceptions of a body all that can be referred to mere sensuous experience—colour, hardness or softness, weight, even impenetrability—the body will then vanish; but the space which it occupied still remains, and this it is utterly impossible to annihilate in thought. Again, if we take away, in like manner, from our empirical conception of any object, corporeal or incorporeal, all properties which mere experience has taught us to connect with it, still we cannot think away those through which we cogitate it as substance, or adhering to substance, although our conception of substance is more determined than that of an object. Compelled, therefore, by that necessity with which the conception of substance forces itself upon us, we must confess that it has its seat in our faculty of cognition *a priori*.

3

Of far more importance than all that has been above said, is the consideration that certain of our cognitions rise completely above the sphere of all possible experience, and by means of conceptions, to which there exists in the whole extent of experience no corresponding object, seem to extend the range of our judgments beyond its bounds. And just in this transcendental or supersensible sphere, where experience affords us neither instruction nor guidance, lie the investigations of *Reason,* which, on account of their importance, we consider far preferable to, and as having a far more elevated aim than, all that the understanding can achieve within the sphere of sensuous phenomena. These unavoidable problems of mere pure reason are God, Freedom (of will), and Immortality. The science which, with all its preliminaries, has for its especial object the solution of these problems is named metaphysics—a science which is at the very outset dogmatical, that is, it confidently takes upon itself the execution of this task without any previous investigation of the ability or inability of reason for such an undertaking.

Instead of thus trying to build without a foundation, it is rather to be expected that we should long ago have put the question, how the understanding can arrive at these *a priori* cognitions, and what is the extent, validity, and worth which they may possess?

4

In all judgments wherein the relation of a subject to the predicate is cogitated, this relation is possible in two different ways. Either the predicate B belongs to the subject A, as somewhat which is contained in the conception A; or the predicate B lies completely out of the conception A, although it stands in connection with it. In the first instance, I term the judgment analytical, in the second, synthetical. Analytical judgments are therefore those in which the connection of the predicate with the subject is cogitated through identity; those in which this connection is cogitated without identity, are called synthetical judgments. The former may be called *explicative,* the latter *augmentative* judgments; because the former add in the predicate nothing to the conception of the subject, but only analyse it into its constituent conceptions, which were thought already in the subject, although in a confused manner; the latter add to our conceptions of the subject a predicate which was not contained in it, and which no analysis could ever have discovered therein.

Judgments of experience, as such, are always synthetical. For it would be absurd to think of grounding an analytical judgment on experience, because in forming such a judgment I need not go out of the sphere of my conceptions, and therefore recourse to the testimony of experience is quite unnecessary.

But to synthetical judgments *a priori,* such aid is entirely wanting. If I go out of and beyond the conception A, in order to recognize another B as connected with it, what foundation have I to rest on, whereby to render the synthesis possible? I have here no longer the advantage of looking out in the sphere of experience for what I want.

5

Mathematical judgments are always synthetical. Hitherto this fact, though incontestably true and very important in its consequences, seems to have escaped the analysts of the human mind, nay, to be in complete opposition to all their conjectures.

Before all, be it observed, that proper mathematical propositions are always judgments *a priori,* and not empirical, because they carry along with them the conception of necessity, which cannot be given by experience. If this be demurred to, it matters not; I will then limit my assertion to *pure* mathematics, the very conception of which implies that it consists of knowledge altogether non-empirical and *a priori.*

The science of Natural Philosophy contains in itself synthetical judgments *a priori,* as principles. I shall adduce two propositions. For instance, the proposition, 'In all changes of the material world, the quantity of matter remains unchanged'; or, that, 'In all communication of motion, action and reaction must always be equal.' In both of these, not only is the necessity, and therefore their origin *a priori* clear, but also that they are synthetical propositions. For in the conception of matter, I do not cogitate its permanency, but merely its presence in space, which it fills. I therefore really go out of and beyond the conception of matter, in order to think on to it something *a priori,* which I did not think in it.

As to Metaphysics, even if we look upon it merely as an attempted science, yet, from the nature of human reason, an indispensable one, we find that it must contain synthetical propositions *a priori.* It is not merely the duty of metaphysics to dissect, and thereby analytically to illustrate the conceptions which we form *a priori* of things; but we seek to widen the range of our *a priori* knowledge. For this purpose, we must avail ourselves of such principles as add something to the original conception— something not identical with, nor contained in it, and by means of synthetical judgments *a priori,* leave far behind us the limits of experience; for example, in the proposition, 'the world must have a beginning,' and such like. Thus metaphysics, according to the proper aim of the science, consists merely of synthetical propositions *a priori.*

6

It is extremely advantageous to be able to bring a number of investigations under the formula of a single problem. For in this manner, we not only facilitate our own labour, inasmuch as we define it clearly to ourselves, but also render it more easy for others to decide whether we have done justice to our undertaking. The proper problem of pure reason, then, is contained in the question: 'How are synthetical judgments *a priori* possible?'

That metaphysical science has hitherto remained in so vacillating a state of uncertainty and contradiction, is only to be attributed to the fact, that this great problem, and perhaps even the difference between analytical and synthetical judgments, did not sooner suggest itself to philosophers. Upon the solution of this problem, or upon sufficient proof of the impossibility of synthetical knowledge *a priori,* depends the existence or downfall of the science of metaphysics.

In the solution of the above problem is at the same time comprehended the possibility of the use of pure reason in the foundation and construction of all sciences which contain theoretical knowledge *a priori* of objects, that is to say, the answer to the following questions:

How is pure mathematical science possible?

How is pure natural science possible?

Respecting these sciences, as they do certainly exist, it may with propriety be asked, *how* they are possible?—for that they must be possible, is shown by the fact of their really existing. But as to metaphysics, the miserable progress it has hitherto made, and the fact that of no one system yet brought forward, as far as regards its true aim, can it be said that this science really exists, leaves any one at liberty to doubt with reason the very possibility of its existence.

We may and must, therefore, regard the attempts hitherto made to establish metaphysical science dogmatically as non-existent. For what of analysis, that is, mere dissection of conceptions, is contained in one or other, is not the aim of, but only a preparation for metaphysics proper, which has for its object the extension, by means of synthesis, of our *a priori* knowledge. And for this purpose, mere analysis is of course useless, because it only shows what is contained in these conceptions, but not how we arrive, *a priori,* at them; and this it is her duty to show, in order to be able afterwards to determine their valid use in regard to all objects of experience, to all knowledge in general.

7

From all that has been said, there results the idea of a particular science, which may be called the *Critique of Pure Reason*. For reason is the faculty which furnishes us with the principles of knowledge *a priori*. Hence, pure reason is the faculty which contains the principles of cognizing anything absolutely *a priori*. I apply the term *transcendental* to all knowledge which is not so much occupied with objects as with the mode of our cognition of these objects, so far as this mode of cognition is possible *a priori*. A system of such conceptions would be called *Transcendental Philosophy*.

Transcendental philosophy is the idea of a science, for which the *Critique of Pure Reason* must sketch the whole plan architectonically, that is, from principles, with a full guarantee for the validity and stability of all the parts which enter into the building. It is the system of all the principles of pure reason. If this *Critique* itself does not assume the title of transcendental philosophy, it is only because, to be a complete system, it ought to contain a full analysis of all human knowledge *a priori*.

To the *Critique of Pure Reason,* therefore, belongs all that constitutes transcendental philosophy; and it is the complete idea of transcendental philosophy, but still not the science itself; because it only proceeds so far with the analysis as is necessary to the power of judging completely of our synthetical knowledge *a priori*.

Transcendental Doctrine of Elements

PART FIRST: TRANSCENDENTAL AESTHETIC

Introductory

IN WHATEVER MODE, or by whatsoever means, our knowledge may relate to objects, it is at least quite clear, that the only manner in which it immediately relates to them, is by means of an intuition. To this as the indispensable groundwork, all thought points. But an intuition can take place only in so far as the object is given to us. This, again, is only possible, to man at least, on condition that the object affect the mind in a certain manner. The capacity for receiving representations (receptivity) through the mode in which we are affected by objects, is called *sensibility*. By means of sensibility, therefore, objects are given to us, and it alone furnishes us with intuitions; by the understanding they are *thought,* and from it arise conceptions. But all thought must directly, or indirectly, by means of certain signs, relate ultimately to intuitions; consequently, with us, to sensibility, because in no other way can an object be given to us.

The effect of an object upon the faculty of representation, so far as we are affected by the said object, is sensation. That sort of intuition which relates to an object by means of sensation, is called an empirical intuition. The undetermined object of an empirical intuition, is called *phenomenon.* That which in the phenomenon corresponds to the sensation, I term its *matter;* but that which effects that the content of the phenomenon can be arranged under certain relations, I call its *form.* But that in which our sensations are merely arranged, and by which they are susceptible of assuming a certain form, cannot be itself sensation. It is, then, the matter of all phenomena that is given to us *a posteriori;* the form must lie ready *a priori* for them in the mind, and consequently can be regarded separately from all sensation.

I call all representations *pure,* in the transcendental meaning of the word, wherein nothing is met with that belongs to sensation. And accordingly we find existing in the mind *a priori,* the pure form of sensuous intuitions in general, in which all the manifold content of the phenomenal world is arranged and viewed under certain relations. This pure form of sensibility I shall call pure intuition. Thus, if I take away from our representation of a body, all that the understanding thinks as belonging to it, as substance, force, divisibility, etc., and also whatever belongs to sensation, as impenetrability, hardness, colour, etc.; yet there is still something left us from this empirical intuition, namely, extension and shape. These belong to pure intuition, which exists *a priori* in the mind, as a mere form of sensibility, and without any real object of the senses or any sensation.

The science of all the principles of sensibility *a priori,* I call Transcendental Aesthetic. There must then, be such a science forming the first part of the transcendental doctrine of elements, in contradistinction to that part which contains the principles of pure thought, and which is called transcendental logic.

I. OF SPACE

Metaphysical Exposition of This Conception

BY MEANS of the external sense, we represent to ourselves objects as without us, and these all in space. Therein alone are their shapes, dimensions, and relations to each other determined or determinable. The internal sense, by means of which the mind contemplates itself or its internal state, gives, indeed, no intuition of the soul as an object; yet there is nevertheless a determinate form, under which alone the contemplation of our internal state is possible, so that all which relates to the inward determinations of the mind is represented in relations of time. Of time we cannot have any external intuition, any more than we can have an internal intuition of space.

Space is not a conception which has been derived from outward experiences. For, in order that certain sensations may relate to something without me; in like manner, in order that I may represent them not merely as without of and near to each other, but also in separate places, the representation of space must already exist as a foundation. Consequently, the representation of space cannot be borrowed from the relations of external phenomena through experience; but, on the contrary, this external experience is itself only possible through the said antecedent representation.

Space then is a necessary representation *a priori,* which serves for the foundation of all external intuitions. We never can imagine or make a representation to ourselves of the non-existence of space, though we may easily enough think that no objects are found in it. It must, therefore, be considered as the condition of the possibility of phenomena, and by no means as a determination dependent on them, and is a representation *a priori,* which necessarily supplies the basis for external phenomena.

Space is no discursive, or as we say, general conception of the relations of things, but a pure intuition. For in the first place, we can only represent to ourselves one space, and when we talk of divers spaces, we mean only parts of one and the same space. Moreover, these parts cannot antecede this one all-embracing space, as the component parts from which the aggregate can be made up, but can be cogitated only as existing in it. Space is essentially one, and multiplicity in it, consequently the general notion of spaces, of this or that space, depends solely upon limitations. Hence it follows that an *a priori* intuition lies at the root of all our conceptions of space.

Space is represented as an infinite given quantity. Now every conception must indeed be considered as a representation which is contained in an infinite multitude of different possible representations, which, therefore, comprises these under itself; but no conception, as such, can be so conceived, as if it contained within itself an infinite multitude of representations. Nevertheless, space is so conceived of, for all parts of space are equally capable of being produced to infinity. Consequently, the original representation of space is an intuition *a priori,* and not a conception.

Conclusions

Space does not represent any property of objects as things in themselves, nor does it represent them in their relations to each other.

Space is nothing else than the form of all phenomena of the external sense, that is, the subjective condition of the sensibility, under which alone external intuition is possible.

II. OF TIME

Metaphysical Exposition of This Conception

TIME is not an empirical conception. For neither co-existence nor succession would be perceived by us, if the representation of time did not exist as a foundation *a priori.* Without this presupposition we could not represent to ourselves that things exist together at one and the same time, or at different times.

Time is a necessary representation, lying at the foundation of all our intuitions. With regard to phenomena in general, we cannot think away time from them, and represent them to ourselves as out of and unconnected with time, but we can quite well represent to ourselves time void of phenomena. Time is therefore given *a priori.*

On this necessity *a priori* is also founded the possibility of apodeictic principles of the relations of time, or axioms of time in general, such as: 'Time has only one dimension,' 'Different times are not co-existent but successive.' These principles cannot be derived from experience, for it would give neither strict universality nor apodeictic certainty.

Time is not a discursive, or as it is called, general conception, but a pure form of the sensuous intuition. Different times are merely parts of one and the same time.

The infinity of time signifies nothing more than that every determined quantity of time is possible only through limitations of one time lying at the foundation. Consequently, the original representation, time, must be given as unlimited.

Conclusions

Time is not something which subsists of itself, or which inheres in things as an objective determination, and therefore remains, when abstraction is made of the subjective conditions of the intuition of things.

Time is nothing else than the form of the internal sense, that is, of the intuitions of self and of our internal state. For time cannot be any determination of outward phenomena. It has to do neither with shape nor position; on the contrary, it determines the relation of representations in our internal state.

Time is the formal condition *a priori* of all phenomena whatsoever. Space, as the pure form of external intuition, is limited as a condition *a priori* to external phenomena alone. On the other hand, because all representations, whether they have or have not external things for their objects, still in themselves, as determinations of the mind, belong to our internal state; and because this internal state is subject to the formal condition of the internal intuition, that is, to time—time is a condition *a priori* of all phenomena whatsoever—the *immediate* condition of all internal, and thereby the *mediate* condition of all external phenomena.

PART SECOND: TRANSCENDENTAL LOGIC

INTRODUCTION: IDEA OF A TRANSCENDENTAL LOGIC

Of Logic in General

OUR KNOWLEDGE springs from two main sources in the mind, the first of which is the faculty or power of receiving representations; the second is the power of cognizing by means of these representations. Through the first an object is given to us; through the second, it is, in relation to the representation, thought. Intuition and conceptions constitute, therefore, the elements of all our knowledge, so that neither conceptions without an intuition in some way corresponding to them, nor intuition without conceptions, can afford us a cognition. Both are either pure or empirical. They are empirical, when sensation is contained in them; and pure, when no sensation is mixed with the representation. Sensations we may call the matter of sensuous cognition. Pure intuition consequently contains merely the form under which something is intuited, and pure conception only the form of the thought of an object. Only pure intuitions and pure conceptions are possible *a priori;* the empirical only *a posteriori.*

We apply the term *sensibility* to the receptivity of the mind for impressions, in so far as it is in some way affected; and, on the other hand, we call the faculty of spontaneously producing representations, or the spontaneity of cognition, *understanding.* Our nature is so constituted, that intuition with us never can be other than sensuous, that is, it contains only the mode in which we are affected by objects. On the other hand, the faculty of thinking the object of sensuous intuition, is the understanding. Neither of these faculties has a preference over the other. Without the sensuous faculty no object would be given to us, and without the understanding no object would be thought. Thoughts without content are void; intuitions without conceptions, blind. Hence it is as necessary for the mind to make its conceptions sensuous, as to make its intuitions intelligible. Neither of these faculties can exchange its proper function. Understanding cannot intuit, and the sensuous faculty cannot think. In no other way than from the united operation of both, can knowledge arise. But no one ought, on this account, to overlook the difference of the elements contributed by each; we have rather great reason carefully to separate and distinguish them. We therefore distinguish the science of the laws of sensibility, that is, Aesthetic, from the science of the laws of the understanding, that is, Logic.

Of Transcendental Logic

General logic, as we have seen, makes abstraction of all content of cognition, that is, of all relation of cognition to its object, and regards only the logical form in the relation of cognitions to each other, that is, the form of thought in general. But as we have both pure and empirical intuitions, in like manner a distinction might be drawn between pure and empirical thought. In this case, there would exist a kind of logic, in which we should not make abstraction of all content of cognition; for that logic which should comprise merely the laws of pure thought, would of course exclude all those cognitions which were of empirical content. This kind of logic would also examine the origin of our cognitions of objects, so far as that origin cannot be ascribed to the objects themselves; while, on the contrary, general logic has nothing to do with the origin of our cognitions, but contemplates our representations, be they given primitively *a priori* in ourselves, or be they only of empirical origin, solely according to the laws which the understanding observes in employing them in the process of thought, in relation to each other. Consequently, general logic treats of the form of the understanding only, which can be applied to representations, from whatever source they may have arisen.

And here I shall make a remark, which the reader must bear well in mind in the course of the following considerations, to wit, that not every cognition *a priori*, but only those through which we cognize that and how certain representations (intuitions or conceptions) are applied or are possible only *a priori;* that is to say, the *a priori* possibility of cognition and the *a priori* use of it are transcendental. Therefore neither is space, nor any *a priori* geometrical determination of space, a transcendental representation, but only the knowledge that such a representation is not of empirical origin, and the possibility of its relating to objects of experience, although itself *a priori,* can be called transcendental. So also, the application of space to objects in general, would be transcendental; but if it be limited to objects of sense, it is empirical. Thus, the distinction of the transcendental and empirical belongs only to the critique of cognitions, and does not concern the relation of these to their object.

Of the Division of Transcendental Logic into Transcendental Analytic and Dialectic

In transcendental logic we isolate the understanding and select from our cognition merely that part of thought which has its origin in the understanding alone. The exercise of this pure cognition, however, depends upon this as its condition, that objects to which it may be applied be given to us in intuition, for without intuition the whole of our cognition is without objects, and is therefore quite void. That part of transcendental logic, then, which treats of the elements of pure cognition of the understanding, and of the principles without which no object at all can be thought, is transcendental analytic, and at the same time a logic of truth. For no cognition can contradict it, without losing at the same time all content, that is, losing all reference to an object, and therefore all truth. But because we are very easily seduced into employing these pure cognitions and principles of the understanding by themselves, and that even beyond the boundaries of experience, which yet is the only source whence we can obtain matter on which those pure conceptions may be employed—understanding runs the risk of making, by means of empty sophisms, a material and objective use of the mere formal principles of the pure understanding, and of passing judgments on objects without distinction—objects which are not given to us, nay, perhaps cannot be given to us in any way. Now, as it ought properly to be only a canon for judging of the empirical use of the understanding, this kind of logic is misused when we seek to employ it as an organon of the universal and unlimited exercise of the understanding, and attempt with the pure understanding alone to judge synthetically, affirm, and determine respecting objects in general. In this case the exercise of the pure understanding becomes dialectical. The second part of our transcendental logic must therefore be a critique of dialectical illusion, and this critique we shall term Transcendental Dialectic—not meaning it as an art of producing dogmatically such illusion, but as a critique of understanding and reason in regard to their hyperphysical use. This critique will expose the groundless nature of the pretensions of these two faculties, and invalidate their claims to the discovery and enlargement of our cognitions merely by means of transcendental principles, and show that the proper employment of these faculties is to test the judgments made by the pure understanding, and to guard it from sophistical delusion.

TRANSCENDENTAL LOGIC

FIRST DIVISION: TRANSCENDENTAL ANALYTIC

TRANSCENDENTAL ANALYTIC is the dissection of the whole of our *a priori* knowledge into the elements of the pure cognition of the understanding. In order to effect our purpose, it is necessary: (1) That the conceptions be pure and not empirical; (2) That they belong not to intuition and sensibility, but to thought and understanding; (3) That they be elementary conceptions, and as such, quite different from deduced or compound conceptions; (4) That our table of these elementary conceptions be complete, and fill up the whole sphere of the pure understanding. Now this completeness of a science cannot be accepted with confidence on the guarantee of a mere estimate of its existence in an aggregate formed only by means of repeated experiments and attempts. The completeness which we require is possible only by means of an idea of the totality of the *a priori* cognition of the understanding, and through the thereby determined division of the conceptions which form the said whole; consequently, only by means of their connection in a system.

Book One: Analytic of Conceptions

By the term 'Analytic of Conceptions,' I do not understand the analysis of these, or the usual process in philosophical investigations of dissecting the conceptions which present themselves, according to their content, and so making them clear; but I mean the hitherto little attempted dissection of the faculty of understanding itself, in order to investigate the possibility of conceptions *a priori,* by looking for them in the understanding alone, as their birthplace, and analysing the pure use of this faculty.

I. Of the Transcendental Clue to the Discovery of All Pure Conceptions of the Understanding

Of the Logical Use of the Understanding in General

THE UNDERSTANDING was defined above only negatively, as a non-sensuous faculty of cognition. Now, independently of sensibility, we cannot possibly have any intuition; consequently, the understanding is no faculty of intuition. But besides intuition there is no other mode of cognition, except through conceptions; consequently, the cognition of every, at least of every human, understanding is a cognition through conceptions —not intuitive, but discursive. All intuitions, as sensuous, depend on affections; conceptions, therefore, upon functions. By the word function I understand the unity of the act of arranging diverse representations under one common representation. Conceptions, then, are based on the spontaneity of thought, as sensuous intuitions are on the receptivity of impressions. Now, the understanding cannot make any other use of these conceptions than to judge by means of them. As no representation, except an intuition, relates immediately to its object, a conception never relates immediately to an object, but only to some other representation thereof, be that an intuition or itself a conception. A judgment, therefore, is the mediate cognition of an object, consequently the representation of a representation of it. In every judgment there is a conception which applies to, and is valid for many other conceptions, and which among these comprehends also a given representation, this last being immediately connected with an object. All judgments, accordingly, are functions of unity in our representations, inasmuch as, instead of an immediate, a higher representation, which comprises this and various others, is used for our cognition of the object, and thereby many possible cognitions are collected into one. But we can reduce all acts of the understanding to judgments, so that *understanding* may be represented as the *faculty of judging*. For it is, according to what has been said above, a faculty of thought. Now thought is cognition by means of conceptions. But conceptions, as predicates of possible judgments, relate to some representation of a yet undetermined object. All the functions of the understanding therefore can be discovered, when we can completely exhibit the functions of unity in judgments. And that this may be effected very easily, the following section will show.

Of the Logical Function of the Understanding in Judgments

If we abstract all the content of a judgment, and consider only the intellectual form thereof, we find that the function of thought in a judgment can be brought under four heads, of which each contains three momenta. These may be conveniently represented in the following table:

I

Quantity of judgments

Universal
Particular
Singular

2		3
Quality		*Relation*
Affirmative		Categorical
Negative		Hypothetical
Infinite		Disjunctive

4
Modality
Problematical
Assertorical
Apodeictical

Of the Pure Conceptions of the Understanding, or Categories

General logic, as has been repeatedly said, makes abstraction of all content of cognition, and expects to receive representations from some other quarter, in order, by means of analysis, to convert them into conceptions. On the contrary, transcendental logic has lying before it the manifold content of *a priori* sensibility, which transcendental aesthetic presents to it in order to give matter to the pure conceptions of the understanding, without which transcendental logic would have no content, and be therefore utterly void. Now space and time contain an infinite diversity of determinations of pure *a priori* intuition, but are nevertheless the condition of the mind's receptivity, under which alone it can obtain representations of objects, and which, consequently, must always affect the conception of these objects. But the spontaneity of thought requires that this diversity be examined after a certain manner, received into the mind, and connected, in order afterwards to form a cognition out of it. This process I call synthesis.

By the word *synthesis,* in its most general signification, I understand the process of joining different representations to each other, and of comprehending their diversity in one cognition. This synthesis is pure when the diversity is not given empirically but *a priori*. Our representations must be given previously to any analysis of them; and no conceptions can arise, *quoad* their content, analytically. But the synthesis of a diversity is the first requisite for the production of a cognition, which in its beginning, indeed, may be crude and confused, and therefore in need of analysis—still, synthesis is that by which alone the elements of our cognitions are collected and united into a certain content, consequently it is the first thing on which we must fix our attention, if we wish to investigate the origin of our knowledge.

Synthesis, generally speaking, is, as we shall afterwards see, the mere operation of the imagination—a blind but indispensable function of the soul, without which we should have no cognition whatever, but of the working of which we are seldom even conscious. But to reduce this synthesis to conceptions is a function of the understanding, by means of which we attain to cognition, in the proper meaning of the term.

Pure synthesis, represented generally, gives us the pure conception of the understanding. But by this pure synthesis, I mean that which rests upon a basis of *a priori* synthetical unity. Thus, our numeration is a synthesis according to conceptions, because it takes place according to a common basis of unity. By means of this conception, therefore, the unity in the synthesis of the manifold becomes necessary.

By means of analysis different representations are brought under one conception—an operation of which general logic treats. On the other hand, the duty of transcendental logic is to reduce to conceptions, not representations, but the pure synthesis of representations. The first thing which must be given to us in order to the *a priori* cognition of all objects, is the diversity of the pure intuition; the synthesis of this diversity by means of the imagination is the second; but this gives, as yet, no cognition. The conceptions which give unity to this pure synthesis, and which consist solely in the representation of this necessary synthetical unity, furnish the third requisite for the cognition of an object, and these conceptions are given by the understanding.

Of the Pure Conceptions of the Understanding, or Categories

IN THIS MANNER, there arise exactly so many pure conceptions of the understanding, applying *a priori* to objects of intuition in general, as there are logical functions in all possible judgments. For there is no other function or faculty existing in the understanding besides those enumerated in that table. These conceptions we shall, with Aristotle, call categories, our purpose being originally identical with his, notwithstanding the great difference in the execution.

TABLE OF THE CATEGORIES

1	2
Of Quantity	*Of Quality*
Unity	Reality
Plurality	Negation
Totality	Limitation

3
Of Relation
Of Inherence and Subsistence (substantia et accidens)
Of Causality and Dependence (cause and effect)
Of Community (reciprocity between the agent and patient)

4
Of Modality
Possibility—Impossibility
Existence—Non-existence
Necessity—Contingence

This, then, is a catalogue of all the originally pure conceptions of the synthesis which the understanding contains *a priori,* and these conceptions alone entitle it to be called a pure understanding; inasmuch as only by them it can render the manifold of intuition conceivable, in other words, think an object of intuition.

II. Of the Deduction of the Pure Conceptions of the Understanding

Of the Principles of a Transcendental Deduction in General

Among the many conceptions which make up the very variegated web of human cognition, some are destined for pure use *a priori,* independent of all experience; and their title to be so employed always requires a deduction, inasmuch as, to justify such use of them, proofs from experience are not sufficient; but it is necessary to know how these conceptions can apply to objects without being derived from experience. I term, therefore, an explanation of the manner in which conceptions can apply *a priori* to objects, the *transcendental deduction* of conceptions, and I distinguish it from the *empirical deduction,* which indicates the mode in which a conception is obtained through experience and reflection thereon; consequently, does not concern itself with the right, but only with the fact of our obtaining conceptions in such and such a manner. We have already seen that we are in possession of two perfectly different kinds of conceptions, which nevertheless agree with each other in this, that they both apply to objects completely *a priori.* These are the conceptions of space and time as forms of sensibility, and the categories as pure conceptions of the understanding. To attempt an empirical deduction of either of these classes would be labour in vain, because the distinguishing characteristic of their nature consists in this, that they apply to their objects, without having borrowed anything from experience towards the representation of them. Consequently, if a deduction of these conceptions is necessary, it must always be transcendental.

But although it is admitted that the only possible deduction of pure *a priori* cognition is a transcendental deduction, it is not, for that reason, perfectly manifest that such a deduction is absolutely necessary. We have already traced to their sources the conceptions of space and time, by means of a transcendental deduction, and we have explained and determined their objective validity *a priori.* Geometry, nevertheless, advances steadily and securely in the province of pure *a priori* cognitions, without needing to ask from Philosophy any certificate as to the pure and legitimate origin of its fundamental conception of space. But the use of the conception in this science extends only to the external world of sense, the pure form of the intuition of which is space; and in *this* world, therefore, all geometrical cognition, because it is founded upon *a priori* intuition, possesses immediate evidence, and the objects of this cognition are given *a priori* in intuition by and through the cognition itself. With the pure conceptions of Understanding, on the contrary, commences the absolute necessity of seeking a transcendental deduction, not only of these conceptions themselves, but likewise of space, because, inasmuch as they make affirmations concerning objects not by means of the predicates of intuition and sensibility, but of pure thought *a priori,* they apply to objects without any of the conditions of sensibility. Besides, not being founded on experience, they are not presented with any object in *a priori* intuition upon which, antecedently to experience, they might base their synthesis. Hence results, not only doubt as to the objective validity and proper limits of their use, but that even our conception of space is rendered equivocal; inasmuch as we are very ready, with the aid of the categories, to carry the use of this conception beyond the conditions of sensuous intuition—and for this reason, we have already found a transcendental deduction of it needful.

Of the Possibility of a Conjunction of the Manifold Representations Given by Sense

The manifold content in our representations can be given in an intuition which is merely sensuous—in other words, is nothing but susceptibility; and the form of this intuition can exist *a priori* in our faculty of representation, without being anything else but the mode in which the subject is affected. But the conjunction of a manifold in intuition never can be given us by the senses; it cannot therefore be contained in the pure form of sensuous intuition, for it is a spontaneous act of the faculty of representation. And as we must, to distinguish it from sensibility, entitle this faculty *understanding;* so all conjunction—whether conscious or unconscious, be it of the manifold in intuition, sensuous or non-sensuous, or of several conceptions—is an act of the understanding. To this act we shall give the general appellation of *synthesis,* thereby to indicate, at the same time, that we cannot represent anything as conjoined in the object without having previously conjoined it ourselves. Of all mental notions, that of conjunction is the only one which cannot be given through objects, but can be originated only by the subject itself, because it is an act of its purely spontaneous activity. The reader will easily enough perceive that the possibility of conjunction must be grounded in the very nature of this act, and that it must be equally valid for all conjunction; and that analysis, which appears to be its contrary, must, nevertheless, always presuppose it; for where the understanding has not previously conjoined, it cannot dissect or analyse, because only as conjoined by it, must that which is to be analysed have been given to our faculty of representation.

But the conception of conjunction includes, besides the conception of the manifold and of the synthesis of it, that of the unity of it also. Conjunction is the representation of the synthetical unity of the manifold.

This idea of unity, therefore, cannot arise out of that of conjunction; much rather does that idea, by combining itself with the representation of the manifold, render the conception of conjunction possible. This unity, which *a priori* precedes all conceptions of conjunction, is not the category of unity; for all the categories are based upon logical functions of judgment, and in these functions we already have conjunction, and consequently unity of given conceptions. It is therefore evident that the category of unity presupposes conjunction. We must therefore look still higher for this unity in that, namely, which contains the ground of the unity of diverse conceptions in judgments, the ground, consequently, of the possibility of the existence of the understanding, even in regard to its logical use.

Of the Originally Synthetical Unity of Apperception

The *I think* must accompany all my representations, for otherwise something would be represented in me which could not be thought; in other words, the representation would either be impossible, or at least be, in relation to me, nothing. That representation which can be given previously to all thought, is called intuition. All the diversity or manifold content of intuition has, therefore, a necessary relation to the *I think,* in the subject in which this diversity is found. But this representation, *I think,* is an act of *spontaneity;* that is to say, it cannot be regarded as belonging to mere sensibility. I call it pure apperception, in order to distinguish it from empirical or primitive apperception, because it is a self-consciousness which, whilst it gives birth to the representation *I think,* must necessarily be capable of accompanying all our representations. It is in all acts of consciousness one and the same, and unaccompanied by it, no representation can exist *for me.* The unity of this apperception I call the transcendental unity of self-consciousness, in order to indicate the possibility of *a priori* cognition arising from it. For the manifold representations which are given in an intuition would not all of them be my representations, if they did not all belong to one self-consciousness, that is, as my representations they must conform to the condition under which alone they can exist together in a common self-consciousness, because otherwise they would not all without exception belong to me.

The Principle of the Synthetical Unity of Apperception Is the Highest Principle of All Exercise of the Understanding

The supreme principle of the possibility of all intuition in relation to sensibility was, according to our transcendental aesthetic, that all the manifold in intuition be subject to the formal conditions of Space and Time. The supreme principle of the possibility of it in relation to the Understanding is: that all the manifold in it be subject to conditions of the originally synthetical Unity of Apperception. To the former of these two principles are subject all the various representations of Intuition, in so far as they are given to us; to the latter, in so far as they must be capable•of conjunction in one consciousness; for without this nothing can be thought or cognized, because the given representations would not have in common the act of the apperception *I think;* and therefore could not be connected in one self-consciousness.

Understanding is, to speak generally, *the faculty of Cognitions.* These consist in the determined relation of given representations to an object. But an object is that, in the conception of which the manifold in a given intuition is united. Now all union of representations requires unity of consciousness in the synthesis of them. Consequently, it is the unity of consciousness alone that constitutes the possibility of representations relating to an object, and therefore of their objective validity, and of their becoming cognitions, and consequently, the possibility of the existence of the understanding itself.

The Logical Form of All Judgments Consists in the Objective Unity of Apperception of the Conceptions Contained Therein

I could never satisfy myself with the definition which logicians give of a judgment. It is, according to them, the representation of a relation between two conceptions. I shall not dwell here on the faultiness of this definition, in that it suits only for categorical and not for hypothetical or disjunctive judgments, these latter containing a relation not of conceptions but of judgments themselves—a blunder from which many evil results have followed. It is more important for our present purpose to observe that this definition does not determine in what the said relation consists.

But if I investigate more closely the relation of given cognitions in every judgment, and distinguish it, as belonging to the understanding, from the relation which is produced according to laws of the reproductive imagination, I find that a judgment is nothing but the mode of bringing given cognitions under the objective unity of apperception. This is plain from our use of the term of relation *is* in judgments, in order to distinguish the objective unity of given representations from the subjective unity. For this term indicates the relation of these representations to the original apperception, and also their *necessary unity,* even although the judgment is empirical, therefore contingent, as in the judgment: 'All bodies are heavy.' I do not mean by this, that these representations do *necessarily* belong to each other in empirical intuition, but that by means of the *necessary unity* of apperception they belong to each other in the synthesis of intuitions, that is to say, they belong to each other according to principles of the objective determination of all our representations, in so far as cognition can arise from them, these principles being all deduced from the main principle of the transcendental unity of apperception. In this way alone can there arise from this relation a *judgment,* that is, a relation which has objective validity, and is perfectly distinct from that relation of the very same representations which has only subjective validity—a relation, to wit, which is produced according to laws of association. According to these laws, I could only say: 'When I hold in my hand or carry a body, I feel an impression of weight'; but I could not say: 'It, the body, is heavy'; for this is tantamount to saying both these representations are conjoined in the object, that is, without distinction as to the condition of the subject, and do not merely stand together in my perception, however frequently the perceptive act may be repeated.

All Sensuous Intuitions Are Subject to the Categories, as Conditions under Which Alone the Manifold Content of Them Can Be United in One Consciousness

The manifold content given in a sensuous intuition comes necessarily under the original synthetical unity of apperception, because thereby alone is the *unity* of intuition possible. But that act of the understanding, by which the manifold content of given representations is brought under one apperception, is the logical function of judgments. All the manifold, therefore, in so far as it is given in one empirical intuition, is *determined* in relation to one of the logical functions of judgment, by means of which it is brought into union in one consciousness. Now the categories are nothing else than these functions of judgment, so far as the manifold in a given intuition is determined in relation to them. Consequently, the manifold in a given intuition is necessarily subject to the categories of the understanding.

In Cognition, Its Application to Objects of Experience Is the Only Legitimate Use of the Category

To think an object and to cognize an object are by no means the same thing. In cognition there are two elements: firstly, the conception, whereby an object is cogitated; and, secondly, the intuition, whereby the object is given. For supposing that to the conception a corresponding intuition could not be given, it would still be a thought as regards its form, but without any object, and no cognition of anything would be possible by means of it, inasmuch as, so far as I knew, there existed and could exist nothing to which my thought could be applied. Now all intuition possible to us is sensuous; consequently, our thought of an object by means of a pure conception of the understanding can become cognition for us only in so far as this conception is applied to objects of the senses. Sensuous intuition is either pure intuition or empirical intuition—of that which is immediately represented in space and time by means of sensation as real. Through the determination of pure intuition we obtain *a priori* cognitions of objects, as in mathematics, but only as regards their form as phenomena; whether there can exist things which must be intuited in this form is not thereby established. All mathematical conceptions, therefore, are not *per se* cognition, except in so far as we presuppose that there exist things which can only be represented conformably to the form of our pure sensuous intuition.

Book Two

INTRODUCTION: OF THE TRANSCENDENTAL FACULTY OF JUDGMENT IN GENERAL

IF UNDERSTANDING in general be defined as the faculty of laws or rules, the faculty of judgment may be termed the faculty of *subsumption* under these rules; that is, of distinguishing whether this or that does or does not stand under a given rule. General logic contains no directions or precepts for the faculty of judgment, nor can it contain any such. For as *it makes abstraction of all content of cognition,* no duty is left for it, except that of exposing analytically the mere form of cognition in conceptions, judgments, and conclusions, and of thereby establishing formal rules for all exercise of the understanding. Now if this logic wished to give some general direction how we should subsume under these rules, that is, how we should distinguish whether this or that did or did not stand under them, this again could not be done otherwise than by means of a rule. But this rule, precisely because it is a rule, requires for itself direction from the faculty of judgment. Thus, it is evident that the understanding is capable of being instructed by rules, but that the judgment is a peculiar talent, which does not, and cannot require tuition, but only exercise.

But although general logic cannot give directions to the faculty of judgment, the case is very different as regards transcendental logic, insomuch that it appears to be the especial duty of the latter to secure and direct, by means of determinate rules, the faculty of judgment in the employment of the pure understanding. For, as a doctrine, that is, as an endeavour to enlarge the sphere of the understanding in regard to pure *a priori* cognitions, philosophy is worse than useless, since from all the attempts hitherto made, little or no ground has been gained. But, as a critique, in order to guard against the mistakes of the faculty of judgment in the employment of the few pure conceptions of the understanding which we possess, although its use is in this case purely negative, philosophy is called upon to apply all its acuteness and penetration.

I. OF THE SCHEMATISM OF THE PURE CONCEPTIONS OF THE UNDERSTANDING

IN ALL SUBSUMPTIONS of an object under a conception, the representation of the object must be homogeneous with the conception; in other words, the conception must contain that which is represented in the object to be subsumed under it. For this is the meaning of the expression: An object is contained under a conception.

But pure conceptions of the understanding, when compared with empirical intuitions, or even with sensuous intuitions in general, are quite heterogeneous, and never can be discovered in any intuition. How then is the *subsumption* of the latter under the former, and consequently the application of the categories to phenomena, possible? This natural and important question forms the real cause of the necessity of a transcendental doctrine of the faculty of judgment, with the purpose, to wit, of showing how pure conceptions of the understanding can be applied to phenomena. In all other sciences, where the conceptions by which the object is thought in the general are not so different and heterogeneous from those which represent the object *in concreto*—as it is given, it is quite unnecessary to institute any special inquiries concerning the application of the former to the latter.

Now it is quite clear that there must be some third thing, which on the one side is homogeneous with the category, and with the phenomenon on the other, and so makes the application of the former to the latter possible. This mediating representation must be pure, and yet must on the one side be *intellectual,* on the other *sensuous.* Such a representation is the *transcendental schema.*

The conception of the understanding contains pure synthetical unity of the manifold in general. Time, as the formal condition of the manifold of the internal sense, consequently of the conjunction of all representations, contains *a priori* a manifold in the pure intuition. Now a transcendental determination of time is so far homogeneous with the *category,* which constitutes the unity thereof, that it is universal, and rests upon a rule *a priori*. On the other hand, it is so far homogeneous with the *phenomenon,* inasmuch as time is contained in every empirical representation of the manifold. Thus an application of the category to phenomena becomes possible, by means of the transcendental determination of time, which, as the schema of the conceptions of the understanding, mediates the subsumption of the latter under the former.

The schema is, in itself, always a mere product of the imagination. But as the synthesis of imagination has for its aim no single intuition, but merely unity in the determination of sensibility, the schema is clearly distinguishable from the image.

In truth, it is not images of objects, but schemata, which lie at the foundation of our pure sensuous conceptions. No image could ever be adequate to our conception of a triangle in general. For the generalness of the conception it never could attain to, as this includes under itself all triangles, whether right-angled, acute-angled, etc., whilst the image would always be limited to a single part of this sphere. The schema of the triangle can exist nowhere else than in thought, and it indicates a rule of the synthesis of the imagination in regard to pure figures in space. Still less is an object of experience, or an image of the object, ever adequate to the empirical conception. On the contrary, the conception always relates immediately to the schema of the imagination, as a rule for the determination of our intuition, in conformity with a certain general conception.

II. System of all Principles of the Pure Understanding

Of the Supreme Principle of All Analytical Judgments

WHATEVER may be the content of our cognition, and in whatever manner our cognition may be related to its object, the universal, although only negative condition of all our judgments is that they do not contradict themselves; otherwise these judgments are in themselves nothing. But although there may exist no contradiction in our judgment, it may nevertheless connect conceptions in such a manner, that they do not correspond to the object, or without any grounds either *a priori* or *a posteriori* for arriving at such a judgment, and thus, without being self-contradictory, a judgment may nevertheless be either false or groundless.

Now, the proposition: 'No subject can have a predicate that contradicts it,' is called the principle of contradiction, and is a universal but purely negative criterion of all truth. But it belongs to logic alone, because it is valid of cognitions, merely as cognitions, and without respect to their content, and declares that the contradiction entirely nullifies them. We can also, however, make a positive use of this principle, that is, not merely to banish falsehood and error, but also for the cognition of truth. For *if the judgment is analytical,* be it affirmative or negative, its truth must always be recognizable by means of the principle of contradiction. For the contrary of that which lies and is cogitated as conception in the cognition of the object will be always properly negatived, but the conception itself must always be affirmed of the object, inasmuch as the contrary thereof would be in contradiction to the object.

We must therefore hold the *principle of contradiction* to be the universal and fully sufficient *principle of all analytical cognition.* But as a sufficient criterion of truth, it has no further utility or authority. For the fact that no cognition can be at variance with this principle without nullifying itself, constitutes this principle the *sine qua non,* but not the determining ground of the truth of our cognition.

Of the Supreme Principle of All Synthetical Judgments

The explanation of the possibility of synthetical judgments is a task with which general Logic has nothing to do; indeed she needs not even be acquainted with its name. But in transcendental Logic it is the most important matter to be dealt with—indeed the only one, if the question is of the possibility of synthetical judgments *a priori,* the conditions and extent of their validity. For when this question is fully decided, it can reach its aim with perfect ease, the determination, to wit, of the extent and limits of the pure understanding.

In an analytical judgment I do not go beyond the given conception, in order to arrive at some decision respecting it. If the judgment is affirmative, I predicate of the conception only that which was already cogitated in it; if negative, I merely exclude from the conception its contrary. But in synthetical judgments, I must go beyond the given conception, in order to cogitate, in relation with it, something quite different from that which was cogitated in it, a relation which is consequently never one either of identity or contradiction, and by means of which the truth or error of the judgment cannot be discerned merely from the judgment itself.

Granted, then, that we must go out beyond a given conception, in order to compare it synthetically with another, a third thing is necessary, in which alone the synthesis of two conceptions can originate. It is only a complex, in which all our representations are contained, the internal sense to wit, and its form *a priori,* Time.

The synthesis of our representations rests upon the imagination; their synthetical unity, upon the unity of apperception. In this, therefore, is to be sought the possibility of synthetical judgments, and as all three contain the sources of *a priori* representations, the possibility of pure synthetical judgments also; nay, they are necessary upon these grounds, if we are to possess a knowledge of objects, which rests solely upon the synthesis of representations.

If a cognition is to have objective reality, that is, to relate to an object, and possess sense and meaning in respect to it, it is necessary that the object be given in some way or another. Without this, our conceptions are empty, and we may indeed have thought by means of them, but by such thinking we have not, in fact, cognized anything, we have merely played with representation. To give an object, if this expression be understood in the sense of to present the object, not mediately but immediately in intuition, means nothing else than to apply the representation of it to experience, be that experience real or only possible. Space and time themselves, pure as these conceptions are from all that is empirical, and certain as it is that they are represented fully *a priori* in the mind, would be completely without objective validity, and without sense and significance, if their necessary use in the objects of experience were not shown. Nay, the representation of them is a mere schema, that always relates to the reproductive imagination, which calls up the objects of experience, without which they have no meaning. And so is it with all conceptions without distinction.

Systematic Representation of All Synthetical Principles Thereof

That principles exist at all is to be ascribed solely to the pure understanding, which is not only the faculty of rules in regard to that which happens, but is even the source of principles according to which everything that can be presented to us as an object is necessarily subject to rules, because without such rules we never could attain to cognition of an object. Even the laws of nature, if they are contemplated as principles of the empirical use of the understanding, possess also a characteristic of necessity, and we may therefore at least expect them to be determined upon grounds which are valid *a priori* and antecedent to all experience. But all laws of nature, without distinction, are subject to higher principles of the understanding, inasmuch as the former are merely applications of the latter to particular cases of experience. These higher principles alone therefore give the conception, which contains the necessary condition, and, as it were, the exponent of a rule; experience, on the other hand, gives the case which comes under the rule.

The table of the categories is naturally our guide to the table of principles, because these are nothing else than rules for the objective employment of the former. Accordingly, all principles of the pure understanding are:

I

Axioms of
INTUITION

2   3
Anticipations   *Analogies*
of   *of*
PERCEPTION   EXPERIENCE

4

Postulates of
EMPIRICAL THOUGHT
in general

These appellations I have chosen advisedly, in order that we might not lose sight of the distinctions in respect of the evidence and the employment of these principles. It will, however, soon appear that—a fact which concerns both the evidence of these principles, and the *a priori* determination of phenomena—according to the categories of *Quantity* and *Quality,* the principles of these categories are distinguishable from those of the two others, inasmuch as the former are possessed of an intuitive, but the latter of a merely discursive, though in both instances a complete certitude. I shall therefore call the former *mathematical* and the latter *dynamical* principles. It must be observed, however, that by these terms I mean, just as little in the one case the principles of mathematics, as those of general dynamics in the other. I have here in view merely the principles of the pure understanding, in their application to the internal sense, by means of which the sciences of mathematics and dynamics become possible. Accordingly, I have named these principles rather with reference to their application, than their content; and I shall now proceed to consider them in the order in which they stand in the table.

1. AXIOMS OF INTUITION

The principle of these is: *All Intuitions are Extensive Quantities.*

PROOF

All phenomena contain, as regards their form, an intuition in space and time, which lies *a priori* at the foundation of all without exception. Phenomena, therefore, cannot be apprehended, that is, received into empirical consciousness, otherwise than through the synthesis of a manifold, through which the representations of a determinate space or time are generated; that is to say, through the composition of the homogeneous, and the consciousness of the synthetical unity of this manifold. Now the consciousness of a homogeneous manifold in intuition, in so far as thereby the representation of an object is rendered possible, is the conception of a quantity. Consequently, even the perception of an object as phenomenon is possible only through the same synthetical unity of the manifold of the given sensuous intuition, through which the unity of the composition of the homogeneous manifold in the conception of a *quantity* is cogitated; that is to say, all phenomena are quantities, and *extensive* quantities, because as intuitions in space or time they must be represented by means of the same synthesis, through which space and time themselves are determined.

An extensive quantity I call that wherein the representation of the parts renders possible the representation of the whole. I cannot represent to myself any line, however small, without drawing it in thought, that is, without generating from a point all its parts one after another, and in this way alone producing this intuition. Precisely the same is the case with every, even the smallest portion of time. I cogitate therein only the successive progress from one moment to another, and hence, by means of the different portions of time and the addition of them, a determinate quantity of time is produced. As the pure intuition in all phenomena is either time or space, so is every phenomenon in its character of intuition an extensive quantity, inasmuch as it can only be cognized in our apprehension by successive synthesis (from part to part). All phenomena are, accordingly, to be considered as aggregates, that is, as a collection of previously given parts; which is not the case with every sort of quantities, but only with those which are represented and apprehended by us as extensive.

2. ANTICIPATIONS OF PERCEPTION

The principle of these is: *In all phenomena the Real, that which is an object of sensation, has Intensive Quantity, that is, has a Degree.*

PROOF

Perception is empirical consciousness, that is to say, a consciousness which contains an element of sensation. Phenomena as objects of perception are not pure, that is, merely formal intuitions, like space and time, for they cannot be perceived in themselves. They contain, then, over and above the intuition, the materials for an object, that is to say, they contain the real of sensation, as a representation merely subjective, which gives us merely the consciousness that the subject is affected, and which we refer to some external object. Now, a gradual transition from empirical consciousness to pure consciousness is possible, inasmuch as the real in this consciousness entirely evanishes, and there remains a merely formal consciousness of the manifold in time and space; consequently there is possible a synthesis also of the production of the quantity of a sensation from its commencement, that is, from the pure intuition=o onwards, up to a certain quantity of the sensation. Now as sensation in itself is not an objective representation, and in it is to be found neither the intuition of space nor of time, it cannot possess any extensive quantity, and yet there does belong to it a quantity, consequently an *intensive quantity*. And thus we must ascribe intensive quantity, that is, a degree of influence on sense to all objects of perception, in so far as this perception contains sensation.

3. ANALOGIES OF EXPERIENCE

The principle of these is: *Experience is possible only through the representation of a necessary connection of perceptions.*

PROOF

Experience is an empirical cognition; that is to say, a cognition which determines an object by means of perceptions. It is therefore a synthesis of perceptions, a synthesis which is not itself contained in perception, but which contains the synthetical unity of the manifold of perception in a consciousness; and this unity constitutes the essential of our cognition of *objects* of the senses, that is, of experience. Now in experience our perceptions come together contingently, so that no character of necessity in their connection appears, or can appear from the perceptions themselves, because apprehension is only a placing together of the manifold of empirical intuition, and no representation of a necessity in the connected existence of the phenomena which apprehension brings together is to be discovered therein. But as experience is a cognition of objects by means of perceptions, it follows that the relation of the existence of the manifold must be represented in experience not as it is put together in time, but as it is objectively in time. And as time itself cannot be perceived, the determination of the existence of objects in time can only take place by means of their connection in time in general, consequently only by means of *a priori* connecting conceptions. Now as these conceptions always possess the character of necessity, experience is possible only by means of a representation of the necessary connection of perception.

The three *modi* of time are *permanence, succession,* and *coexistence.* Accordingly, there are three rules of all relations of time in phenomena, according to which the existence of every phenomenon is determined in respect of the unity of all time, and these antecede all experience, and render it possible.

The general principle of all three analogies rests on the necessary *unity* of apperception in relation to all possible empirical consciousness *at every time,* consequently, as this unity lies *a priori* at the foundation of all mental operations, the principle rests on the synthetical unity of all phenomena according to their relation in time. For the original apperception relates to our internal sense, and indeed relates *a priori* to its form, that is to say, the relation of the manifold empirical consciousness in time. Now this manifold must be combined in original apperception according to relations of time—a necessity imposed by the *a priori* transcendental unity of apperception, to which is subjected all that can belong to my cognition, and therefore all that can become an object for me. This synthetical and *a priori* determined unity in relation of perceptions in time is therefore the rule: 'All empirical determinations of time must be subject to rules of the general determination of time'; and the analogies of experience, of which we are now about to treat, must be rules of this nature.

4. The Postulates of Empirical Thought

1. That which agrees with the formal conditions of experience is *possible.*

2. That which coheres with the material conditions of experience is *real.*

3. That whose coherence with the real is determined according to universal conditions of experience is *necessary.*

The categories of modality possess this peculiarity, that they do not in the least determine the object, or enlarge the conception to which they are annexed as predicates, but only express its relation to the faculty of cognition. Though my conception of a thing is in itself complete, I am still entitled to ask whether the object of it is merely possible, or whether it is also real, or, if the latter, whether it is also necessary. But hereby the object itself is not more definitely determined in thought, but the question is only in what relation it, including all its determinations, stands to the understanding and its employment in experience, to the empirical faculty of judgment, and to the reason in its application to experience.

For this very reason, too, the categories of modality are nothing more than explanations of the conceptions of possibility, reality, and necessity, as employed in experience, and at the same time, restrictions of all the categories to empirical use alone, not authorizing the transcendental employment of them. For if they are to have something more than a merely logical significance, and to be something more than a mere analytical expression of the form of *thought,* and to have a relation to *things* and their possibility, reality, or necessity, they must concern possible experience and its synthetical unity, in which alone objects of cognition can be given.

The postulate of the possibility of things requires also, that the conception of the things agree with the formal conditions of our experience in general. But this, that is to say, the objective form of experience, contains all the kinds of synthesis which are requisite for the cognition of objects. A conception which contains a synthesis must be regarded as empty and without reference to an object, if its synthesis does not belong to experience—either as borrowed from it, and in this case it is called an *empirical conception,* or such as is the ground and *a priori* condition of experience (its form), and in this case it is a *pure conception,* a conception which nevertheless belongs to experience, inasmuch as its object can be found in this alone. For where shall we find the criterion or character of the possibility of an object which is cogitated by means of an *a priori* synthetical conception, if not in the synthesis which constitutes the form of empirical cognition of objects? That in such a conception no contradiction exists is indeed a necessary logical condition, but very far from being sufficient to establish the objective reality of the conception, that is, the possibility of such an object as is thought in the conception. Thus, in the conception of a figure which is contained within two straight lines, there is no contradiction, for the conceptions of two straight lines and of their junction contain no negation of a figure. The impossibility in such a case does not rest upon the conception in itself, but upon the construction of it in space, that is to say, upon the conditions of space and its determinations. But these have themselves objective reality, that is, they apply to possible things, because they contain *a priori* the form of experience in general.

III. Of the Ground of the Division of All Objects Into Phenomena and Noumena

We have seen that everything which the understanding draws from itself, without borrowing from experience, it nevertheless possesses only for the behoof and use of experience. The principles of the pure understanding, whether constitutive *a priori,* or merely regulative, contain nothing but the pure schema, as it were, of possible experience. For experience possesses its unity from the synthetical unity which the understanding, originally and from itself, imparts to the synthesis of the imagination in relation to apperception, and in *a priori* relation to and agreement with which phenomena, as data for a possible cognition, must stand. But although these rules of the understanding are not only *a priori* true, but the very source of all truth, that is, of the accordance of our cognition with objects, and on this ground, that they contain the basis of the possibility of experience, as the *ensemble* of all cognition, it seems to us not enough to propound what is true—we desire also to be told what we want to know. If, then, we learn nothing more by this critical examination than what we should have practised in the merely empirical use of the understanding, without any such subtle inquiry, the presumption is, that the advantage we reap from it is not worth the labour bestowed upon it. It may certainly be answered, that no rash curiosity is more prejudicial to the enlargement of our knowledge than that which must know beforehand the utility of this or that piece of information which we seek, before we have entered on the needful investigations, and before one could form the least conception of its utility, even though it were placed before our eyes. But there is one advantage in such transcendental inquiries which can be made comprehensible to the dullest and most reluctant learner—this, namely, that the understanding which is occupied merely with empirical exercise, and does not reflect on the sources of its own cognition, may exercise its functions very well and very successfully, but is quite unable to do one thing, and that of very great importance, to determine, namely, the bounds that limit its employment, and to know what lies within or without its own sphere. This purpose can be obtained only by such profound investigations as we have instituted. But if it cannot distinguish whether certain questions lie within its horizon or not, it can never be sure either as to its claims or possessions, but must lay its account with many humiliating corrections, when it transgresses, as it unavoidably will, the limits of its own territory, and loses itself in fanciful opinions and blinding illusions.

That the understanding, therefore, cannot make of its *a priori* principles, or even of its conceptions, other than an empirical use, is a proposition which leads to the most important results. A transcendental use is made of a conception in a fundamental proposition or principle when it is referred to things *in general* and considered as things *in themselves;* an empirical use, when it is referred merely to *phenomena,* that is, to objects of a possible *experience.* That the latter use of a conception is the only admissible one, is evident from the reasons following. For every conception are requisite, firstly, the logical form of a conception in general; and, secondly, the possibility of presenting to this an object to which it may apply. Failing this latter, it has no sense, and is utterly void of content, although it may contain the logical function for constructing a conception from certain data. Now object cannot be given to a conception otherwise than by intuition, and, even if a pure intuition antecedent to the object is *a priori* possible, this pure intuition can itself obtain objective validity only from empirical intuition, of which it is itself but the form. All conceptions, therefore, and with them all principles, however high the degree of their *a priori* possibility, relate to empirical intuitions, that is, to data towards a possible experience. Without this they possess no objective validity, but are mere play of imagination or of understanding with images or notions.

TRANSCENDENTAL LOGIC

SECOND DIVISION: TRANSCENDENTAL DIALECTIC

Introduction

It is not at present our business to treat of empirical illusory appearance, which occurs in the empirical application of otherwise correct rules of the understanding, and in which the judgment is misled by the influence of imagination. Our purpose is to speak of *transcendental illusory appearance,* which influences principles—that are not even applied to experience, for in this case we should possess a sure test of their correctness—but which leads us, in disregard of all the warnings of criticism, completely beyond the empirical employment of the categories, and deludes us with the chimera of an extension of the sphere of the *pure understanding.* We shall term those principles, the application of which is confined entirely within the limits of possible experience, *immanent;* those, on the other hand, which transgress these limits, we shall call *transcendent* principles. But by these latter I do not understand principles of the *transcendental* use or misuse of the categories, which is in reality a mere fault of the judgment when not under due restraint from criticism, and therefore not paying sufficient attention to the limits of the sphere in which the pure understanding is allowed to exercise its functions; but real principles which exhort us to break down all those barriers, and to lay claim to a perfectly new field of cognition, which recognizes no line of demarcation. Thus *transcendental* and *transcendent* are not identical terms. The principles of the pure understanding, which we have already propounded, ought to be of empirical and not of transcendental use, that is, they are not applicable to any object beyond the sphere of experience. A principle which removes these limits, nay, which authorizes us to overstep them, is called *transcendent.* If our criticism can succeed in exposing the illusion in these pretended principles, those which are limited in their employment to the sphere of experience may be called, in opposition to the others, *immanent* principles of the pure understanding.

Logical illusion, which consists merely in the imitation of the form of reason, arises entirely from a want of due attention to logical rules. So soon as the attention is awakened to the case before us, this illusion totally disappears. Transcendental illusion, on the contrary, does not cease to exist, even after it has been exposed, and its nothingness clearly perceived by means of transcendental criticism.

Transcendental dialectic will therefore content itself with exposing the illusory appearance in transcendental judgments, and guarding us against it; but to make it, as in the case of logical illusion, entirely disappear and cease to be illusion, is utterly beyond its power. For we have here to do with a *natural* and unavoidable illusion, which rests upon subjective principles, and imposes these upon us as objective, while logical dialectic, in the detection of sophisms, has to do merely with an error in the logical consequence of the propositions, or with an artificially constructed illusion, in imitation of the natural error. There is, therefore, a natural and unavoidable dialectic of pure reason—not that in which the bungler, from want of the requisite knowledge, involves himself, nor that which the sophist devises for the purpose of misleading, but that which is an inseparable adjunct of human reason, and which, even after its illusions have been exposed, does not cease to deceive, and continually to lead reason into momentary errors, which it becomes necessary continually to remove.

Book One: Of the Conceptions of Pure Reason

THE CONCEPTIONS of pure reason—we do not here speak of the possibility of them—are not obtained by reflection, but by inference or conclusion. The conceptions of understanding are also cogitated *a priori* antecedently to experience, and render it possible; but they contain nothing but the unity of reflection upon phenomena, in so far as these must necessarily belong to a possible empirical consciousness. Through them alone are cognition and the determination of an object possible. It is from them, accordingly, that we receive material for reasoning, and antecedently to them we possess no *a priori* conceptions of objects from which they might be deduced. On the other hand, the sole basis of their objective reality consists in the necessity imposed on them, as containing the intellectual form of all experience, of restricting their application and influence to the sphere of experience.

But the term, *conception of reason* or rational conception, itself indicates that it does not confine itself within the limits of experience, because its object-matter is a cognition, of which every empirical cognition is but a part—nay, the whole of possible experience may be itself but a part of it—a cognition to which no actual experience ever fully attains, although it does always pertain to it. The aim of rational conceptions is the *comprehension,* as that of the conceptions of understanding is the *understanding* of perceptions. If they contain the unconditioned, they relate to that to which all experience is subordinate, but which is never itself an object of experience—that towards which reason tends in all its conclusions from experience, and by the standard of which it estimates the degree of their empirical use, but which is never itself an element in an empirical synthesis. If, notwithstanding, such conceptions possess objective validity, they may be called *conceptus ratiocinati;* in cases where they do not, they have been admitted on account of having the appearance of being correctly concluded, and may be called *conceptus ratiocinantes.* But as this can only be sufficiently demonstrated in that part of our treatise which relates to the dialectical conclusions of reason, we shall omit any consideration of it in this place. As we called the pure conceptions of the understanding categories, we shall also distinguish those of pure reason by a new name, and call them transcendental ideas. These terms, however, we must in the first place explain and justify.

Of Ideas in General

Spite of the great wealth of words which European languages possess, the thinker finds himself often at a loss for an expression exactly suited to his conception, for want of which he is unable to make himself intelligible either to others or to himself.

For this reason, when it happens that there exists only a single word to express a certain conception, and this word, in its usual acceptation, is thoroughly adequate to the conception, the accurate distinction of which from related conceptions is of great importance, we ought not to employ the expression improvidently, or, for the sake of variety and elegance of style, use it as a synonym for other cognate words. It is our duty, on the contrary, carefully to preserve its peculiar signification, as otherwise it easily happens that when the attention of the reader is no longer particularly attracted to the expression, and it is lost amid the multitude of other words of very different import, the thought which it conveyed, and which it alone conveyed, is lost with it.

Plato employed the expression *Idea* in a way that plainly showed he meant by it something which is never derived from the senses, but which far transcends even the conceptions of the understanding, inasmuch as in experience nothing perfectly corresponding to them could be found. Ideas are, according to him, archetypes of things themselves, and not merely keys to possible experiences, like the categories.

Of Transcendental Ideas

Transcendental analytic showed us how the mere logical form of our cognition can contain the origin of pure conceptions *a priori,* conceptions which represent objects antecedently to all experience, or rather, indicate the synthetical unity which alone renders possible an empirical cognition of objects. The form of judgments—converted into a conception of the synthesis of intuitions—produced the categories, which direct the employment of the understanding in experience. This consideration warrants us to expect that the form of syllogisms, when applied to synthetical unity of intuitions, following the rule of the categories, will contain the origin of particular *a priori* conceptions, which we may call pure conceptions of reason or transcendental ideas, and which will determine the use of the understanding in the totality of experience according to principles.

The function of reason in arguments consists in the universality of a cognition according to conceptions, and the syllogism itself is a judgment which is determined *a priori* in the whole extent of its condition.

Hence, in the conclusion of a syllogism we restrict a predicate to a certain object, after having thought it in the major in its whole extent under a certain condition. This complete quantity of the extent in relation to such a condition is called *universality.* To this corresponds *totality* of conditions in the synthesis of intuitions. The transcendental conception of reason is therefore nothing else than the conception of the *totality of the conditions* of a given conditioned. Now as the *unconditioned* alone renders possible totality of conditions, and, conversely, the totality of conditions is itself always unconditioned; a pure rational conception in general can be defined and explained by means of the conception of the unconditioned, in so far as it contains a basis for the synthesis of the conditioned.

To the number of modes of relation which the understanding cogitates by means of the categories, the number of pure rational conceptions will correspond. We must therefore seek for, first, an *unconditioned* of the *categorical* synthesis in a *subject;* secondly, of the *hypothetical* synthesis of the members of a *series;* thirdly, of the *disjunctive* synthesis of parts in a *system.*

There are exactly the same number of modes of syllogisms, each of which proceeds through prosyllogisms to the unconditioned—one to the subject which cannot be employed as predicate, another to the presupposition which supposes nothing higher than itself, and the third to an aggregate of the members of the complete division of a conception. Hence the pure rational conceptions of totality in the synthesis of conditions have a necessary foundation in the nature of human reason—at least as modes of elevating the unity of the understanding to the unconditioned. They may have no valid application, corresponding to their transcendental employment, *in concreto,* and be thus of no greater utility than to direct the understanding how, while extending them as widely as possible, to maintain its exercise and application in perfect consistence and harmony.

Now the transcendental conception of reason has for its object nothing else than absolute totality in the synthesis of conditions, and does not rest satisfied till it has attained to the absolutely, that is, in all respects and relations, unconditioned. For pure reason leaves to the understanding everything that immediately relates to the object of intuition or rather to their synthesis in imagination. The former restricts itself to the absolute totality in the employment of the conceptions of the understanding, and aims at carrying out the synthetical unity which is cogitated in the category, even to the unconditioned. This unity may hence be called the *rational unity* of phenomena, as the other, which the category expresses, may be termed the *unity of the understanding.* Reason, therefore, has an immediate relation to the use of the understanding, not indeed in so far as the latter contains the ground of possible experience, but solely for the purpose of directing it to a certain unity, of which the understanding has no conception, and the aim of which is to collect into an *absolute whole* all acts of the understanding. Hence the objective employment of the pure conceptions of reason is always *transcendent,* while that of the pure conceptions of the understanding must, according to their nature, be always *immanent,* inasmuch as they are limited to possible experience.

I understand by idea a necessary conception of reason, to which no corresponding object can be discovered in the world of sense. Accordingly, the pure conceptions of reason at present under consideration are *transcendental ideas.* They are conceptions of pure reason, for they regard all empirical cognition as determined by means of an absolute totality of conditions. They are not mere fictions, but natural and necessary products of reason, and have hence a necessary relation to the whole sphere of the exercise of the understanding. And finally, they are transcendent, and overstep the limits of all experience, in which, consequently, no object can ever be presented that would be perfectly adequate to a transcendental idea.

System of Transcendental Ideas

We are not at present engaged with a logical dialectic which makes complete abstraction of the content of cognition, and aims only at unveiling the illusory appearance in the form of syllogisms. Our subject is transcendental dialectic, which must contain, completely *a priori,* the origin of certain cognitions drawn from pure reason, and the origin of certain deduced conceptions, the object of which cannot be given empirically, and which therefore lie beyond the sphere of the faculty of understanding.

Now the most general relations which can exist in our representations are: 1st, the relation to the subject; 2nd, the relation to objects, either as phenomena, or as objects of thought in general. If we connect this subdivision with the main division, all the relations of our representations, of which we can form either a conception or an idea, are threefold: 1. The relation to the subject; 2. The relation to the manifold of the object as a phenomenon; 3. The relation to all things in general.

Now all pure conceptions have to do in general with the synthetical unity of representations; conceptions of pure reason, on the other hand, with the unconditional synthetical unity of all conditions. It follows that all transcendental ideas arrange themselves in three classes, the *first* of which contains the absolute *unity of the thinking subject,* the *second* the absolute *unity of the series of the conditions* of a phenomenon, the *third* the absolute *unity of the conditions of all objects of thought* in general.

The thinking subject is the object-matter of *Psychology;* the sum total of all phenomena is the object-matter of *Cosmology;* and the thing which contains the highest condition of the possibility of all that is cogitable is the object-matter of all *Theology.* Thus pure reason presents us with the idea of a transcendental doctrine of the soul, of a transcendental science of the world, and finally of a transcendental doctrine of God. Understanding cannot originate even the outline of any of these sciences, even when connected with the highest logical use of reason, that is, all cogitable syllogisms—for the purpose of proceeding from one object to all others, even to the utmost limits of the empirical synthesis. They are, on the contrary, pure and genuine products, or problems, of pure reason.

An *objective deduction,* such as we were able to present in the case of the categories, is impossible as regards these transcendental ideas. For they have, in truth, no relation to any object, in experience, for the very reason that they are only ideas.

Book Two: Of the Dialectical Procedure of Pure Reason

IT MAY BE SAID that the object of a merely transcendental idea is something of which we have no conception, although the idea may be a necessary product of reason according to its original laws. For, in fact, a conception of an object that is adequate to the idea given by reason, is impossible. For such an object must be capable of being presented and intuited in a possible experience. But we should express our meaning better, and with less risk of being misunderstood, if we said that we can have no knowledge of an object, which perfectly corresponds to an idea, although we may possess a problematical conception thereof.

Now the transcendental reality at least of the pure conceptions of reason rests upon the fact that we are led to such ideas by a necessary procedure of reason. There must therefore be syllogisms which contain no empirical premisses, and by means of which we conclude from something that we do know, to something of which we do not even possess a conception, to which we, nevertheless, by an unavoidable illusion, ascribe objective reality. Such arguments are, as regards their result, rather to be termed sophisms than syllogisms, although indeed, as regards their origin, they are very well entitled to the latter name, inasmuch as they are not fictions or accidental products of reason, but are necessitated by its very nature. They are sophisms, not of men, but of pure reason herself, from which the wisest cannot free himself. After long labour he may be able to guard against the error, but he can never be thoroughly rid of the illusion which continually mocks and misleads him.

I. OF THE PARALOGISMS OF PURE REASON

THE LOGICAL PARALOGISM consists in the falsity of an argument in respect of its form, be the content what it may. But a transcendental paralogism has a transcendental foundation, and concludes falsely, while the form is correct and unexceptionable. In this manner the paralogism has its foundation in the nature of human reason, and is the parent of an unavoidable, though not insoluble, mental illusion.

The dialectical illusion in rational psychology arises from our confounding an idea of reason with the conception—in every respect undetermined—of a thinking being in general. I cogitate myself in behalf of a possible experience, at the same time making abstraction of all actual experience; and infer therefrom that I can be conscious of myself apart from experience and its empirical conditions. I consequently confound the possible *abstraction* of my empirically determined existence with the supposed consciousness of a possible *separate* existence of my thinking self; and I believe that I cognize what is substantial in myself as a transcendental subject, when I have nothing more in thought than the unity of consciousness, which lies at the basis of all determination of cognition.

The task of explaining the community of the soul with the body does not properly belong to the psychology of which we are here speaking; because it proposes to prove the personality of the soul apart from this communion, and is therefore *transcendent* in the proper sense of the word, although occupying itself with an object of experience—only in so far, however, as it ceases to be an object of experience. But a sufficient answer may be found to the question in our system. The difficulty which lies in the execution of this task consists, as is well known, in the presupposed heterogeneity of the object of the internal sense and the objects of the external senses; inasmuch as the formal condition of the intuition of the one is time, and of that of the other space also. But if we consider that both kinds of objects do not differ internally, but only in so far as the one *appears* externally to the other—consequently, that what lies at the basis of phenomena, as a thing in itself, may not be heterogeneous—this difficulty disappears. There then remains no other difficulty than is to be found in the question—how a community of substances is possible; a question which lies out of the region of psychology, and which the reader, after what in our Analytic has been said of primitive forces and faculties, will easily judge to be also beyond the region of human cognition.

II. The Antinomy of Pure Reason

We showed in the introduction to this part of our work that all transcendental illusion of pure reason arose from dialectical arguments, the schema of which logic gives us in its three formal species of syllogisms— just as the categories find their logical schema in the four functions of all judgments. The first kind of these sophistical arguments related to the unconditioned unity of the *subjective* conditions of all representations in general, in correspondence with the *categorical* syllogisms, the major of which, as the principle, enounces the relation of a predicate to a subject. The second kind of dialectical argument will therefore be concerned, following the analogy with *hypothetical* syllogisms, with the unconditioned unity of the objective conditions in the phenomenon; and, in this way, the theme of the third kind to be treated of in the following chapter, will be the unconditioned unity of the objective conditions of the possibility of objects in general.

But it is worthy of remark that the transcendental paralogism produced in the mind only a one-sided illusion, in regard to the idea of the subject of our thought; and the conceptions of reason gave no ground to maintain the contrary proposition. The advantage is completely on the side of Pneumatism; although this theory itself passes into naught, in the crucible of pure reason.

Very different is the case when we apply reason to the *objective synthesis* of phenomena. Here, certainly, reason establishes, with much plausibility, its principle of unconditioned unity; but it very soon falls into such contradictions, that it is compelled, in relation to cosmology, to renounce its pretensions.

For here a new phenomenon of human reason meets us—a perfectly natural antithetic, which does not require to be sought for by subtle sophistry, but into which reason of itself unavoidably falls. It is thereby preserved, to be sure, from the slumber of a fancied conviction—which a merely one-sided illusion produces; but it is at the same time compelled, either, on the one hand, to abandon itself to a despairing scepticism, or, on the other, to assume a dogmatical confidence and obstinate persistence in certain assertions, without granting a fair hearing to the other side of the question. Either is the death of a sound philosophy, although the former might perhaps deserve the title of the Euthanasia of pure reason.

System of Cosmological Ideas

That we may be able to enumerate with systematic precision these ideas according to a principle, we must remark, *in the first place,* that it is from the understanding alone that pure and transcendental conceptions take their origin; that the reason does not properly give birth to any conception, but only frees the conception of the understanding from the unavoidable limitation of a possible experience, and thus endeavours to raise it above the empirical, though it must still be in connection with it. This happens from the fact, that for a given conditioned, reason demands absolute totality on the side of the conditions, and thus makes of the category a transcendental idea. This it does that it may be able to give absolute completeness to the empirical synthesis, by continuing it to the unconditioned. Reason requires this according to the principle: *If the conditioned is given, the whole of the conditions, and consequently the absolutely unconditioned, is also given,* whereby alone the former was possible. *First,* then, the transcendental ideas are properly nothing but categories elevated to the unconditioned; and they may be arranged in a table according to the titles of the latter. But, *secondly,* all the categories are not available for this purpose, but only those in which the synthesis constitutes a series—of conditions subordinated to, not co-ordinated with, each other.

There are, accordingly, only four cosmological ideas, corresponding with the four titles of the categories. For we can select only such as necessarily furnish us with a series in the synthesis of the manifold.

I

The absolute Completeness
of the
COMPOSITION
of the given totality of all phenomena

2

The absolute Completeness
of the
DIVISION
of a given totality
in a phenomenon

3

The absolute Completeness
of the
ORIGINATION
of a phenomenon

4

The absolute Completeness
of the DEPENDENCE *of the* EXISTENCE
of what is changeable in a phenomenon

Antithetic of Pure Reason

Thetic is the term applied to every collection of dogmatical propositions. By antithetic I do not understand dogmatical assertions of the opposite, but the self-contradiction of seemingly dogmatical cognitions, in none of which we can discover any decided superiority. Antithetic is not therefore occupied with one-sided statements, but is engaged in considering the contradictory nature of the general cognitions of reason, and its causes. Transcendental antithetic is an investigation into the antinomy of pure reason, its causes and result. If we employ our reason not merely in the application of the principles of the understanding to objects of experience, but venture with it beyond these boundaries, there arise certain sophistical propositions or theorems. These assertions have the following peculiarities: They can find neither confirmation nor confutation in experience; and each is in itself not only self-consistent, but possesses conditions of its necessity in the very nature of reason—only that, unluckily, there exist just as valid and necessary grounds for maintaining the contrary proposition.

The questions which naturally arise in the consideration of this dialectic of pure reason, are therefore: 1st. In what propositions is pure reason unavoidably subject to an antinomy? 2nd. What are the causes of this antinomy? 3rd. Whether and in what way can reason free itself from this self-contradiction?

A dialectical proposition or theorem of pure reason must, according to what has been said, be distinguishable from all sophistical propositions, by the fact that it is not an answer to an arbitrary question, which may be raised at the mere pleasure of any person, but to one which human reason must necessarily encounter in its progress. In the second place, a dialectical proposition, with its opposite, does not carry the appearance of a merely artificial illusion, which disappears as soon as it is investigated, but a natural and unavoidable illusion, which, even when we are no longer deceived by it, continues to mock us, and, although rendered harmless, can never be completely removed.

This dialectical doctrine will not relate to the unity of understanding in empirical conceptions, but to the unity of reason in pure ideas. The conditions of this doctrine are—inasmuch as it must, as a synthesis according to rules, be conformable to the understanding, and at the same time as the absolute unity of the synthesis, to the reason—that, if it is adequate to the unity of reason, it is too great for the understanding, if according with the understanding, it is too small for the reason. Hence arises a mutual opposition, which cannot be avoided, do what we will.

FIRST CONFLICT OF THE TRANSCENDENTAL IDEAS

Thesis	*Antithesis*
The world has a beginning in time, and is also limited in regard to space.	The world has no beginning, and no limits in space, but is, in relation both to time and space, infinite.
PROOF	PROOF
Granted, that the world has no beginning in time; up to every given moment of time, an eternity must have elapsed, and therewith passed away an infinite series of successive conditions or states of things in the world. Now the infinity of a series consists in the fact, that it never can	For let it be granted, that it has a beginning. A beginning is an existence which is preceded by a time in which the thing does not exist. On the above supposition, it follows that there must have been a time in which the world did not exist, that is, a void time. But in a void time

be completed by means of a successive synthesis. It follows that an infinite series already elapsed is impossible, and that consequently a beginning of the world is a necessary condition of its existence. And this was the first thing to be proved.

As regards the second, let us take the opposite for granted. In this case, the world must be an infinite given total of coexistent things. Now we cannot cogitate the dimensions of a quantity, which is not given within certain limits of an intuition, in any other way than by means of the synthesis of its parts, and the total of such a quantity only by means of a completed synthesis, or the repeated addition of unity to itself. Accordingly, to cogitate the world, which fills all spaces, as a whole, the successive synthesis of the parts of an infinite world must be looked upon as completed, that is to say, an infinite time must be regarded as having elapsed in the enumeration of all coexisting things; which is impossible. For this reason an infinite aggregate of actual things cannot be considered as a given whole, consequently, not as a contemporaneously given whole. The world is consequently, as regards extension in space, *not infinite,* but enclosed in limits. And this was the second thing to be proved.

the origination of a thing is impossible; because no part of any such time contains a distinctive condition of being, in preference to that of non-being. Consequently, many series of things may have a beginning in the world, but the world itself cannot have a beginning, and is, therefore, in relation to past time, infinite.

As regards the second statement, let us first take the opposite for granted—that the world is finite and limited in space; it follows that it must exist in a void space, which is not limited. We should therefore meet not only with a relation of things *in space,* but also a relation of things *to space.* Now, as the world is an absolute whole, out of and beyond which no object of intuition, and consequently no correlate to which can be discovered, this relation of the world to a void space is merely a relation to *no object.* But such a relation, and consequently the limitation of the world by void space, is nothing. Consequently, the world, as regards space, is not limited, that is, it is infinite in regard to extension.

SECOND CONFLICT OF THE TRANSCENDENTAL IDEAS

Thesis	*Antithesis*
Every composite substance in the world consists of simple parts; and there exists nothing that is not either itself simple, or composed of simple parts.	No composite thing in the world consists of simple parts; and there does not exist in the world any simple substance.

PROOF

For, grant that composite substances do not consist of simple parts; in this case, if all combination or composition were annihilated in thought, no composite part and no simple part would exist. Consequently, no substance; consequently, nothing would exist. Either, then, it is impossible to annihilate composition in thought; or, after such annihilation, there must remain something that subsists without composition, that is, something that is simple. But in the former case the composite could not itself consist of substances, because with substances composition is merely a contingent relation, apart from which they must still exist as self-subsistent beings. Now, as this case contradicts the supposition, the second must contain the truth —that the substantial composite in the world consists of simple parts.

It follows as an immediate inference, that the things in the world are all, without exception, simple beings—that composition is merely an external condition pertaining to them—and that, although we never can separate and isolate the ele-

PROOF

Let it be supposed that a composite thing consists of simple parts. Inasmuch as all external relation, consequently all composition of substances, is possible only in space; the space, occupied by that which is composite, must consist of the same number of parts as is contained in the composite. But space does not consist of simple parts, but of spaces. Therefore, every part of the composite must occupy a space. But the absolutely primary parts of what is composite are simple. It follows that what is simple occupies a space. Now, as everything real that occupies a space, contains a manifold the parts of which are external to each other, and is consequently composite— and a real composite, not of accidents, but of substances—it follows that the simple must be a substantial composite, which is self-contradictory.

The second proposition of the antithesis—that there exists in the world nothing that is simple—is here equivalent to the following: The existence of the absolutely simple cannot be demonstrated

mentary substances from the state of composition, reason must cogitate these as the primary subjects of all composition, and consequently, as prior thereto—and as simple substances.

from any experience or perception either external or internal; and the absolutely simple is a mere idea, the objective reality of which cannot be demonstrated in any possible experience; it is consequently, in the exposition of phenomena, without application and object. For, let us take for granted that an object may be found in experience for this transcendental idea; the empirical intuition of such an object must then be recognized to contain absolutely no manifold with its parts external to each other, and connected into unity. Now, as we cannot reason from the non-consciousness of such a manifold to the impossibility of its existence in the intuition of an object, and as the proof of this impossibility is necessary for the establishment and proof of absolute simplicity; it follows, that this simplicity cannot be inferred from any perception whatever. As, therefore, an absolutely simple object cannot be given in any experience, and the world of sense must be considered as the sum total of all possible experiences: nothing simple exists in the world. This second proposition has a more extended aim than the first. The first merely banishes the simple from the intuition of the composite; while the second drives it entirely out of nature. Hence we were unable to demonstrate it from the conception of a given object of external intuition, but we were obliged to prove it from the relation of a given object to a possible experience in general.

THIRD CONFLICT OF TRANSCENDENTAL IDEAS

Thesis

Causality according to the laws of nature, is not the only causality operating to originate the phenomena of the world. A causality of freedom is also necessary to account fully for these phenomena.

PROOF

Let it be supposed, that there is no other kind of causality than that according to the laws of nature. Consequently, everything that happens presupposes a previous condition, which it follows with absolute certainty, in conformity with a rule. But this previous condition must itself be something that has happened, for, if it has always been in existence, its consequence or effect would not thus originate for the first time, but would likewise have always existed. The causality, therefore, of a cause, whereby something happens, is itself a thing that has *happened*. Now this again presupposes, in conformity with the law of nature, a previous condition and its causality, and this another anterior to the former, and so on. If, then, everything happens solely in accordance with the laws of nature, there cannot be any real first beginning of things, but only a subaltern or comparative beginning. There cannot, therefore, be a completeness of series on the side of the causes which originate the one from the other. But the law of nature is, that

Antithesis

There is no such thing as freedom, but everything in the world happens solely according to the laws of nature.

PROOF

Granted, that there does exist *freedom* in the transcendental sense, as a peculiar kind of causality, operating to produce events in the world —a faculty, that is to say, of originating a state, and consequently a series of consequences from that state. In this case, not only the series originated by this spontaneity, but the determination of this spontaneity itself to the production of the series, that is to say, the causality itself must have an absolute commencement, such, that nothing can precede to determine this action according to unvarying laws. But every beginning of action presupposes in the acting cause a state of inaction; and a dynamically primal beginning of action presupposes a state, which has no connection—as regards causality—with the preceding state of the cause—which does not, that is, in any wise result from it. Transcendental freedom is therefore opposed to the natural law of cause and effect, and such a conjunction of successive states in effective causes is destructive of the possibility of unity in experience, nothing can happen without a sufficient *a priori* determined cause. The proposition, therefore—if all causality is possible only in accordance with the laws of nature—is, when stated in this unlimited and general manner, self-contradictory. It follows that this cannot be the only kind of causality.

From what has been said, it follows that a causality must be admitted, by means of which something happens, without its cause being determined according to necessary laws by some other cause preceding. That is to say, there must exist an *absolute spontaneity* of cause, which of itself originates a series of phenomena which proceeds according to natural laws—consequently transcendental freedom, without which even in the course of nature the succession of phenomena on the side of causes is never complete.

and for that reason not to be found in experience—is consequently a mere fiction of thought.

We have, therefore, nothing but nature to which we must look for connection and order in cosmical events. Freedom—independence of the laws of nature—is certainly a deliverance from restraint, but it is also a relinquishing of the guidance of law and rule. For it cannot be alleged, that, instead of the laws of nature, laws of freedom may be introduced into the causality of the course of nature. For, if freedom were determined according to laws, it would be no longer freedom, but merely nature. Nature, therefore, and transcendental freedom are distinguishable as conformity to law and lawlessness. The former imposes upon understanding the difficulty of seeking the origin of events ever higher and higher in the series of causes, inasmuch as causality is always conditioned thereby; while it compensates this labour by the guarantee of a unity complete and in conformity with law. The latter, on the contrary, holds out to the understanding the promise of a point of rest in the chain of causes, by conducting it to an unconditioned causality, which professes to have the power of spontaneous origination, but which, in its own utter blindness, deprives it of the guidance of rules, by which alone a completely connected experience is possible.

FOURTH CONFLICT OF THE TRANSCENDENTAL IDEAS

Thesis	*Antithesis*
There exists either in, or in connection with the world—either as a part of it, or as the cause of it —an absolutely necessary being.	An absolutely necessary being does not exist, either in the world, or out of it—as its cause.

PROOF

The world of sense, as the sum total of all phenomena, contains a series of changes. For, without such a series, the mental representation of the series of time itself, as the condition of the possibility of the sensuous world, could not be presented to us. But every change stands under its condition, which precedes it in time and renders it necessary. Now the existence of a given condition presupposes a complete series of conditions up to the absolutely unconditioned, which alone is absolutely necessary. It follows that something that is absolutely necessary must exist, if change exists as its consequence. But this necessary thing itself belongs to the sensuous world. For suppose it to exist out of and apart from it, the series of cosmical changes would receive from it a beginning, and yet this necessary cause would not itself belong to the world of sense. But this is impossible. For, as the beginning of a series in time is determined only by that which precedes it in time, the supreme condition of the beginning of a series of changes must exist in the time in which this series itself did not exist;

PROOF

Grant that either the world itself is necessary, or that there is contained in it a necessary existence. Two cases are possible. *First,* there must either be in the series of cosmical changes a beginning, which is unconditionally necessary, and therefore uncaused—which is at variance with the dynamical law of the determination of all phenomena in time; or *secondly,* the series itself is without beginning, and, although contingent and conditioned in all its parts, is nevertheless absolutely necessary and unconditioned as a whole—which is self-contradictory. For the existence of an aggregate cannot be necessary, if no single part of it possesses necessary existence.

Grant, on the other hand, that an absolutely necessary cause exists out of and apart from the world. This cause, as the highest member in the series of the causes of cosmical changes, must originate or begin the existence of the latter and their series. In this case it must also begin to act, and its causality would therefore belong to time, and consequently to the sum total of phenomena, that is, to the world. It for a beginning supposes a time preceding, in which the thing that begins to be was not in existence. The causality of the necessary cause of changes, and consequently the cause itself, must for these reasons belong to time—and to phenomena, time being possible only as the form of phenomena. Consequently, it cannot be cogitated as separated from the world of sense—the sum total of all phenomena. There is, therefore, contained in the world, something that is absolutely necessary—whether it be the whole cosmical series itself, or only a part of it.

follows that the cause cannot be out of the world; which is contradictory to the hypothesis. Therefore, neither in the world, nor out of it, does there exist any absolutely necessary being.

Of the Interest of Reason in These Self-Contradictions

We have thus completely before us the dialectical procedure of the cosmological ideas. No possible experience can present us with an object adequate to them in extent. Nay, more, reason itself cannot cogitate them as according with the general laws of experience. And yet they are not arbitrary fictions of thought. On the contrary, reason, in its uninterrupted progress in the empirical synthesis, is necessarily conducted to them, when it endeavours to free from all conditions and to comprehend in its unconditioned totality, that which can only be determined conditionally in accordance with the laws of experience. These dialectical propositions are so many attempts to solve four natural and unavoidable problems of reason. There are neither more, nor can there be less, than this number, because there are no other series of synthetical hypotheses, limiting a priori the empirical synthesis.

The brilliant claims of reason striving to extend its dominion beyond the limits of experience have been represented above only in dry formulae, which contain merely the grounds of its pretensions. They have, besides, in conformity with the character of a transcendental philosophy, been freed from every empirical element; although the full splendour of the promises they hold out, and the anticipations they excite, manifests itself only when in connection with empirical cognitions. In the application of them, however, and in the advancing enlargement of the employment of reason, while struggling to rise from the region of experience and to soar to those sublime ideas, philosophy discovers a value and a dignity, which, if it could but make good its assertions, would raise it far above all other departments of human knowledge—professing, as it does, to present a sure foundation for our highest hopes and the ultimate aims of all the exertions of reason. The questions: whether the world has a beginning and a limit to its extension in space; whether there exists any-where, or perhaps, in my own thinking Self, an indivisible and inde-structible unity—or whether nothing but what is divisible and transitory exists; whether I am a free agent, or, like other beings, am bound in the chains of nature and fate; whether, finally, there is a supreme cause of the world, or all our thought and speculation must end with nature and the order of external things—are questions for the solution of which the mathematician would willingly exchange his whole science; for in it there is no satisfaction for the highest aspirations and most ardent desires of humanity. Nay, it may even be said that the true value of mathematics —that pride of human reason—consists in this: that she guides reason to the knowledge of nature—in her greater, as well as in her less manifesta-tions—in her beautiful order and regularity—guides her, moreover, to an insight into the wonderful unity of the moving forces in the opera-tions of nature, far beyond the expectations of a philosophy building only on experience; and that she thus encourages philosophy to extend the province of reason beyond all experience, and at the same time provides it with the most excellent materials for supporting its investigations, in so far as their nature admits, by adequate and accordant intuitions.

Of the Necessity Imposed upon Pure Reason of Presenting a Solution of Its Transcendental Problems

To avow an ability to solve all problems and to answer all questions, would be a profession certain to convict any philosopher of extravagant boasting and self-conceit, and at once to destroy the confidence that might otherwise have been reposed in him. There are, however, sciences so constituted, that every question arising within their sphere must necessarily be capable of receiving an answer from the knowledge already possessed, for the answer must be received from the same sources whence the question arose. In such sciences it is not allowable to excuse ourselves on the plea of necessary and unavoidable ignorance; a solution is absolutely requisite. The rule of *right* and *wrong* must help us to the knowledge of what is right or wrong in all possible cases; otherwise, the idea of obligation or duty would be utterly null, for we cannot have any obliga-tion to that *which we cannot know*. On the other hand, in our investiga-tions of the phenomena of nature, much must remain uncertain, and many questions continue insoluble; because what we know of nature is far from being sufficient to explain all the phenomena that are presented to our observation. Now the question is: Whether there is in transcendental philosophy any question, relating to an object presented to pure reason, which is unanswerable by this reason; and whether we must regard the subject of the question as quite uncertain—so far as our knowledge extends, and must give it a place among those subjects, of which we have just so much conception as is sufficient to enable us to raise a question—faculty or materials failing us, however, when we attempt an answer.

Now I maintain, that among all speculative cognition, the peculiarity of transcendental philosophy is, that there is no question, relating to an object presented to pure reason, which is insoluble by this reason; and that the profession of unavoidable ignorance—the problem being alleged to be beyond the reach of our faculties—cannot free us from the obligation to present a complete and satisfactory answer. For the very conception, which enables us to raise the question, must give us the power of answering it; inasmuch as the object, as in the case of right and wrong, is not to be discovered out of the conception.

Sceptical Exposition of the Cosmological Problems Presented in the Four Transcendental Ideas

We should be quite willing to desist from the demand of a dogmatical answer to our questions, if we understood beforehand that, be the answer what it may, it would only serve to increase our ignorance, to throw us from one incomprehensibility into another, from one obscurity into another still greater, and perhaps lead us into irreconcilable contradictions. If a dogmatical affirmative or negative answer is demanded, is it at all prudent to set aside the probable grounds of a solution which lie before us, and to take into consideration what advantage we shall gain, if the answer is to favour the one side or the other? If it happens that in both cases the answer is mere nonsense, we have in this an irresistible summons to institute a critical investigation of the question, for the purpose of discovering whether it is based on a groundless presupposition, and relates to an idea, the falsity of which would be more easily exposed in its application and consequences, than in the mere representation of its content. This is the great utility of the sceptical mode of treating the questions addressed by pure reason to itself. By this method we easily rid ourselves of the confusions of dogmatism, and establish in its place a temperate criticism, which, as a genuine cathartic, will successfully remove the presumptuous notions of philosophy and their consequence—the vain pretension to universal science.

If, then, I could understand the nature of a cosmological idea, and perceive, before I entered on the discussion of the subject at all, that, whatever side of the question regarding the unconditioned of the regressive synthesis of phenomena it favoured, it must either be *too great* or *too small* for every *conception of the understanding*—I would be able to comprehend how the idea, which relates to an object of experience—an experience which must be adequate to and in accordance with a possible conception of the understanding—must be completely void and without significance, inasmuch as its object is inadequate, consider it as we may. And this is actually the case with all cosmological conceptions, which, for the reason above mentioned, involve reason, so long as it remains attached to them, in an unavoidable antinomy. For suppose:

First, that *the world has no beginning*—in this case it is too large for our conception; for this conception, which consists in a successive regress, cannot overtake the whole eternity that has elapsed. Grant that *it has a beginning,* it is then too small for the conception of the understanding. For, as a beginning presupposes a time preceding, it cannot be unconditioned; and the law of the empirical employment of the understanding imposes the necessity of looking for a higher condition of time; and the world is, therefore, evidently too small for this law.

Secondly, if every phenomenon in space consists of an *infinite number of parts,* the regress of the division is always too great for our conception; and if the *division* of space must *cease* with some member of the division, it is too small for the idea of the unconditioned. For the member at which we have discontinued our division still admits a regress to many more parts contained in the object.

Thirdly, suppose that every event in the world happens in accordance with the laws of nature; the causality of a cause must itself be an event, and necessitates a regress to a still higher cause, and consequently the unceasing prolongation of the series of conditions *a parte priori.* Operative nature is therefore too large for every conception we can form in the synthesis of cosmical events.

Fourthly, if we assume the existence of an *absolutely necessary being* —whether it be the world or something in the world, or the cause of the world; we must place it in a time at an infinite distance from any given moment; for, otherwise, it must be dependent on some other and higher existence. Such an existence is, in this case, too large for our empirical conception, and unattainable by the continued regress of any synthesis.

But if we believe that everything in the world—be it condition or conditioned—is *contingent;* every given existence is too small for our conception. For in this case we are compelled to seek for some other existence upon which the former depends.

Transcendental Idealism as the Key to the Solution of Pure Cosmological Dialectic

In the transcendental aesthetic we proved, that everything intuited in space and time—all objects of a possible experience, are nothing but phenomena, that is, mere representations; and that these, as presented to us—as extended bodies, or as series of changes—have no self-subsistent existence apart from human thought. This doctrine I call *Transcendental Idealism.* The realist in the transcendental sense regards these modifications of our sensibility—these mere representations, as things subsisting in themselves.

Transcendental idealism allows that the objects of external intuition —as intuited in space, and all changes in time—as represented by the internal sense, are real. For, as space is the form of that intuition which we call external, and without objects in space, no empirical representation could be given us; we can and ought to regard extended bodies in it as real. The case is the same with representations in time. But time and space, with all phenomena therein, are not in themselves *things.* They are nothing but representations, and cannot exist out of and apart from the mind. Nay, the sensuous internal intuition of the mind, the determination of which is represented by the succession of different states in time, is not the real, proper self, as it exists in itself—not the transcendental subject, but only a phenomenon, which is presented to the sensibility of this, to us, unknown being. This internal phenomenon cannot be admitted to be a self-subsisting thing; for its condition is time, and time cannot be the condition of a thing in itself. But the empirical truth of phenomena in space and time is guaranteed beyond the possibility of doubt, and sufficiently distinguished from the illusion of dreams or fancy—although both have a proper and thorough connection in an experience according to empirical laws. The objects of experience then are not things in themselves, but are given only in experience, and have no existence apart from and independently of experience. That there may be inhabitants in the moon, although no one has ever observed them, must certainly be admitted; but this assertion means only, that we may in the possible progress of experience discover them at some future time. For that, which stands in connection with a perception according to the laws of the progress of experience, is real. They are therefore really existent, if they stand in empirical connection with my actual or real consciousness, although they are not in themselves real, that is, apart from the progress of experience.

There is nothing actually given—we can be conscious of nothing as real, except a perception and the empirical progression from it to other possible perceptions. For phenomena, as mere representations, are real only in perception; and perception is, in. fact, nothing but the reality of an empirical representation, that is, a phenomenon. To call a phenomenon a real thing prior to perception, means either that we must meet with this phenomenon in the progress of experience, or it means nothing at all. For I can say only of a thing in itself that it exists without relation to the senses and experience. But we are speaking here merely of phenomena in space and time, both of which are determinations of sensibility, and not of things in themselves. It follows that phenomena are not things in themselves, but are mere representations, which, if not given in us— in perception, are non-existent.

Critical Solution of the Cosmological Problem

The antinomy of pure reason is based upon the following dialectical argument: If that which is conditioned is given, the whole series of its conditions is also given; but sensuous objects are given as conditioned; consequently . . . This syllogism, the major of which seems so natural and evident, introduces as many cosmological ideas as there are different kinds of conditions in the synthesis of phenomena, in so far as these conditions constitute a series. These ideas require absolute totality in the series, and thus place reason in inextricable embarrassment. Before proceeding to expose the fallacy in this dialectical argument, it will be necessary to have a correct understanding of certain conceptions that appear in it.

In the first place, the following proposition is evident, and indubitably certain: If the conditioned is given, a regress in the series of all its conditions is thereby imperatively *required*. For the very conception of a conditioned is a conception of something related to a condition, and, if this condition is itself conditioned, to another condition—and so on through all the members of the series. This proposition is, therefore, analytical, and has nothing to fear from transcendental criticism. It is a logical postulate of reason: to pursue, as far as possible, the connection of a conception with its conditions.

If, in the second place, both the conditioned and the condition are things in themselves, and if the former is given, not only is the regress to the latter requisite, but the latter is really *given with* the former. Now, as this is true of all the members of the series, the entire series of conditions, and with them the unconditioned, is at the same time given in the very fact of the conditioned, the existence of which is possible only in and through that series, being given. In this case, the synthesis of the conditioned with its condition, is a synthesis of the understanding merely, which represents things *as they are,* without regarding whether and how we can cognize them. But if I have to do with phenomena, which, in their character of mere representations, are not given, if I do not attain to a cognition of them, I am not entitled to say: If the conditioned is given, all its conditions (as phenomena) are also given. I cannot, therefore, from the fact of a conditioned being given, infer the absolute totality of the series of its conditions. For phenomena are nothing but an empirical synthesis in apprehension or perception, and are therefore given only in it. Now, in speaking of phenomena, it does not follow, that, if the conditioned is given, the synthesis which constitutes its empirical condition is also thereby given and presupposed; such a synthesis can be established only by an actual regress in the series of conditions. But we are entitled to say in this case: that a *regress* to the conditions of a conditioned, in other words, that a continuous empirical synthesis is enjoined; that, if the conditions are not *given,* they are at least *required;* and that we are certain to discover the conditions in this regress.

We can now see that the major in the above cosmological syllogism, takes the conditioned in the transcendental signification which it has in the pure category, while the minor speaks of it in the empirical signification which it has in the category as applied to phenomena. There is, therefore, a dialectical fallacy in the syllogism—a *sophisma figurae dictionis.* But this fallacy is not a consciously devised one, but a perfectly natural illusion of the common reason of man. For, when a thing is given as conditioned, we presuppose in the major its conditions and their series, unperceived, as it were, and unseen; because this is nothing more than the logical requirement of complete and satisfactory premises for a given conclusion. In this case, time is altogether left out in the connection of the conditioned with the condition; they are supposed to be given in themselves, and *contemporaneously.* It is, moreover, just as natural to regard phenomena (in the minor) as things in themselves and as objects presented to the pure understanding, as in the major, in which complete abstraction was made of all conditions of intuition. But it is under these conditions alone that objects are given. Now we overlooked a remarkable distinction between the conceptions. The synthesis of the conditioned with its condition, and the complete series of the latter are not limited by time, and do not contain the conception of succession. On the contrary, the empirical synthesis, and the series of conditions in the phenomenal world—subsumed in the minor—are necessarily successive, and given in time alone. It follows that I cannot presuppose in the minor, as I did in the major, the absolute *totality* of the synthesis and of the series therein represented; for in the major all the members of the series are given as things in themselves—without any limitations or conditions of time, while in the minor they are possible only in and through a successive regress, which cannot exist, except it be actually carried into execution in the world of phenomena.

Regulative Principle of Pure Reason in Relation to the Cosmological Ideas

The cosmological principle of totality could not give us any certain knowledge in regard to the *maximum* in the series of conditions in the world of sense, considered as a thing in itself. The actual regress in the series is the only means of approaching this maximum. This principle of pure reason, therefore, may still be considered as valid—not as an *axiom* enabling us to cogitate totality in the object as actual, but as a *problem* for the understanding, which requires it to institute and to continue, in conformity with the idea of totality in the mind, the regress in the series of the conditions of a given conditioned. For in the world of sense, that is, in space and time, every condition which we discover in our investigation of phenomena is itself conditioned; because sensuous objects are not things in themselves, but are merely empirical representations, the conditions of which must always be found in intuition. The principle of reason is therefore properly a mere rule—prescribing a regress in the series of conditions for given phenomena, and prohibiting any pause or rest on an absolutely unconditioned. It is, therefore, not a principle of the possibility of experience or of the empirical cognition of sensuous objects—consequently not a principle of the understanding; for every experience is confined within certain proper limits determined by the given intuition. Still less is it a *constitutive principle* of reason authorizing us to extend our conception of the sensuous world beyond all possible experience. It is merely a principle for the enlargement and extension of experience as far as is possible for human faculties. It forbids us to consider any empirical limits as absolute. It is, hence, a principle of reason, which, as a *rule,* dictates how we ought to proceed in our empirical regress, but is unable to *anticipate* or indicate prior to the empirical regress what is given in the object itself. I have termed it for this reason a *regulative* principle of reason; while the principle of the absolute totality of the series of conditions, as existing in itself and given in the object, is a constitutive cosmological principle. This distinction will at once demonstrate the falsehood of the constitutive principle, and prevent us from attributing objective reality to an idea, which is valid only as a rule.

*Of the Empirical Use of the Regulative Principle of Reason with
Regard to the Cosmological Ideas*

We have shown that no transcendental use can be made either of
the conceptions of reason or of understanding. We have shown, likewise,
that the demand of absolute totality in the series of conditions in the
world of sense arises from a transcendental employment of reason, rest-
ing on the opinion that phenomena are to be regarded as things in themselves. It follows that we are not required to answer the question respecting the absolute quantity of a series—whether it is *in itself* limited or unlimited. We are only called upon to determine how far we must proceed
in the empirical regress from condition to condition, in order to discover,
in conformity with the rule of reason, a full and correct answer to the
question proposed by reason itself.

This principle of reason is hence valid only as a rule for the *extension*
of a possible experience—its invalidity as a principle constitutive of
phenomena in themselves having been sufficiently demonstrated. And
thus, too, the antinomial conflict of reason with itself is completely put
an end to; inasmuch as we have not only presented a critical solution
of the fallacy lurking in the opposite statements of reason, but have shown
the true meaning of the ideas which gave rise to these statements. The
dialectical principle of reason has, therefore, been changed into a *doctrinal*
principle. But in fact, if this principle, in the subjective signification
which we have shown to be its only true sense, may be guaranteed as a
principle of the unceasing extension of the employment of our understanding, its influence and value are just as great as if it were an axiom
for the *a priori* determination of objects. For such an axiom could not
exert a stronger influence on the extension and rectification of our knowledge, otherwise than by procuring for the principles of the understanding
the most widely expanded employment in the field of experience.

I. SOLUTION OF THE COSMOLOGICAL IDEA OF THE TOTALITY OF THE COMPOSITION OF PHENOMENA IN THE UNIVERSE

Here, as well as in the case of the other cosmological problems, the
ground of the regulative principle of reason is the proposition, that in
our empirical regress *no experience of an absolute limit,* and consequently
no experience of a condition, which is itself *absolutely unconditioned,* is
discoverable. And the truth of this proposition itself rests upon the consideration, that such an experience must represent to us phenomena as

limited by nothing or the mere void, on which our continued regress by means of perception must abut—which is impossible.

Now this proposition, which declares that every condition attained in the empirical regress must itself be considered empirically conditioned, contains the rule *in terminis,* which requires me, to whatever extent I may have proceeded in the ascending series, always to look for some higher member in the series—whether this member is to become known to me through experience, or not.

Nothing further is necessary, then, for the solution of the first cosmological problem, than to decide whether, in the regress to the unconditioned quantity of the universe, this never limited ascent ought to be called a *regressus in infinitum* or *in indefinitum.*

The general representation which we form in our minds of the series of all past states or conditions of the world, or of all the things which at present exist in it, is itself nothing more than a *possible* empirical regress, which is cogitated—although in an undetermined manner—in the mind, and which gives rise to the conception of a series of conditions for a given object. Now I have a conception of the universe, but not an intuition—that is, not an intuition of it as a whole. Thus I cannot infer the magnitude of the regress from the quantity or magnitude of the world, and determine the former by means of the latter; on the contrary, I must first of all form a conception of the quantity or magnitude of the world from the magnitude of the empirical regress. But of this regress I know nothing more, than that I ought to proceed from every given member of the series of conditions to one still higher. But the quantity of the universe is not thereby determined, and we cannot affirm that this regress proceeds *in infinitum.* Such an affirmation would *anticipate* the members of the series which have not yet been reached, and represent the number of them as beyond the grasp of any empirical synthesis; it would consequently *determine* the cosmical quantity prior to the regress—which is impossible. For the world is not given in its totality in any intuition: consequently, its quantity cannot be given prior to the regress. It follows that we are unable to make any declaration respecting the cosmical quantity in itself—not even that the regress in it is a regress *in infinitum;* we must only endeavour to attain to a conception of the quantity of the universe, in conformity with the rule which determines the empirical regress in it. But this rule merely requires us never to admit an absolute limit to our series—how far soever we may have proceeded in it, but always, on the contrary, to subordinate every phenomenon to some other as its condition, and consequently to proceed to this higher phenomenon. Such a regress is, therefore, the *regressus in indefinitum,* which, as not determining a quantity in the object, is clearly distinguishable from the *regressus in infinitum.*

It follows from what we have said that we are not justified in declaring the world to be infinite in space, or as regards past time. For this conception of an infinite given quantity is empirical; but we cannot apply the conception of an infinite quantity to the world as an object of the senses. I cannot say, the regress from a given perception to everything limited either in space or time, proceeds *in infinitum*—for this presupposes an infinite cosmical quantity; neither can I say, it is *finite*—for an absolute limit is likewise impossible in experience. It follows that I am not entitled to make any assertion at all respecting the whole object of experience—the world of sense; I must limit my declarations to the rule, according to which experience or empirical knowledge is to be attained.

To the question, therefore, respecting the cosmical quantity, the first and negative answer is: The world has no beginning in time, and no absolute limit in space.

For, in the contrary case, it would be limited by a void time on the one hand, and by a void space on the other. Now, since the world, as a phenomenon, cannot be thus limited in itself—for a phenomenon is not a thing in itself; it must be possible for us to have a perception of this limitation by a void time and a void space. But such a perception —such an experience is impossible; because it has no content. Consequently, an absolute cosmical limit is empirically, and therefore absolutely, impossible.

From this follows the *affirmative* answer: The regress in the series of phenomena—as a determination of the cosmical quantity, proceeds *in indefinitum*. This is equivalent to saying—the world of sense has no absolute quantity, but the empirical regress rests upon a rule, which requires it to proceed from every member of the series—as conditioned, to one still more remote, and not to cease at any point in this extension of the possible empirical employment of the understanding. And this is the proper and only use which reason can make of its principles.

II. SOLUTION OF THE COSMOLOGICAL IDEA OF THE TOTALITY OF THE DIVISION
OF A WHOLE GIVEN IN INTUITION

When I divide a whole which is given in intuition, I proceed from a conditioned to its conditions. The division of the parts of the whole is a regress in the series of these conditions. The absolute totality of this series would be actually attained and given to the mind, if the regress could arrive at *simple* parts. But if all the parts in a continuous decomposition are themselves divisible, the division, that is to say, the regress, proceeds from the conditioned to its conditions *in infinitum;* because the conditions are themselves contained in the conditioned, and, as the latter is given in a limited intuition, the former are all given along with it. This regress cannot, therefore, be called a *regressus in indefinitum,* as happened in the case of the preceding cosmological idea, the regress in which proceeded from the conditioned to the conditions not given contemporaneously and along with it, but discoverable only through the empirical regress. We are not, however, entitled to affirm of a whole of this kind, which is divisible *in infinitum,* that *it consists of an infinite number of parts.* For, although all the parts are contained in the intuition of the whole, the *whole division* is not contained therein. The division is contained only in the progressing decomposition—in the regress itself, which is the condition of the possibility and actuality of the series. Now, as this regress is infinite, all the members to which it attains must be contained in the given whole as an *aggregate.* But the complete *series of division* is not contained therein. For this series, being infinite in succession and always incomplete, cannot represent an infinite number of members, and still less a composition of these members into a whole.

To apply this remark to space. Every limited part of space presented to intuition is a whole, the parts of which are always spaces—to whatever extent subdivided. Every limited space is hence divisible to infinity.

III. SOLUTION OF THE COSMOLOGICAL IDEA OF THE TOTALITY OF THE DEDUCTION OF COSMICAL EVENTS FROM THEIR CAUSES

There are only two modes of causality cogitable—the causality of *nature,* or of *freedom.* The first is the conjunction of a particular state with another preceding it in the world of sense, the former following the latter by virtue of a law. Now, as the causality of phenomena is subject to conditions of time, and the preceding state, if it had always existed, could not have produced an effect which would make its first appearance at a particular time, the causality of a cause must itself be an effect—must itself have *begun to be,* and therefore, according to the principle of the understanding, itself requires a cause.

We must understand, on the contrary, by the term freedom, in the cosmological sense, a faculty of the *spontaneous* origination of a state; the causality of which, therefore, is not subordinated to another cause determining it in time. Freedom is in this sense a pure transcendental idea, which, in the first place, contains no empirical element; the object of which, in the second place, cannot be given or determined in any experience, because it is a universal law of the very possibility of experience, that everything which happens must have a cause, that consequently the causality of a cause, being itself something that has *hap-*

pened, must also have a cause. In this view of the case, the whole field
of experience, how far soever it may extend, contains nothing that is not
subject to the laws of nature. But, as we cannot by this means attain to
an absolute totality of conditions in reference to the series of causes and
effects, reason creates the idea of a spontaneity, which can begin to act
of itself, and without any external cause determining it to action, according to the natural law of causality.

IV. SOLUTION OF THE COSMOLOGICAL IDEA OF THE TOTALITY OF THE
DEPENDENCE OF PHENOMENAL EXISTENCES

In the preceding remarks, we considered the changes in the world
of sense as constituting a dynamical series, in which each member is
subordinated to another—as its cause. Our present purpose is to avail
ourselves of this series of states or conditions as a guide to an existence
which may be the highest condition of all changeable phenomena, that is,
to a *necessary being.* Our endeavour is to reach, not the unconditioned
causality, but the unconditioned existence, of substance. The series before
us is therefore a series of conceptions, and not of intuitions (in which
the one intuition is the condition of the other).

But it is evident that, as all phenomena are subject to change, and
conditioned in their existence, the series of dependent existences cannot
embrace an unconditioned member, the existence of which would be
absolutely necessary. It follows that, if phenomena were things in themselves, and—as an immediate consequence from this supposition—condition and conditioned belonged to the same series of phenomena, the
existence of a necessary being, as the condition of the existence of sensuous
phenomena, would be perfectly impossible.

An important distinction, however, exists between the dynamical
and the mathematical regress. The latter is engaged solely with the combination of parts into a whole, or with the division of a whole into its
parts; and therefore are the conditions of its series parts of the series,
and to be consequently regarded as homogeneous, and for this reason,
as consisting, without exception, of phenomena. In the former regress,
on the contrary, the aim of which is not to establish the possibility of
an unconditioned whole consisting of given parts, or of an unconditioned
part of a given whole, but to demonstrate the possibility of the deduction of a certain state from its cause, or of the contingent existence of
substance from that which exists necessarily, it is not requisite that the
condition should form part of an empirical series along with the conditioned.

In the case of the apparent antinomy with which we are at present dealing, there exists a way of escape from the difficulty; for it is not impossible that both of the contradictory statements may be true in different relations. All sensuous phenomena may be contingent, and consequently possess only an empirically conditioned existence, and yet there may also exist a non-empirical condition of the whole series, or, in other words, a necessary being. For this necessary being, as an intelligible condition, would not form a member—not even the highest member— of the series; the whole world of sense would be left in its empirically determined existence uninterfered with and uninfluenced. This would also form a ground of distinction between the modes of solution employed for the third and fourth antinomies. For, while in the consideration of freedom in the former antinomy, the thing itself—the cause was regarded as belonging to the series of conditions, and only its *causality* to the intelligible world—we are obliged in the present case to cogitate this necessary being as purely intelligible and as existing entirely apart from the world of sense; for otherwise it would be subject to the phenomenal law of contingency and dependence.

In relation to the present problem, therefore, the *regulative principle* of reason is that everything in the sensuous world possesses an empirically conditioned existence—that no property of the sensuous world possesses unconditioned necessity—that we are bound to expect, and, so far as is possible, to seek for the empirical condition of every member in the series of conditions—and that there is no sufficient reason to justify us in deducing any existence from a condition which lies out of and beyond the empirical series, or in regarding any existence as independent and self-subsistent; although this should not prevent us from recognizing the possibility of the whole series being based upon a being which is intelligible, and for this reason free from all empirical conditions.

III. The Ideal of Pure Reason

Of the Ideal in General

WE HAVE SEEN that pure conceptions do not present objects to the mind, except under sensuous conditions; because the conditions of objective reality do not exist in these conceptions, which contain, in fact, nothing but the mere form of thought. They may, however, when applied to phenomena, be presented *in concreto;* for it is phenomena that present to them the materials for the formation of empirical conceptions, which are nothing more than concrete forms of the conceptions of the understanding. But *ideas* are still further removed from objective reality than *categories;* for no phenomenon can ever present them to the human mind *in concreto.* They contain a certain perfection, attainable by no possible empirical cognition; and they give to reason a systematic unity, to which the unity of experience attempts to approximate, but can never completely attain.

But still further removed than the idea from objective reality is the *Ideal,* by which term I understand the idea, not *in concreto,* but *in individuo*—as an individual thing, determinable or determined by the idea alone. The idea of humanity in its complete perfection supposes not only the advancement of all the powers and faculties, which constitute our conception of human nature, to a complete attainment of their final aims, but also everything which is requisite for the complete determination of the idea; for of all contradictory predicates, only one can conform with the idea of the perfect man. What I have termed an ideal, was in Plato's philosophy an *idea of the divine mind*—an individual object present to its pure intuition, the most perfect of every kind of possible beings, and the archetype of all phenomenal existences.

Without rising to these speculative heights, we are bound to confess that human reason contains not only ideas, but ideals, which possess, not, like those of Plato, creative, but certainly *practical* power—as regulative principles, and form the basis of the perfectibility of certain *actions.* Moral conceptions are not perfectly pure conceptions of reason, because an empirical element—of pleasure or pain—lies at the foundation of them. In relation, however, to the principle, whereby reason sets bounds to a freedom which is in itself without law, and consequently when we attend merely to their form, they may be considered as pure conceptions of reason. Virtue and wisdom in their perfect purity are ideas. But the wise man of the Stoics is an ideal, that is to say, a human being existing only in thought, and in complete conformity with the idea of wisdom. As the idea provides a rule, so the ideal serves as an *archetype* for the perfect and complete determination of the copy. Thus the conduct of this wise and divine man serves us as a standard of action, with which we may compare and judge ourselves, which may help us to reform ourselves, although the perfection it demands can never be attained by us. Although we cannot concede objective reality to these ideals, they are not to be considered as chimeras; on the contrary, they provide reason with a standard, which enables it to estimate, by comparison, the degree of incompleteness in the objects presented to it. But to aim at realizing the ideal in an example in the world of experience—to describe, for instance, the character of the perfectly wise man in a romance, is impracticable. Nay more, there is something absurd in the attempt; and the result must be little edifying, as the natural limitations which are continually breaking in upon the perfection and completeness of the idea, destroy the illusion in the story, and throw an air of suspicion even on what is good in the idea, which hence appears fictitious and unreal.

Of the Transcendental Ideal

Every conception is, in relation to that which is not contained in it, undetermined and subject to the principle of *determinability*. This principle is, that of *every two* contradictorily opposed predicates, only one can belong to a conception. It is a purely logical principle, itself based upon the principle of contradiction; inasmuch as it makes complete abstraction of the content, and attends merely to the logical form of the cognition.

But again, everything, as it regards its possibility, is also subject to the principle of complete determination, according to which one of *all the possible contradictory predicates* of things must belong to it. This principle is not based merely upon that of contradiction; for, in addition to the relation between two contradictory predicates, it regards everything as standing in a relation to the *sum of possibilities,* as the sum-total of all predicates of things, and, while presupposing this sum as an *a priori* condition, presents to the mind everything as receiving the possibility of its individual existence from the relation it bears to, and the share it possesses in the aforesaid sum of possibilities. The principle of complete determination relates therefore to the content and not to the logical form. It is the principle of the synthesis of all the predicates which are required to constitute the complete conception of a thing, and not a mere principle of analytical representation, which enounces that one of two contradictory predicates must belong to a conception. It contains, moreover, a transcendental presupposition—that, namely, of the material for *all possibility,* which must contain *a priori* the data for this or that *particular possibility.*

The proposition, *Everything which exists is completely determined,* means not only that one of every pair of *given* contradictory attributes, but that one of all *possible* attributes, is always predicable of the thing; in it the predicates are not merely compared logically with each other, but the thing itself is transcendentally compared with the sum-total of all possible predicates. The proposition is equivalent to saying: To attain to a complete knowledge of a thing, it is necessary to possess a knowledge of everything that is possible, and to determine it thereby in a positive or negative manner. The conception of complete determination is consequently a conception which cannot be presented in its totality *in concreto,* and is therefore based upon an idea, which has its seat in the reason

—the faculty which prescribes to the understanding the laws of its harmonious and perfect exercise.

Now, although this idea of the *sum-total of all possibility,* in so far as it forms the condition of the complete determination of everything, is itself undetermined in relation to the predicates which may constitute this sum-total, and we cogitate in it merely the sum-total of all possible predicates—we nevertheless find, upon closer examination, that this idea, as a primitive conception of the mind, excludes a large number of predicates—those deduced and those irreconcilable with others, and that it is evolved as a conception completely determined *a priori.* Thus it becomes the conception of an individual object, which is completely determined by and through the mere idea, and must consequently be termed an ideal of pure reason.

When we consider all possible predicates, not merely logically, but transcendentally, that is to say, with reference to the content which may be cogitated as existing in them *a priori,* we shall find that some indicate a being, others merely a non-being. The logical negation expressed in the word *not,* does not properly belong to a conception, but only to the relation of one conception to another in a judgment, and is consequently quite insufficient to present to the mind the content of a conception. The expression *not mortal* does not indicate that a non-being is cogitated in the object; it does not concern the content at all. A transcendental negation, on the contrary, indicates non-being in itself, and is opposed to transcendental affirmation, the conception of which of itself expresses a being. Hence this affirmation indicates a reality, because in and through it objects are considered to be something—to be things; while the opposite negation, on the other hand, indicates a mere want, or privation, or absence, and, where such negations alone are attached to a representation, the non-existence of anything corresponding to the representation.

Now a negation cannot be cogitated as determined, without cogitating at the same time the opposite affirmation. The man born blind has not the least notion of darkness, because he has none of light; the vagabond knows nothing of poverty, because he has never known what it is to be in comfort; the ignorant man has no conception of his ignorance, because he has no conception of knowledge. All conceptions of negatives are accordingly derived or deduced conceptions; and realities contain the *data,* and, so to speak, the material or transcendental content of the possibility and complete determination of all things.

If, therefore, a transcendental substratum lies at the foundation of the complete determination of things—a substratum which is to form the fund from which all possible predicates of things are to be supplied, this substratum cannot be anything else than the idea of a sum-total of reality. In this view, negations are nothing but *limitations*—a term which could not, with propriety, be applied to them, if the unlimited did not form the true basis of our conception.

Of the Arguments Employed by Speculative Reason in Proof of the Existence of a Supreme Being

Notwithstanding the pressing necessity which reason feels, to form some presupposition that shall serve the understanding as a proper basis for the complete determination of its conceptions, the idealistic and factitious nature of such a presupposition is too evident to allow reason for a moment to persuade itself into a belief of the objective existence of a mere creation of its own thought. But there are other considerations which compel reason to seek out some resting-place in the regress from the conditioned to the unconditioned, which is not given as an actual existence from the mere conception of it, although it alone can give completeness to the series of conditions. And this is the natural course of every human reason, even of the most uneducated, although the path at first entered it does not always continue to follow. It does not begin from conceptions, but from common experience, and requires a basis in actual existence. But this basis is insecure, unless it rests upon the immovable rock of the absolutely necessary. And this foundation is itself unworthy of trust, if it leave under and above it empty space, if it do not fill all, and leave no room for a *why* or a *wherefore,* if it be not, in one word, infinite in its reality.

If we admit the existence of some one thing, whatever it may be, we must also admit that there is something which exists *necessarily.* For what is contingent exists only under the condition of some other thing, which is its cause; and from this we must go on to conclude the existence of a cause which is not contingent, and which consequently exists necessarily and unconditionally. Such is the argument by which reason justifies its advances towards a primal being.

Now reason looks round for the conception of a being that may be admitted, without inconsistency, to be worthy of the attribute of absolute necessity, not for the purpose of inferring *a priori,* from the conception of such a being, its objective existence, but for the purpose of discovering, among all our conceptions of possible things, that conception which possesses no element inconsistent with the idea of absolute necessity. For that there must be some absolutely necessary existence, it regards as a truth already established. Now, if it can remove every existence incapable of supporting the attribute of absolute necessity, excepting one—this must be the absolutely necessary being, whether its necessity is comprehensible by us, that is, deducible from the conception of it alone, or not.

Of the Impossibility of an Ontological Proof of the Existence of God

It is evident from what has been said, that the conception of an absolutely necessary being is a mere idea, the objective reality of which is far from being established by the mere fact that it is a need of reason. On the contrary, this idea serves merely to indicate a certain unattainable perfection, and rather limits the operations than, by the presentation of new objects, extends the sphere of the understanding. But a strange anomaly meets us at the very threshold; for the inference from a given existence in general to an absolutely necessary existence, seems to be correct and unavoidable, while the conditions of the *understanding* refuse to aid us in forming any conception of such a being.

Philosophers have always talked of an *absolutely necessary* being, and have nevertheless declined to take the trouble of conceiving, whether—and how—a being of this nature is even cogitable, not to mention that its existence is actually demonstrable. A verbal definition of the conception is certainly easy enough: it is something, the non-existence of which is impossible. But does this definition throw any light upon the conditions which render it impossible to cogitate the non-existence of a thing—conditions which we wish to ascertain, that we may discover whether we think anything in the conception of such a being or not? For the mere fact that I throw away, by means of the word *Unconditioned,* all the conditions which the understanding habitually requires in order to regard anything as necessary, is very far from making clear whether by means of the conception of the unconditionally necessary I think of something, or really of nothing at all.

Nay, more, this chance-conception, now become so current, many have endeavoured to explain by examples which seemed to render any inquiries regarding its intelligibility quite needless. Every geometrical proposition—a triangle has three angles—it was said, is absolutely necessary; and thus people talked of an object which lay out of the sphere of our understanding as if it were perfectly plain what the conception of such a being meant.

All the examples adduced have been drawn, without exception, from *judgments,* and not from *things.* But the unconditioned necessity of a judgment does not form the absolute necessity of a thing. On the contrary, the absolute necessity of a judgment is only a conditioned necessity of a thing, or of the predicate in a judgment. The proposition above mentioned does not enounce that three angles necessarily exist, but, upon condition that a triangle exists, three angles must necessarily exist—in it. And thus this logical necessity has been the source of the greatest delusions. Having formed an *a priori* conception of a thing, the content of which was made to embrace existence, we believed ourselves safe in concluding that, because existence belongs necessarily to the object of the conception, the existence of the thing is also posited necessarily, and that it is therefore absolutely necessary—merely because its existence has been cogitated in the conception.

If, in an identical judgment, I annihilate the predicate in thought, and retain the subject, a contradiction is the result; and hence I say, the former belongs necessarily to the latter. But if I suppress both subject and predicate in thought, no contradiction arises; for there *is nothing* at all, and therefore no means of forming a contradiction. To suppose the existence of a triangle and not that of its three angles, is self-contradictory; but to suppose the non-existence of both triangle and angles is perfectly admissible. And so is it with the conception of an absolutely necessary being. Annihilate its existence in thought, and you annihilate the thing itself with all its predicates; how then can there be any room for contradiction? Externally, there is nothing to give rise to a contradiction, for a thing cannot be necessary externally; nor internally, for, by the annihilation or suppression of the thing itself, its internal properties are also annihilated. God is omnipotent—that is a necessary judgment. His omnipotence cannot be denied, if the existence of a Deity is posited—the existence, that is, of an infinite being, the two conceptions being identical. But when you say, *God does not exist,* neither omnipotence nor any other predicate is affirmed; they must all disappear with the subject, and in this judgment there cannot exist the least self-contradiction.

Of the Impossibility of a Cosmological Proof of the Existence of God

It was by no means a natural course of proceeding, but, on the contrary, an invention entirely due to the subtlety of the schools, to attempt to draw from a mere idea a proof of the existence of an object corresponding to it. Such a course would never have been pursued, were it not for that need of reason which requires it to suppose the existence of a necessary being as a basis for the empirical regress, and that, as this necessity must be unconditioned and *a priori,* reason is bound to discover a conception which shall satisfy, if possible, this requirement, and enable us to attain to the *a priori* cognition of such a being. This conception was thought to be found in the idea of an *ens realissimum,* and thus this idea was employed for the attainment of a better defined knowledge of a necessary being, of the existence of which we were convinced, or persuaded, on other grounds. Thus reason was seduced from her natural course; and, instead of concluding with the conception of an *ens realissimum,* an attempt was made to begin with it, for the purpose of inferring from it that idea of a necessary existence which it was in fact called in to complete. Thus arose that unfortunate ontological argument, which neither satisfies the healthy common sense of humanity, nor sustains the scientific examination of the philosopher.

The *cosmological proof,* which we are about to examine, retains the connection between absolute necessity and the highest reality; but, instead of reasoning from this highest reality to a necessary existence, like the preceding argument, it concludes from the given unconditioned necessity of some being its unlimited reality. The track it pursues, whether rational or sophistical, is at least natural, and not only goes far to persuade the common understanding, but shows itself deserving of respect from the speculative intellect; while it contains, at the same time, the outlines of all the arguments employed in natural theology—arguments which always have been, and still will be, in use and authority. These, however adorned, and hid under whatever embellishments of rhetoric and sentiment, are at bottom identical with the arguments we are at present to discuss. This proof, termed by Leibnitz the *argumentum a contingentia mundi,* I shall now lay before the reader, and subject to a strict examination.

It is framed in the following manner: If something exists, an absolutely necessary being must likewise exist. Now I, at least, exist. Consequently, there exists an absolutely necessary being. The minor contains an experience, the major reasons from a general experience to the existence of a necessary being. Thus this argument really begins at experience, and is not completely *a priori,* or ontological. The object of all possible experience being the world, it is called the *cosmological* proof. It contains no reference to any peculiar property of sensuous objects, by which this world of sense might be distinguished from other possible worlds; and in this respect it differs from the physico-theological proof, which is based upon the consideration of the peculiar constitution of our sensuous world.

The proof proceeds thus: A necessary being can be determined only in one way, that is, it can be determined by only one of all possible opposed predicates; consequently, it must be *completely* determined in and by its conception. But there is only a single conception of a thing possible, which completely determines the thing *a priori:* that is, the conception of the *ens realissimum.* It follows that the conception of the *ens realissimum* is the only conception by and in which we can cogitate a necessary being. Consequently, a Supreme Being necessarily exists.

In this cosmological argument are assembled so many sophistical propositions, that speculative reason seems to have exerted in it all her dialectical skill to produce a transcendental illusion of the most extreme character. We shall postpone an investigation of this argument for the present, and confine ourselves to exposing the stratagem by which it imposes upon us an old argument in a new dress, and appeals to the agreement of two witnesses, the one with the credentials of pure reason, and the other with those of empiricism; while, in fact, it is only the former who has changed his dress and voice, for the purpose of passing himself off for an additional witness. That it may possess a secure foundation, it bases its conclusions upon experience, and thus appears to be completely distinct from the ontological argument, which places its confidence entirely in pure *a priori* conceptions. But this experience merely aids reason in making one step—to the existence of a necessary being. What the properties of this being are, cannot be learned from experience; and therefore reason abandons it altogether, and pursues its inquiries in the sphere of pure conceptions, for the purpose of discovering what the properties of an absolutely necessary being ought to be, that is, what among all possible things contain the conditions of absolute necessity. Reason believes that it has discovered these requisites in the conception of an *ens realissimum*—and in it alone, and hence concludes: The *ens realissimum* is an absolutely necessary being. But it is evident that reason has here presupposed that the conception of an *ens realissimum* is perfectly adequate to the conception of a being of absolute necessity, that is, that we may infer the existence of the latter from that of the former—a proposition which formed the basis of the ontological argument, and which is now employed in the support of the cosmological argument, contrary to the wish and professions of its inventors. For the existence of an absolutely necessary being is given in conceptions alone. But if I say—the conception of the *ens realissimum* is a conception of this kind, and in fact the only conception which is adequate to our idea of a necessary being, I am obliged to admit, that the latter may be inferred from the former. Thus it is properly the ontological argument which figures in the cosmological, and constitutes the whole strength of the latter; while the spurious basis of experience has been of no further use than to conduct us to the conception of absolute necessity, being utterly insufficient to demonstrate the presence of this attribute in any determinate existence or thing. For when we propose to ourselves an aim of this character, we must abandon the sphere of experience, and rise to that of pure conceptions, which we examine with the purpose of discovering whether any one contains the conditions of the possibility of an absolutely necessary being. But if the possibility of such a being is thus demonstrated, its existence is also proved; for we may then assert that, of all possible beings there is one which possesses the attribute of necessity—in other words, this being possesses an absolutely necessary existence.

All illusions in an argument are more easily detected when they are presented in the formal manner employed by the schools, which we now proceed to do.

If the proposition: Every absolutely necessary being is likewise an *ens realissimum,* is correct, it must, like all affirmative judgments, be capable of conversion—the *conversio per accidens,* at least. It follows, then, that some *entia realissima* are absolutely necessary beings. But no *ens realissimum* is in any respect different from another, and what is valid of some, is valid of all. In this present case, therefore, I may employ simple conversion, and say: Every *ens realissimum* is a necessary being. But as this proposition is determined *a priori* by the conceptions contained in it, the mere conception of an *ens realissimum* must possess the additional attribute of absolute necessity. But this is exactly what was maintained in the ontological argument, and not recognized by the cosmological, although it formed the real ground of its disguised and illusory reasoning.

Thus the second mode employed by speculative reason of demonstrating the existence of a Supreme Being is not only, like the first, illusory and inadequate, but possesses the additional blemish of an *ignoratio elenchi*—professing to conduct us by a new road to the desired goal, but bringing us back, after a short circuit, to the old path which we had deserted at its call.

Of the Impossibility of a Physico-Theological Proof

If, then, neither a pure conception nor the general experience of an existing being can provide a sufficient basis for the proof of the existence of the Deity, we can make the attempt by the only other mode—that of grounding our argument upon a *determinate experience* of the phenomena of the present world, their constitution and disposition, and discover whether we can thus attain to a sound conviction of the existence of a Supreme Being. This argument we shall term the *physico-theological* argument. If it is shown to be insufficient, speculative reason cannot present us with any satisfactory proof of the existence of a being corresponding to our transcendental idea.

The world around us opens before our view so magnificent a spectacle of order, variety, beauty, and conformity to ends, that whether we pursue our observations into the infinity of space in the one direction, or into its illimitable divisions in the other, whether we regard the world in its greatest or its least manifestations—even after we have attained to the highest summit of knowledge which our weak minds can reach, we find that language in the presence of wonders so inconceivable has lost its force, and number its power to reckon, nay, even thought fails to conceive adequately, and our conception of the whole dissolves into an astonishment without the power of expression—all the more eloquent that it is dumb. Everywhere around us we observe a chain of causes and effects, of means and ends, of death and birth; and, as nothing has entered of itself into the condition in which we find it, we are constantly referred to some other thing, which itself suggests the same inquiry regarding its cause, and thus the universe must sink into the abyss of nothingness, unless we admit that, besides this infinite chain of contingencies, there exists something that is primal and self-subsistent—something which, as the cause of this phenomenal world, secures its continuance and preservation.

This highest cause—what magnitude shall we attribute to it? Of the content of the world we are ignorant; still less can we estimate its magnitude by comparison with the sphere of the possible. But this supreme cause being a necessity of the human mind, what is there to prevent us from attributing to it such a degree of perfection as to place it above the sphere of *all that* is possible? This we can easily do, although only by the aid of the faint outline of an abstract conception, by representing this being to ourselves as containing in itself, as an individual substance, all possible perfection—a conception which satisfies that requirement of reason which demands parsimony in principles, which is free from self-contradiction, which even contributes to the extension of the employment of reason in experience, by means of the guidance afforded by this idea to order and system, and which in no respect conflicts with any law of experience.

I maintain, then, that the physico-theological argument is insufficient of itself to prove the existence of a Supreme Being, that it must entrust this to the ontological argument—to which it serves merely as an introduction, and that, consequently, this argument contains the *only possible ground of proof* for the existence of this being.

Transcendental Doctrine of Method

I UNDERSTAND by the transcendental doctrine of method, the determination of the formal conditions of a complete system of pure reason. We shall accordingly have to treat of the *Discipline,* the *Canon,* the *Architectonic,* and, finally, of the *History* of pure reason. This part of our *Critique* will accomplish, from the transcendental point of view, what has been usually attempted, but miserably executed, under the name of *practical logic.* It has been badly executed, I say, because general logic, not being limited to any particular kind of cognition, nor to any particular objects, it cannot, without borrowing from other sciences, do more than present merely the titles or signs of *possible methods* and the technical expressions, which are employed in the systematic parts of all sciences; and thus the pupil is made acquainted with names, the meaning and application of which he is to learn only at some future time.

I. The Discipline of Pure Reason

NEGATIVE JUDGMENTS—those which are so not merely as regards their logical form, but in respect of their content—are not commonly held in especial respect. They are, on the contrary, regarded as jealous enemies of our insatiable desire for knowledge; and it almost requires an apology to induce us to tolerate, much less to prize and to respect them.

But where the limits of our possible cognition are very much contracted, the attraction to new fields of knowledge great, the illusions to which the mind is subject of the most deceptive character, and the evil consequences of error of no inconsiderable magnitude—the *negative* element in knowledge, which is useful only to guard us against error, is of far more importance than much of that positive instruction which makes additions to the sum of our knowledge. The *restraint* which is employed to repress, and finally to extirpate the constant inclination to depart from certain rules, is termed *Discipline.*

Reason, when employed in the field of experience, does not stand in need of criticism, because its principles are subjected to the continual test of empirical observations. Nor is criticism requisite in the sphere of mathematics, where the conceptions of reason must always be presented *in concreto* in pure intuition, and baseless or arbitrary assertions are discovered without difficulty. But where reason is not held in a plain track by the influence of empirical or of pure intuition, that is, when it is employed in the transcendental sphere of pure conceptions, it stands in great need of discipline, to restrain its propensity to overstep the limits of possible experience, and to keep it from wandering into error. In fact, the utility of the philosophy of pure reason is entirely of this negative character.

The Discipline of Pure Reason in the Sphere of Dogmatism

Philosophical cognition is the *cognition* of *reason* by means of *conceptions;* mathematical cognition is cognition by means of the *construction* of conceptions. The *construction* of a conception is the presentation *a priori* of the intuition which corresponds to the conception. For this purpose a *non-empirical* intuition is requisite, which, as an intuition, is an *individual* object; while, as the construction of a conception, it must be seen to be universally valid for all the possible intuitions which rank under that conception.

Philosophical cognition, accordingly, regards the particular only in the general; mathematical the general in the particular, nay, in the individual. This is done, however, entirely *a priori* and by means of pure reason, so that, as this individual figure is determined under certain universal conditions of construction, the object of the conception, to which this individual figure corresponds as its schema, must be cogitated as universally determined.

The essential difference of these two modes of cognition consists, therefore, in this formal quality; it does not regard the difference of the matter or objects of both. Those thinkers who aim at distinguishing philosophy from mathematics by asserting that the former has to do with *quality* merely, and the latter with *quantity,* have mistaken the effect for the cause. The reason why mathematical cognition can relate only to quantity, is to be found in its form alone. For it is the conception of quantities only that is capable of being constructed, that is, presented *a priori* in intuition; while qualities cannot be given in any other than an empirical intuition. Hence the cognition of qualities by reason is possible only through conceptions. No one can find an intuition which shall correspond to the conception of reality, except in experience; it cannot be presented to the mind *a priori,* and antecedently to the empirical consciousness of a reality.

Now, what is the cause of this difference in the fortune of the philosopher and the mathematician, the former of whom follows the path of conceptions, while the latter pursues that of intuitions, which he represents, *a priori,* in correspondence with his conceptions? The cause is evident from what has been already demonstrated in the introduction to this *Critique.* We do not, in the present case, want to discover analytical propositions, which may be produced merely by analysing our conceptions—for in this the philosopher would have the advantage over his rival; we aim at the discovery of synthetical propositions—such synthetical propositions, moreover, as can be cognized *a priori.* I must not confine myself to that which I actually cogitate in my conception of a triangle, for this is nothing more than the mere definition; I must try to go beyond that, and to arrive at properties which are not contained in, although they belong to, the conception. Now, this is impossible, unless I determine the object present to my mind according to the conditions, either of empirical, or of pure intuition. In the former case, I should have an empirical proposition, which would possess neither universality nor necessity; but that would be of no value. In the latter, I proceed by geometrical construction, by means of which I collect, in a pure intuition, just as I would in an empirical intuition, all the various properties which belong to the schema of a triangle in general, and consequently to its conception, and thus construct synthetical propositions which possess the attribute of universality.

All our knowledge relates, finally, to possible intuitions, for it is these alone that present objects to the mind. An *a priori* or non-empirical conception contains either a pure intuition—and in this case it can be constructed; or it contains nothing but the synthesis of possible intuitions, which are not given *a priori*. In this latter case, it may help us to form synthetical *a priori* judgments, but only in the discursive method, by conceptions, not in the intuitive, by means of the construction of conceptions.

The only *a priori* intuition is that of the pure form of phenomena—space and time. A conception of space and time as *quanta* may be presented *a priori* in intuition, that is, constructed, either alone with their quality, or as pure quantity, by means of number. But the matter of phenomena, by which *things* are given in space and time, can be presented only in perception, *a posteriori*. The only conception which represents *a priori* this empirical content of phenomena, is the conception of a *thing* in general; and the *a priori* synthetical cognition of this conception can give us nothing more than the rule for the synthesis of that which may be contained in the corresponding *a posteriori* perception; it is utterly inadequate to present an *a priori* intuition of the real object, which must necessarily be empirical.

Synthetical propositions, which relate to *things* in general, an *a priori* intuition of which is impossible, are transcendental. For this reason transcendental propositions cannot be framed by means of the construction of conceptions; they are *a priori,* and based entirely on conceptions themselves. They contain merely the rule, by which we are to seek in the world of perception or experience the synthetical unity of that which cannot be intuited *a priori*. But they are incompetent to present any of the conceptions which appear in them in an *a priori* intuition; these can be given only *a posteriori,* in experience, which, however, is itself possible only through these synthetical principles.

The Discipline of Pure Reason in Polemics

By the polemic of pure reason I mean the defence of its propositions made by reason, in opposition to the dogmatical counter-propositions advanced by other parties. The question here is not whether its own statements may not also be false; it merely regards the fact that reason proves that the opposite cannot be established with demonstrative certainty, nor even asserted with a higher degree of probability. Reason does not hold her possessions upon sufferance; for, although she cannot show a perfectly satisfactory title to them, no one can prove that she is *not* the rightful possessor.

It is a melancholy reflection, that reason, in its highest exercise, falls into an antithetic; and that the supreme tribunal for the settlement of differences should not be at union with itself. It is true that we had to discuss the question of an apparent antithetic, but we found that it was based upon a misconception. In conformity with the common prejudice, phenomena were regarded as things in themselves, and thus an absolute completeness in their synthesis was required in the one mode or in the other; a demand entirely out of place in regard to phenomena. There was, then, no real self-contradiction of reason in the propositions—The series of phenomena *given in themselves* has an absolutely first beginning, and, This series is absolutely and *in itself* without beginning. The two propositions are perfectly consistent with each other, because phenomena as phenomena are *in themselves* nothing, and consequently the hypothesis that they are things in themselves, must lead to self-contradictory inferences.

But there are cases in which a similar misunderstanding cannot be provided against, and the dispute must remain unsettled. Take, for example, the theistic proposition: There is a Supreme Being; and on the other hand, the atheistic counter-statement: There exists no Supreme Being; or, in psychology: Everything that thinks, possesses the attribute of absolute and permanent unity, which is utterly different from the transitory unity of material phenomena; and the counter-proposition: The soul is not an immaterial unity, and its nature is transitory, like that of phenomena. The objects of these questions contain no heterogeneous or contradictory elements, for they relate to *things in themselves,* and not to phenomena. There would arise, indeed, a real contradiction, if reason came forward with a statement on the negative side of these questions alone. As regards the criticism to which the grounds of proof on the affirmative side must be subjected, it may be freely admitted, without necessitating the surrender of the affirmative propositions, which have, at least, the interest of reason in their favour—an advantage which the opposite party cannot lay claim to.

Everything in nature is good for some purpose. Even poisons are serviceable; they destroy the evil effects of other poisons generated in our system, and must always find a place in every complete pharmacopoeia. The objections raised against the fallacies and sophistries of speculative reason, are objections given by the nature of this reason itself, and must therefore have a destination and purpose which can only be for the good of humanity. For what purpose has Providence raised many objects, in which we have the deepest interest, so far above us, that we vainly try to cognize them with certainty, and our powers of mental vision are rather excited than satisfied by the glimpses we may chance to seize? It is very doubtful whether it is for our benefit to advance bold affirmations regarding subjects involved in such obscurity; perhaps it would even be detrimental to our best interests. But it is undoubtedly always beneficial to leave the investigating, as well as the critical reason, in perfect freedom, and permit it to take charge of its own interests, which are advanced as much by its limitation, as by its extension of its views, and which always suffer by the interference of foreign powers forcing it, against its natural tendencies, to bend to certain preconceived designs.

The Discipline of Pure Reason in Hypothesis

Imagination may be allowed, under the strict surveillance of reason, to invent suppositions; but, these must be based on something that is perfectly certain—and that is the *possibility* of the object. If we are well assured upon this point, it is allowable to have recourse to supposition in regard to the reality of the object; but this supposition must, unless it is utterly groundless, be connected, as its ground of explanation, with that which is really given and absolutely certain. Such a supposition is termed a *hypothesis*.

It is beyond our power to form the least conception *a priori* of the possibility of dynamical connection in phenomena; and the category of the pure understanding will not enable us to excogitate any such connection, but merely helps us to understand it, when we meet with it in experience. For this reason we cannot, in accordance with the categories, imagine or invent any object or any property of an object not given, or that may not be given in experience, and employ it in a hypothesis; otherwise, we should be basing our chain of reasoning upon mere chimerical fancies, and not upon conceptions of things. Thus, we have no right to assume the existence of new powers, not existing in nature—for example, an understanding with a non-sensuous intuition, a force of attraction without contact, or some new kind of substances occupying space, and yet without the property of impenetrability; and, consequently, we cannot assume that there is any other kind of community among substances than that observable in experience, any kind of presence than that in space, or any kind of duration than that in time. In one word, the conditions of possible experience are for reason the only conditions of the possibility of things; reason cannot venture to form, independently of these conditions, any conceptions of things, because such conceptions, although not self-contradictory, are without object and without application.

Transcendental hypotheses are therefore inadmissible; and we cannot use the liberty of employing, in the absence of physical, hyperphysical grounds of explanation. And this for two reasons; first, because such hypotheses do not advance reason, but rather stop it in its progress; secondly, because this licence would render fruitless all its exertions in its own proper sphere, which is that of experience. For, when the explanation of natural phenomena happens to be difficult, we have constantly at hand a transcendental ground of explanation, which lifts us above the necessity of investigating nature; and our inquiries are brought to a close, not because we have obtained all the requisite knowledge, but because we abut upon a principle, which is incomprehensible, and which, indeed, is so far back in the track of thought, as to contain the conception of the absolutely primal being.

The next requisite for the admissibility of a hypothesis is its sufficiency. That is, it must determine *a priori* the consequences which are given in experience, and which are supposed to follow from the hypothesis itself. If we require to employ auxiliary hypotheses, the suspicion naturally arises that they are mere fictions; because the necessity for each of them requires the same justification as in the case of the original hypothesis, and thus their testimony is invalid. If we suppose the existence of an infinitely perfect cause, we possess sufficient grounds for the explanation of the conformity to aims, the order and the greatness which we observe in the universe; but we find ourselves obliged, when we observe the evil in the world and the exceptions to these laws, to employ new hypotheses in support of the original one. We employ the idea of the simple nature of the human soul as the foundation of all the theories we may form of its phenomena; but when we meet with difficulties in our way, when we observe in the soul phenomena similar to the changes which take place in matter, we require to call in new auxiliary hypotheses. These may, indeed, not be false, but we do not know them to be true, because the only witness to their certitude is the hypothesis which they themselves have been called in to explain.

But, although hypotheses are inadmissible in answers to the questions of pure speculative reason, they may be employed in the defence of these answers. That is to say, hypotheses are admissible in polemic, but not in the sphere of dogmatism. By the defence of statements of this character, I do not mean an attempt at discovering new grounds for their support, but merely the refutation of the arguments of opponents. All *a priori* synthetical propositions possess the peculiarity, that, although the philosopher who maintains the reality of the ideas contained in the proposition, is not in possession of sufficient knowledge to establish the certainty of his statements, his opponent is as little able to prove the truth of the opposite. This equality of fortune does not allow the one party to be superior to the other in the sphere of speculative cognition; and it is this sphere accordingly that is the proper arena of these endless speculative conflicts. But we shall afterwards show that, in relation to its *practical exercise,* Reason has the right of admitting what, in the field of pure speculation, she would not be justified in supposing, except upon perfectly sufficient grounds; because all such suppositions destroy the necessary completeness of speculation—a condition which the practical reason, however, does not consider to be requisite. In this sphere, therefore, Reason is mistress of a possession, her title to which she does not require to prove—which, in fact, she could not do. The burden of proof accordingly rests upon the opponent. But as he has just as little knowledge regarding the subject discussed, and is as little able to prove the non-existence of the object of an idea, as the philosopher on the other side is to demonstrate its reality, it is evident that there is an advantage on the side of the philosopher who maintains his proposition as a practically necessary supposition. For he is at liberty to employ, in self-defence, the same weapons as his opponent makes use of in attacking him; that is, he has a right to use hypotheses not for the purpose of supporting the arguments in favour of his own propositions, but to show that his opponent knows no more than himself regarding the subject under discussion, and cannot boast of any speculative advantage.

Hypotheses are, therefore, admissible in the sphere of pure reason, only as weapons for self-defence, and not as supports to dogmatical assertions. But the opposing party we must always seek for in ourselves. For speculative reason is, in the sphere of transcendentalism, dialectical *in its own nature.* The difficulties and objections we have to fear lie in ourselves. They are like old but never superannuated claims; and we must seek them out, and settle them once and for ever, if we are to expect a permanent peace. External tranquillity is hollow and unreal. The root of these contradictions, which lies in the nature of human reason, must be destroyed; and this can only be done by giving it, in the first instance, freedom to grow, nay, by nourishing it, that it may send out shoots, and thus betray its own existence. It is our duty, therefore, to try to discover new objections, to put weapons in the hands of our opponent, and to grant him the most favourable position in the arena that he can wish. We have nothing to fear from these concessions; on the contrary, we may rather hope that we shall thus make ourselves master of a possession which no one will ever venture to dispute.

The Discipline of Pure Reason in Relation to Proofs

It is a peculiarity which distinguishes the proofs of transcendental synthetical propositions from those of all other *a priori* synthetical cognitions, that reason, in the case of the former, does not apply its conceptions directly to an object, but is first obliged to prove, *a priori,* the objective validity of these conceptions and the possibility of their syntheses. This is not merely a prudential rule, it is essential to the very possibility of the proof of a transcendental proposition. If I am required to pass, *a priori,* beyond the conception of an object, I find that it is utterly impossible without the guidance of something which is not contained in the conception. In mathematics, it is *a priori* intuition that guides my synthesis; and, in this case, all our conclusions may be drawn immediately from pure intuition. In transcendental cognition, so long as we are dealing only with conceptions of the understanding, we are guided by possible experience. That is to say, a proof in the sphere of transcendental cognition does not show that the given conception leads directly to another conception—for this would be a *saltus* which nothing can justify; but it shows that experience itself, and consequently the object of experience, is impossible without the connection indicated by these conceptions. It follows that such a proof must demonstrate the possibility of arriving, synthetically and *a priori,* at a certain knowledge of things, which was not contained in our conceptions of these things. Unless we pay particular attention to this requirement, our proofs, instead of pursuing the straight path indicated by reason, follow the tortuous road of mere subjective association. The illusory conviction, which rests upon subjective causes of association, and which is considered as resulting from the perception of a real and objective natural affinity, is always open to doubt and suspicion. For this reason, all the attempts which have been made to prove the principle of sufficient reason, have, according to the universal admission of philosophers, been quite unsuccessful; and, before the appearance of transcendental criticism, it was considered better, as this principle could not be abandoned, to appeal boldly to the common sense of mankind, rather than attempt to discover new dogmatical proofs.

But, if the proposition to be proved is a proposition of pure reason, and if I aim at passing beyond my empirical conceptions by the aid of mere ideas, it is necessary that the proof should first show that such a step in synthesis is possible (which it is not), before it proceeds to prove the truth of the proposition itself. The so-called proof of the simple nature of the soul from the unity of apperception, is a very plausible one. But it contains no answer to the objection, that, as the notion of absolute simplicity is not a conception which is directly applicable to a perception, but is an idea which must be inferred—if at all—from observation, it is by no means evident, how the mere fact of consciousness, which is contained *in all thought,* although in so far a simple representation, can conduct me to the consciousness and cognition of a thing which is purely a thinking substance. When I represent to my mind the power of my body as in motion, my body in this thought is so far absolute unity, and my representation of it is a simple one; and hence I can indicate this representation by the motion of a point, because I have made abstraction of the size or volume of the body. But I cannot hence infer that, given merely the moving power of a body, the body may be cogitated as simple substance, merely because the representation in my mind takes no account of its content in space, and is consequently simple. The simple, in abstraction, is very different from the objectively simple; and hence the Ego, which is simple in the first sense, may, in the second sense, as indicating the soul itself, be a very complex conception, with a very various content. Thus it is evident that in all such arguments there lurks a paralogism. We guess at the presence of the paralogism by keeping ever before us a criterion of the possibility of those synthetical propositions which aim at proving more than experience can teach us. This criterion is obtained from the observation that such proofs do not lead us directly from the subject of the proposition to be proved to the required predicate, but find it necessary to presuppose the possibility of extending our cognition *a priori* by means of ideas. We must, accordingly, always use the greatest caution; we require, before attempting any proof, to consider how it is possible to extend the sphere of cognition by the operations of pure reason, and from what source we are to derive knowledge, which is not obtained from the analysis of conceptions, nor relates, by anticipation, to possible experience. We shall thus spare ourselves much severe and fruitless labour, by not expecting from reason what is beyond its power, or rather by subjecting it to discipline, and teaching it to moderate its vehement desires for the extension of the sphere of cognition.

The first rule for our guidance is, therefore, not to attempt a transcendental proof, before we have considered from what source we are to derive the principles upon which the proof is to be based, and what right we have to expect that our conclusions from these principles will be veracious. If they are principles of the understanding, it is vain to expect that we should attain by their means to ideas of pure reason; for these principles are valid only in regard to objects of possible experience. If they are principles of pure reason, our labour is alike in vain. The second peculiarity of transcendental proof is, that a transcendental proposition cannot rest upon more than *a single* proof. If I am drawing conclusions, not from conceptions, but from intuition corresponding to a conception, be it pure intuition, as in mathematics, or empirical, as in natural science, the intuition which forms the basis of my inferences, presents me with materials for many synthetical propositions, which I can connect in various modes, while, as it is allowable to proceed from different points in the intention, I can arrive by different paths at the same proposition.

The third rule for the guidance of pure reason in the conduct of a proof is, that all transcendental proofs must never be *apagogic* or indirect, but always ostensive or direct. The direct or ostensive proof not only establishes the truth of the proposition to be proved, but exposes the grounds of its truth; the apagogic, on the other hand, may assure us of the truth of the proposition, but it cannot enable us to comprehend the grounds of its possibility. The latter is, accordingly, rather an auxiliary to an argument, than a strictly philosophical and rational mode of procedure. In one respect, however, they have an advantage over direct proofs, from the fact that the mode of arguing by contradiction, which they employ, renders our understanding of the question more clear, and approximates the proof to the certainty of an intuitional demonstration.

II. The Canon of Pure Reason

I UNDERSTAND by a canon a list of the *a priori* principles of the proper employment of certain faculties of cognition. Thus general logic, in its analytical department, is a formal canon for the faculties of understanding and reason. In the same way, Transcendental Analytic was seen to be a canon of the pure *understanding;* for it alone is competent to enounce true *a priori* synthetical cognitions. But, when no proper employment of a faculty of cognition is possible, no canon can exist. But the synthetical cognition of pure speculative *reason* is, as has been shown, completely impossible. There cannot, therefore, exist any canon for the speculative exercise of this faculty—for its speculative exercise is entirely dialectical; and consequently, transcendental logic, in this respect, is merely a discipline, and not a canon. If, then, there is any proper mode of employing the faculty of pure reason—in which case there must be a canon for this faculty—this canon will relate, not to the speculative, but to the *practical use of reason*. This canon we now proceed to investigate.

Of the Ultimate End of the Pure Use of Reason

The transcendental speculation of reason relates to three things: the freedom of the will, the immortality of the soul, and the existence of God. The speculative interest which reason has in those questions is very small; and, for its sake alone, we should not undertake the labour of transcendental investigation—a labour full of toil and ceaseless struggle. We should be loth to undertake this labour, because the discoveries we might make would not be of the smallest use in the sphere of concrete or physical investigation. We may find out that the will is free, but this knowledge only relates to the intelligible cause of our volition. As regards the phenomena or expressions of this will, that is, our actions, we are bound, in obedience to an inviolable maxim, without which reason cannot be employed in the sphere of experience, to explain these in the same way as we explain all the other phenomena of nature, that is to say, according to its unchangeable laws. We may have discovered the spirituality and immortality of the soul, but we cannot employ this knowledge to explain the phenomena of this life, nor the peculiar nature of the future, because our conception of an incorporeal nature is purely negative and does not add anything to our knowledge, and the only inferences to be drawn from it are purely fictitious. If, again, we prove the existence of a supreme intelligence, we should be able from it to make the conformity to aims existing in the arrangement of the world comprehensible; but we should not be justified in deducing from it any particular arrangement or disposition, or, inferring any, where it is not perceived. For it is a necessary rule of the speculative use of reason, that we must not overlook natural causes, or refuse to listen to the teaching of experience, for the sake of deducing what we know and perceive from something that transcends all our knowledge. In one word, these three propositions are, for the speculative reason, always transcendent, and cannot be employed as immanent principles in relation to the objects of experience; they are, consequently, of no use to us in this sphere, being but the valueless results of the severe but unprofitable efforts of reason.

If, then, the actual *cognition* of these three cardinal propositions is perfectly useless, while Reason uses her utmost endeavours to induce us to admit them, it is plain that their real value and importance relate to our *practical,* and not to our speculative interest.

I term all that is possible through free will, practical. But if the conditions of the exercise of free volition are empirical, reason can have only a regulative, and not a constitutive, influence upon it, and is serviceable merely for the introduction of unity into its empirical laws. In the moral philosophy of prudence, for example, the sole business of reason is to bring about a union of all the ends, which are aimed at by our inclinations, into one ultimate end—that of *happiness,* and to show the agreement which should exist among the means of attaining that end. In this sphere, accordingly, reason cannot present to us any other than *pragmatical* laws of free action, for our guidance towards the aims set up by the senses, and is incompetent to give us laws which are pure and determined completely *a priori.* On the other hand, pure practical laws, the ends of which have been given by reason entirely *a priori,* and which are not empirically conditioned, but are, on the contrary, absolutely imperative in their nature, would be products of pure reason. Such are the *moral* laws; and these alone belong to the sphere of the practical exercise of reason, and admit of a canon.

All the powers of reason, in the sphere of what may be termed pure philosophy, are, in fact, directed to the three above-mentioned problems alone. These again have a still higher end—the answer to the question, *what we ought to do,* if the will is free, if there is a God, and a future world. Now, as this problem relates to our conduct, in reference to the highest aim of humanity, it is evident that the ultimate intention of nature, in the constitution of our reason, has been directed to the *moral* alone. This faculty, accordingly, enounces laws, which are imperative or objective *laws of freedom,* and which tell us what *ought to take place,* thus distinguishing themselves from the *laws of nature,* which relate to that which *does take place.* The laws of freedom or of free will are hence termed practical laws.

Whether reason is not itself, in the actual delivery of these laws, determined in its turn by other influences, and whether the action which, in relation to sensuous impulses, we call free, may not, in relation to higher and more remote operative causes, really form a part of *nature*—these are questions which do not here concern us. They are purely speculative questions; and all we have to do, in the practical sphere, is to inquire into the *rule* of conduct which reason has to present. Experience demonstrates to us the existence of practical freedom as one of the causes which exist in nature, that is, it shows the causal power of reason in the determination of the will. The idea of transcendental freedom, on the contrary, requires that reason—in relation to its causal power of commencing a series of phenomena—should be independent of all sensuous determining causes; and thus it seems to be in opposition to the law of nature and to all possible experience. It therefore remains a problem for the human mind. But this problem does not concern reason in its practical use; and we have, therefore, in a canon of pure reason, to do with only two questions, which relate to the practical interest of pure reason—Is there a God? and, Is there a future life? The question of transcendental freedom is purely speculative, and we may therefore set it entirely aside when we come to treat of practical reason. Besides, we have already fully discussed this subject in the antinomy of pure reason.

Of the Ideal of the Summum Bonum *as a Determining Ground of the Ultimate End of Pure Reason*

The whole interest of reason, speculative as well as practical, is centred in the three following questions:

1. WHAT CAN I KNOW?
2. WHAT OUGHT I TO DO?
3. WHAT MAY I HOPE?

The first question is purely speculative. We have, as I flatter myself, exhausted all the replies of which it is susceptible, and have at last found the reply with which reason must content itself, and with which it ought to be content, so long as it pays no regard to the practical. But from the two great ends to the attainment of which all these efforts of pure reason were in fact directed, we remain just as far removed as if we had consulted our ease, and declined the task at the outset. So far, then, as *knowledge* is concerned, thus much, at least, is established, that, in regard to those two problems, it lies beyond our reach.

The second question is purely practical. As such it may indeed fall within the province of pure reason, but still it is not transcendental, but moral, and consequently cannot in itself form the subject of our criticism.

The third question: If I act as I ought to do, what may I then hope? —is at once practical and theoretical. The practical forms a clue to the answer of the theoretical, and—in its highest form—speculative question. For all *hoping* has happiness for its object, and stands in precisely the same relation to the practical and the law of morality, as *knowing* to the theoretical cognition of things and the law of nature. The former arrives finally at the conclusion that *something is,* because *something ought to take place;* the latter, that *something is,* because *something does take place.*

Happiness is the satisfaction of all our desires; *extensive,* in regard to their multiplicity; *intensive,* in regard to their degree; and *protensive,* in regard to their duration. The practical law based on the motive of *happiness,* I term a pragmatical law; but that law, assuming such to exist, which has no other motive than the *worthiness of being happy,* I term a moral or ethical law. The first tells us what we have to do, if we wish to become possessed of happiness; the second dictates how we ought to act, in order to deserve happiness. The first is based upon empirical principles; for it is only by experience that I can learn either what inclinations exist which desire satisfaction, or what are the natural means of satisfying them. The second takes no account of our desires or the means of satisfying them, and regards only the freedom of a rational being, and the necessary conditions under which alone this freedom can harmonize with the distribution of happiness according to principles. This second law may therefore rest upon mere ideas of pure reason, and may be cognized *a priori.*

I call the world *a moral world,* in so far as it may be in accordance with all the ethical laws—which, by virtue of the *freedom* of reasonable beings, it *can* be, and according to the necessary laws of *morality* it *ought to be.* But this world must be conceived only as an intelligible world, inasmuch as abstraction is therein made of all conditions, and even of all impediments to morality. So far, then, it is a mere idea—though still a practical idea—which may have, and ought to have, an influence on the world of sense, so as to bring it as far as possible into conformity with itself. The idea of a moral world has, therefore, objective reality, not as referring to an object of intelligible intuition—for of such an object we can form no conception whatever—but to the world of sense—conceived, however, as an object of pure reason in its practical use—and to a *corpus mysticum* of rational beings in it, in so far as the *liberum arbitrium* of the individual is placed, under and by virtue of moral laws, in complete systematic unity both with itself, and with the freedom of all others.

That is the answer to the first of the two questions of pure reason which relate to its practical interest: *Do that which will render thee worthy of happiness.* The second question is this: If I conduct myself so as not to be unworthy of happiness, may I hope thereby to obtain happiness? In order to arrive at the solution of this question, we must inquire whether the principles of pure reason, which prescribe *a priori* the law, necessarily also connect this hope with it.

I say, then, that just as the moral principles are necessary according to reason in its *practical* use, so it is equally necessary according to reason in its *theoretical* use, to assume that every one has ground to hope for happiness in the measure in which he has made himself worthy of it in his conduct, and that therefore the system of morality is inseparably connected with that of happiness.

Now in an intelligible, that is, in the moral world, in the conception of which we make abstraction of all the impediments to morality, such a system of happiness, connected with and proportioned to morality, may be conceived as necessary, because freedom of volition—partly incited, and partly restrained by moral laws—would be itself the cause of general happiness; and thus rational beings, under the guidance of such principles, would be themselves the authors both of their own enduring welfare and that of others. But such a system of self-rewarding morality is only an idea, the carrying out of which depends upon the condition that every one acts as he ought; in other words, that all actions of reasonable beings be such as they would be if they sprung from a Supreme Will, comprehending in, or under, itself all particular wills. But since the moral law is binding on each individual in the use of his freedom of volition, even if others should not act in conformity with this law, neither the nature of things, nor the causality of actions and their relation to morality, determine how the consequences of these actions will be related to happiness; and the necessary connection of the hope of happiness with the unceasing endeavour to become worthy of happiness, cannot be cognized by reason, if we take nature alone for our guide. This connection can be hoped for only on the assumption that the cause of nature is a supreme reason, which governs according to moral laws.

I term the idea of an intelligence in which the morally most perfect will, united with supreme blessedness, is the cause of all happiness in the world, so far as happiness stands in strict relation to morality, *the Ideal of the Supreme Good*. It is only, then, in the ideal of the supreme *original* good, that pure reason can find the ground of the practically necessary connection of both elements of the highest *derivative* good, and accordingly of an intelligible, that is, *moral* world. Now since we are necessitated by reason to conceive ourselves as belonging to such a world, while the senses present to us nothing but a world of phenomena, we must assume the former as a consequence of our conduct in the world of sense, and therefore as future in relation to us. Thus God and a future life are two hypotheses which, according to the principles of pure reason, are inseparable from the obligation which this reason imposes upon us.

Morality *per se* constitutes a system. But we can form no system of happiness, except in so far as it is dispensed in strict proportion to morality. But this is only possible in the intelligible world, under a wise author and ruler. Such a ruler, together with life in such a world, which we must look upon as future, reason finds itself compelled to assume; or it must regard the moral laws as idle dreams, since the necessary consequence which this same reason connects with them must, without this hypothesis, fall to the ground. Hence also the moral laws are universally regarded as *commands,* which they could not be, did they not connect *a priori* adequate consequences with their dictates, and thus carry with them *promises* and *threats*. But this, again, they could not do, did they not reside in a necessary being, as the Supreme Good, which alone can render such a teleological unity possible.

Happiness, therefore, in exact proportion with the morality of rational beings, constitutes alone the supreme good of a world into which we absolutely must transport ourselves according to the commands of pure but practical reason. This world is, it is true, only an intelligible world; for of such a systematic unity of ends as it requires, the world of sense gives us no hint. Its reality can be based on nothing else but the hypothesis of a supreme original good. In it independent reason, equipped with all the sufficiency of a supreme cause, founds, maintains, and fulfils the universal order of things, with the most perfect teleological harmony, however much this order may be hidden from us in the world of sense.

This moral theology has the peculiar advantage, in contrast with speculative theology, of leading inevitably to the conception of a *sole, perfect,* and *rational* First Cause, whereof speculative theology does not give us any *indication* on objective grounds, far less any convincing *evidence*. For we find neither in transcendental nor in natural theology, however far reason may lead us in these, any ground to warrant us in assuming the existence of *one only* Being, which stands at the head of all natural causes, and on which these are entirely dependent. On the other hand, if we take our stand on moral unity as a necessary law of the universe, and from this point of view consider what is necessary to give this law adequate efficiency and, for us, obligatory force, we must come to the conclusion that there is one only supreme will, which comprehends all these laws in itself. For how, under different wills, should we find complete unity of ends? This will must be omnipotent, that all nature and its relation to morality in the world may be subject to it; omniscient, that it may have knowledge of the most secret feelings and their moral worth; omnipresent, that it may be at hand to supply every necessity to which the highest weal of the world may give rise; eternal, that this harmony of nature and liberty may never fail; and so on.

But this systematic unity of ends in this world of intelligences—which, as mere nature, is only a world of sense, but as a system of freedom of volition, may be termed an intelligible, that is, moral world—leads inevitably also to the teleological unity of all things which constitute this great whole, according to universal natural laws—just as the unity of the former is according to universal and necessary moral laws—and unites the practical with the speculative reason. The world must be represented as having originated from an idea, if it is to harmonize with that use of reason without which we cannot even consider ourselves as worthy of reason—namely, the moral use, which rests entirely on the idea of the supreme good. Hence the investigation of nature receives a teleological direction, and becomes, in its widest extension, physico-theology. But this, taking its rise in moral order as a unity founded on the essence of freedom, and not accidentally instituted by external commands, establishes the teleological view of nature on grounds which must be inseparably connected with the internal possibility of things. This gives rise to a *transcendental theology,* which takes the ideal of the highest ontological perfection as a principle of systematic unity; and this principle connects all things according to universal and necessary natural laws, because all things have their origin in the absolute necessity of the one only Primal Being.

Of Opinion, Knowledge, and Belief

The holding of a thing to be true is a phenomenon in our understanding which may rest on objective grounds, but requires, also, subjective causes in the mind of the person judging. If a judgment is valid for every rational being, then its ground is objectively sufficient, and it is termed a *conviction.* If, on the other hand, it has its ground in the particular character of the subject, it is termed a *persuasion.*

Persuasion, accordingly, cannot be *subjectively* distinguished from conviction, that is, so long as the subject views its judgment simply as a phenomenon of its own mind. But if we inquire whether the grounds of our judgment, which are valid for us, produce the same effect on the reason of others as on our own, we have then the means, though only subjective means, not, indeed, of producing conviction, but of detecting the merely private validity of the judgment; in other words, of discovering that there is in it the element of mere persuasion.

If we can, in addition to this, develop the *subjective causes* of the judgment, which we have taken for its *objective grounds,* and thus explain the deceptive judgment as a phenomenon in our mind, apart altogether from the objective character of the object, we can then expose the illusion and need be no longer deceived by it, although, if its subjective cause lies in our nature, we cannot hope altogether to escape its influence.

I can only *maintain,* that is, affirm as necessarily valid for every one, that which produces conviction. Persuasion I may keep for myself, if it is agreeable to me; but I cannot, and ought not, to attempt to impose it as binding upon others.

Holding for true, or the subjective validity of a judgment in relation to conviction, has the three following degrees: *Opinion, Belief,* and *Knowledge.* Opinion is a consciously insufficient judgment, subjectively as well as objectively. Belief is subjectively sufficient, but is recognized as being objectively insufficient. Knowledge is both subjectively and objectively sufficient. Subjective sufficiency is termed *conviction;* objective sufficiency is termed *certainty.* I need not dwell longer on the explanation of such simple conceptions.

I must never venture to *be of opinion,* without *knowing* something, at least, by which my judgment, in itself merely problematical, is brought into connection with the truth—which connection, although not perfect, is still something more than an arbitrary fiction. Moreover, the law of such a connection must be certain. For if, in relation to this law, I have nothing more than opinion, my judgment is but a play of the imagination, without the least relation to truth. In the judgments of pure reason, opinion has no place. For as they do not rest on empirical grounds, and as the sphere of pure reason is that of necessary truth and *a priori* cognition, the principle of connection in it requires universality and necessity, and consequently perfect certainty—otherwise we should have no guide to the truth at all. Hence it is absurd to have an opinion in pure mathematics; we must know, or abstain from forming a judgment altogether. The case is the same with the maxims of morality. For we must not hazard an action on the mere opinion that it is allowed, but we must know it to be so.

In the transcendental sphere of reason, on the other hand, the term opinion is too weak, while the word knowledge is too strong. From the merely speculative point of view, therefore, we cannot form a judgment at all. For the subjective grounds of a judgment, such as produce belief, cannot be admitted in speculative inquiries, inasmuch as they cannot stand without empirical support, and are incapable of being communicated to others in equal measure.

Now, in cases where we cannot enter upon any course of action in reference to some object, and where, accordingly, our judgment is purely theoretical, we can still represent to ourselves, in thought, the possibility of a course of action, for which we suppose that we have sufficient grounds, if any means existed of ascertaining the truth of the matter. Thus we find in purely theoretical judgments an *analogon* of practical judgments, to which the word *belief* may properly be applied, and which we may term *doctrinal belief*. I should not hesitate to stake my all on the truth of the proposition—if there were any possibility of bringing it to the test of experience—that, at least, some one of the planets, which we see, is inhabited. Hence I say that I have not merely the opinion, but the strong belief, on the correctness of which I would stake even many of the advantages of life, that there are inhabitants in other worlds.

Now we must admit that the doctrine of the existence of God belongs to doctrinal belief. For, although in respect to the theoretical cognition of the universe I do not require to form any theory which necessarily involves this idea, as the condition of my explanation of the phenomena which the universe presents, but, on the contrary, am rather bound so to use my reason as if everything were mere nature, still teleological unity is so important a condition of the application of my reason to nature, that it is impossible for me to ignore it—especially since, in addition to these considerations, abundant examples of it are supplied by experience. But the sole condition, so far as my knowledge extends, under which this unity can be my guide in the investigation of nature, is the assumption that a supreme intelligence has ordered all things according to the wisest ends.

It is quite otherwise with *moral belief*. For in this sphere action is absolutely necessary, that is, I must act in obedience to the moral law in all points. The end is here incontrovertibly established, and there is only one condition possible, according to the best of my perception, under which this end can harmonize with all other ends, and so have practical validity—namely, the existence of a God and of a future world. I know also, to a certainty, that no one can be acquainted with any other conditions which conduct to the same unity of ends under the moral law. But since the moral precept is, at the same time, my maxim, I am irresistibly constrained to believe in the existence of God and in a future life; and I am sure that nothing can make me waver in this belief, since I should thereby overthrow my moral maxims, the renunciation of which would render me hateful in my own eyes.

Thus, while all the ambitious attempts of reason to penetrate beyond the limits of experience end in disappointment, there is still enough left to satisfy us in a practical point of view. No one, it is true, will be able to boast that he knows that there is a God and a future life; for, if he knows this, he is just the man whom I have long wished to find. All knowledge, regarding an object of mere reason, can be communicated; and I should thus be enabled to hope that my own knowledge would receive this wonderful extension, through the instrumentality of his instruction. No, my conviction is not *logical,* but *moral* certainty; and since it rests on subjective grounds, I must not even say: *It is* morally certain that there is a God, etc., but: *I am* morally certain, that is, my belief in God and in another world is so interwoven with my moral nature, that I am under as little apprehension of having the former torn from me as of losing the latter.